Level 1
BOOKKEEPING

David Cox

Michael Fardon

Sheila Robinson

osborne
BOOKS

Published by Osborne Books Limited
Unit 1B Everoak Estate
Bromyard Road
Worcester WR2 5HP
Tel 01905 748071
Email books@osbornebooks.co.uk
Website www.osbornebooks.co.uk

Printed by the Bath Press, Bath
Cover design Jon Moore

British Library Cataloguing in Publication Data
A catalogue record for this book is available from the British Library

ISBN 1 872962 87 4

CONTENTS

ACKNOWLEDGEMENTS

The authors wish to thank the following for their help with the reading and production of this book: Debbie Board, Jean Cox, Mike Gilbert, Claire McCarthy, Jon Moore, Roger Petheram, Malcolm Robinson and Liz Smith. The publisher is very grateful to the staff at OCR, and in particular would like to thank Jacqui Handle, Toby McKechnie and Simon Richards, who have provided invaluable advice and support during the course of this project.

THE AUTHORS

David Cox has more than twenty years' experience teaching accountancy students over a wide range of levels. Formerly with the Management and Professional Studies Department at Worcester College of Technology, he now lectures on a freelance basis and carries out educational consultancy work in accountancy studies. He is author and joint author of a number of textbooks in the areas of accounting, finance and banking.

Michael Fardon has extensive teaching experience of a wide range of banking, business and accountancy courses at Worcester College of Technology. He now specialises in writing business and financial texts and is General Editor at Osborne Books. He is also an educational consultant and has worked extensively in the areas of vocational business curriculum development.

Sheila Robinson worked for a firm of accountants before gaining extensive teaching experience at Stockport College of Higher and Further Education, where, as Senior Lecturer, she taught on accounting and management courses. She is a well-established author of book-keeping and accountancy books and, as a training consultant, she lectures in both the private and public sectors. Sheila is a Council Member of the Association of Accounting Technicians.

INTRODUCTION

the textbook

Level 1 Bookkeeping has been written as a practical guide for students studying the three units of the OCR Level 1 Certificate in Bookkeeping which deal with the manual aspects of bookkeeping:

Unit 1	Posting to Accounts
Unit 2	Maintaining Petty Cash
Unit 3	Maintaining the Cash Book

The book assumes no previous knowledge of bookkeeping and is an ideal introduction for people who are interested in preparing for a job in a bookkeeping role. It is also suitable for people already carrying out bookkeeping activities who want to acquire a knowledge of the theory of bookkeeping.

The text of *Level 1 Bookkeeping* contains:

- clear and practical explanations
- step-by-step Case Studies
- Key Terms and Chapter Summaries for revision
- practical Student Activities, many with answers at the back of the book (the remaining answers are given in the Tutor Pack – see below)

completing accounts and documents

A large part of the OCR course involves the completion of accounts and documents. To help with this, Osborne Books has printed suitable account formats and financial documents in the book. Tutors and students are welcome to photocopy these, as indicated in the text. Alternatively, photocopiable material is available as a free download from the resources section of the Osborne Books website: www.osbornebooks.co.uk and also in the Tutor Pack (see below).

Tutor Pack

The Tutor Pack for this text contains photocopiable account formats and documents, together with practice exams and assignments based on the OCR model. It also contains the answers to this assessment material and to some of the questions in this book. If you are interested in a Tutor Pack, please call Osborne Books Customer Services on 01905 748071.

1 BUSINESS AND BOOKKEEPING

this chapter covers . . .

The object of this chapter is to give a short introduction which shows the importance of bookkeeping to a person starting up in business.

The chapter also outlines how the buying and selling process works, and explains a number of important trading terms. The main areas covered are:

- raising money and investing money when starting in business

- the basics of the business trading process

- the need to keep bookkeeping records

- people who need to know about bookkeeping records

- basic forms of business organisation

OCR LEARNING OUTCOMES

Knowledge and Understanding

This chapter does not cover any of the specific Assessment Objectives of Units 1 to 3 of the Level 1 Bookkeeping course, but instead concentrates on a number of the underlying Knowledge and Understanding requirements:

- importance of business record keeping

- difference between suppliers and customers

- difference between credit and cash transactions

- importance of accuracy

The chapter also introduces the theory which underlies some of the ledger accounts, including: expenses, revenues, assets, liabilities and capital.

STARTING IN BUSINESS

bookkeeping in context

In order to make the most of your bookkeeping studies it is important to see how the function of bookkeeping 'fits in' with the way an organisation is run.

A bookkeeper is a person who 'keeps the books' of an organisation.

The **organisation** might be a business, a charity or a local sports club. These organisations buy and sell goods, produce goods for sale or provide a service and aim to make a profit. The **bookkeeper** might be the owner of the business or it may be someone employed to undertake this work. All financial transactions are entered in the 'books of account' and the information recorded in them can provide important data for the business.

starting a business – money in and money out

Starting in business involves money in two ways:

- raising money
- using the money to get the business going

We will look at these two aspects in turn, using the example of Ronaldo Antoni, who starts up a pizza home delivery business.

raising money for business

A business can raise money from two different sources:

- **capital** – the money put in by the owner or owners
- **liabilities** – money borrowed and owed to others

Ronaldo

In this case the pizza delivery business started by Ronaldo Antoni needs to raise £50,000, which will come from:

savings	(capital)	£20,000
bank loan	(liability)	£20,000
loan from brother Carlo	(liability)	£10,000
		£50,000

using the money raised

When the money has been raised (£50,000 in this case) it can then be invested in business assets. **Assets** are items owned by a business. Ronaldo will use his £50,000 for items such as:

- pizza-making equipment
- pizza-making ingredients – flour, oil, toppings

- pizza packaging (boxes)
- a motor bike for delivery of the pizzas
- money in the bank for paying wages, advertising, insurance and all the other outgoings of a business

The function of the bookkeeper here is to record all the financial transactions of the business in an accurate and organised way.

making a profit

profit comes in slices

Nothing ever stands still in business. As Ronaldo starts trading and the pizza business takes off, he will have money to pay into the bank and will also be busy writing cheques. He will deal with:

- **revenue** – money coming into the business from the sale of his pizzas
- **expenses** – money spent on day-to-day requirements: cooking ingredients, pizza boxes, wages, electricity, insurance, telephone costs, advertising

Because Ronaldo is successful in his business, his revenue is greater than his expenses and so he is making a **profit** and is providing an income for himself and his family.

The function of the bookkeeper here is to record revenue (sales) and expenses so that profit can be calculated.

customers and suppliers

Ronaldo depends on his **customers,** the people he sells to, for his revenue. He is also dependent on buying ingredients and pizza boxes from his **suppliers**. He must pay them promptly, or they may stop supplying him.

cash and credit trading

Ronaldo also learns that he can take advantage of selling for cash. When he sells his pizzas, he is paid straightaway. This is known as **cash** settlement. Here cash does not mean 'notes and coins' – although they may be used – but immediate payment by cash, cheque, debit card and credit card. He can bank the money straightaway, which helps him to meet his bills.

When it comes to paying his suppliers for pizza ingredients and packaging, he can negotiate to pay at a later date, usually 30 days later. These terms for payment at a later date are known as **credit** terms. They are very useful because he is paid by his customers before he has to pay his suppliers for the materials for the pizzas. Remember:

cash settlement = paying straightaway

credit terms = paying at a later date

discounts

Ronaldo will also be able to reduce his expenses by negotiating **discounts** from his suppliers. A discount is a percentage reduction in the selling price. This discount might be:

- **trade discount** – a discount given by suppliers to regular customers
- **cash discount** – a discount given by suppliers to customers who pay up earlier than the agreed 30 days, for example

We will explain discounts in greater detail in later chapters.

dealing with the bank

Ronaldo will need to pay in his takings and make payment for his expenses. A bank account is essential for running a business. One of the important roles of the bookkeeper is to record all the banking transactions – payments in and payments out – in a cash book, and then to check the transactions when the bank statement is received. Businesses often keep some cash on the premises to meet small payments, and it will be the role of the bookkeeper to record these '**petty cash**' transactions.

what the bookkeeper does – a summary

The role of the bookkeeper is to record financial transactions in 'accounts' which record:

- money raised by the business
  - capital invested by the owner
  - liabilities, eg loans from the bank and family
- money spent by the business
  - assets bought, eg equipment
  - expenses, eg wages and insurance

The role of the bookkeeper in the buying and selling process is to record:

- cash sales made to customers
- credit sales made – and what is owed by customers at any one time
- cash purchases from suppliers
- credit purchases from suppliers – and what is owed to suppliers

Banking transactions are central to any business and one of the main activities of the bookkeeper will be to write up the cash book, which records:

- all payments received
- all payments made

As you can see, the bookkeeper's role is critically important for the efficient running of a business.

WHO NEEDS TO KNOW?

Recording financial transactions is a complex business. As a bookkeeper, you have to maintain accounts to keep track of:

- who owes you what, and when the payment is due to be received
- amounts that you owe, and when the payment is due to be made

You have to record what you pay into the bank and what you draw out. You need to record the amounts paid in wages to each employee.

We will not at this stage explore in any detail how these financial transactions are recorded – these areas will be covered later in the book. But it is worth noting that if these transactions are not recorded accurately, nobody will know how the business is doing.

Who needs to know?

- the **owner** of the business will need to know if the business is profitable
- the **bank**, which may be lending money, will need to know if the borrowing is likely to be repaid
- the **Inland Revenue** will need to know if they are due any tax on the profits of the business and the **VAT authorities** (HM Customs & Excise) will need to know if VAT is due to be paid to them

an accurate, honest and discreet bookkeeper

The bookkeeper in a business may be the owner or it may be someone employed by the owner to 'write up the books' – ie to record financial transactions. The records themselves may be manual (handwritten) account books, or they may be computerised. The format of manual accounts will be covered in later chapters of this book.

The bookkeeper must be **accurate**, be **honest** and keep the bookkeeping records **confidential.**

Mistakes in the 'books' can lead to wrong information, which can have serious consequences, for example:

- the bank account going overdrawn because the bookkeeper has overstated the amount held in the bank account
- the business sending out a letter demanding money from a customer because the bookkeeper has muddled up two customer accounts

It almost goes without saying that a bookkeeper must not 'fiddle' the books, nor must the bookkeeper make unauthorised disclosures about the business to a third party – eg how much money the business has, or which customers may be bad payers. Discretion is very important.

BOOKKEEPERS AND ACCOUNTANTS

As the business grows in size, the volume of financial transactions will increase and the bookkeeping function will expand and become part of the work of a department, possibly an Accounts Department.

The basic principles of bookkeeping, will, however, remain exactly the same. There will be more staff involved in the recording of financial transactions, and they will provide information for the accountants.

There is a difference between a **bookkeeper** and an **accountant**. A **bookkeeper** is responsible for writing up the accounting records from financial transactions. An **accountant**, on the other hand, is employed to interpret and present the accounting records to provide answers to questions that the business managers and owners might ask, such as:

'How much profit did my business make last year?'

'How much will it cost me to produce and deliver each pizza?'

We will now put the bookkeeping role into the context of different types of business.

BUSINESS ORGANISATIONS

There are three main forms of business organisation:

sole trader

A sole trader is an individual trading in his/her own name, or under a trading name.

The majority of businesses are sole traders. A sole trader will need a wide variety of skills; he or she will be in charge of buying and selling goods and services, hiring and firing of staff and will often, unless an outside book-keeper is employed, 'keep the books' – ie maintain the accounts.

Ronaldo (see page 3) sets up as a sole trader and writes up the books himself.

partnership

A partnership is a group of individuals trading in business, aiming to make a profit.

The partnership is clearly a step up from the sole trader: more people are involved in the business and so more expertise and money will be available.

If Ronaldo's brother Carlo joined the business and helped Ronaldo run it, they would become a partnership.

Examples of partnerships (normally from 2 to 20 people) include electricians, caterers, small shops, dentists and building firms. The need to keep accurate accounting records is therefore very important. It may be that one of the partners will take responsibility for the financial management of the business. As in the case of a sole trader, one of the partners may write up the books, or alternatively an outside bookkeeper may be employed.

limited company

A limited company is a separate legal body, owned by shareholders and managed by directors.

The largest business organisations are usually limited companies. A limited company is quite different from a sole trader and a partnership in that it exists as a business in its own right. It exists separately from its owners, the shareholders, who will not be called upon to pay up if the company goes into liquidation (goes 'bust'). The shareholders have what is known as *limited liability*: all they can lose is the money they have invested in the company. The need for the keeping of accounting records by limited companies is strictly regulated in law. Many limited companies will have an Accounts Department which will carry out all the bookkeeping and accounting functions.

If Ronaldo and Carlo develop their business over the years, they may form a limited company.

Very large limited companies may take the step of becoming public limited companies, which will enable them to have their shares quoted on the Stock Exchange. PizzaExpress is an example of a public limited company, which may have originally started as a small business like Ronaldo's.

CHAPTER SUMMARY

- If you start a business, you will need to raise money, either from your own resources (capital), or by borrowing from other sources such as the bank or friends (liabilities).

- The money raised will be spent on items which the business will own (assets) or kept in the bank to pay for running expenses.

- A business needs to make a profit in order to survive. Profit is the difference between revenue (income) and expenses.

- A business is very dependent on its customers for its revenue, and on its suppliers in order to be able to produce its product or service.

- Suppliers often give credit to their customers (ie 'buy now, pay later') and sometimes allow discounts.

- The business bank account is central to the bookkeeping system, and the bookkeeper will record payments in and out of the bank account.

- It is important to record financial transactions accurately in the bookkeeping records of the business so that the owner and other interested parties, such as the bank and the tax authorities, know how the business is getting on.

- The bookkeeper must be accurate and honest and must not reveal confidential details about the business.

- The role of the bookkeeper is to record the financial transactions and the role of the accountant is to use the information to report on how the business has performed and how much it costs to run.

- The three main forms of business are sole trader, partnership and limited company. The larger the business, the more likely it is to have an Accounts Department which will carry out the bookkeeping function.

capital	money invested in a business by the owner(s)
liability	money borrowed to finance a business
asset	an item owned by a business – including money in the bank
revenue	money received by a business from the sale of its products or services
profit	the difference between revenue and expenses
customer	the person to whom a business sells its products
supplier	the person from whom a business buys the resources it needs to produce its products or services
cash settlement	paying straightaway for products purchased
credit settlement	paying at a later date for products purchased

trade discount	a percentage reduction in the selling price given by a supplier to regular customers
cash discount	a percentage reduction in the selling price given by a supplier to customers who pay up early
bookkeeper	a person who writes up the financial transactions of a business in the accounting records
accountant	a person who uses the accounting records to provide information to the business owner(s)
sole trader	an individual trading in his/her own name in business
partnership	a group of individuals trading together in business
limited company	a separate legal body, owned by shareholders and run by directors

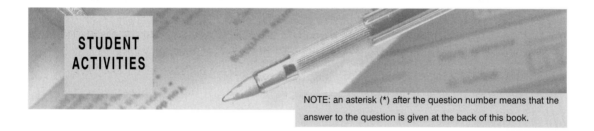

STUDENT ACTIVITIES

NOTE: an asterisk (*) after the question number means that the answer to the question is given at the back of this book.

1.1* Explain the difference between:

(a)   liabilities and capital

(b)   liabilities and assets

1.2* Explain the difference between:

(a)   cash settlement and credit terms

(b)   cash discount and trade discount

1.3* Explain the difference between a bookkeeper and an accountant.

1.4* What is meant by the term 'petty cash'?

1.5*   A friend of yours is thinking of training as a bookkeeper. She wants to know what sort of transactions she would have to record in the accounts.

Write down ten types of transaction the bookkeeper may have to record.

1.6*   Keeping the accounts of a business accurately is important because a number of interested parties may need the financial information which they contain.

Explain why the following would be interested:

(a)   the owner(s) of the business

(b)   the bank which is lending money to the business

(c)   the Inland Revenue

(d)   the VAT authorities

1.7   Another person you know works in a bookkeeping role in a large accounts office and tells you the following in a coffee bar after work one day:

(a)   "Bookkeeping is really easy. I can't always get my accounts to add up properly, but I always change an unimportant figure so that they do. It seems to do the trick."

(b)   "It is a good thing being a bookkeeper. If you are ever short of cash on a Friday you can always 'borrow' cash from the office petty cash tin. I don't think they mind as long as you give it back again. I usually do."

(c)   "We have one customer, R M Consultancy, who never pay up on time, and sometimes not at all. The bosses think the customer is going bust."

What would be your reaction to these three statements from a professional bookkeeper?

Make a list of the qualities of a good bookkeeper.

2 DOCUMENTS FOR SALES AND PURCHASES

this chapter covers . . .

In the last chapter we described the way in which businesses trade on credit – in other words the arrangement by which a buyer can buy now and pay at a later date.

This chapter explains the business documentation involved in this process. The main documents examined are:

- the invoice – which is issued by the seller and sets out what is owed and when it is due for payment

- the credit note – which is also issued by the seller and sets out any refund due on the transaction

- the cheque – which is used to make payment to the seller

In the next chapter we will see how the details from the invoice and the credit note are entered by the bookkeeper in the accounts of the business.

OCR LEARNING OUTCOMES

Knowledge and Understanding – Unit 1 Posting to Accounts

This chapter does not cover any of the specific Assessment Objectives of Unit 1 of the Level 1 Bookkeeping course, but instead concentrates on the underlying Knowledge and Understanding required when entering transactions from financial documents into the accounts:

- difference between suppliers and customers

- difference between credit and cash transactions

- transaction details – amount, correct date, reference number, narrative

- invoices

- credit notes

The way in which financial transactions are entered in the accounting records is covered in detail in the next chapter.

FINANCIAL DOCUMENTS – BUYING AND SELLING ON CREDIT

When a business sells or buys goods or services, it uses a number of different financial documents. These are shown in the diagram below, which shows the **flow of documents** between the buyer and the seller of goods on credit. In this chapter we will concentrate on three of these documents:

- the **invoice** – which is issued by the seller and sets out what is owed by the buyer and when it is due for payment
- the **credit** note – which is also issued by the seller and sets out any refund due to the buyer on the transaction
- the **cheque** – used to pay for what is owed

There are, of course, other documents involved in the process, and we will describe them briefly, as they are important to the process.

Now study the diagram below and follow the credit sales transaction through.

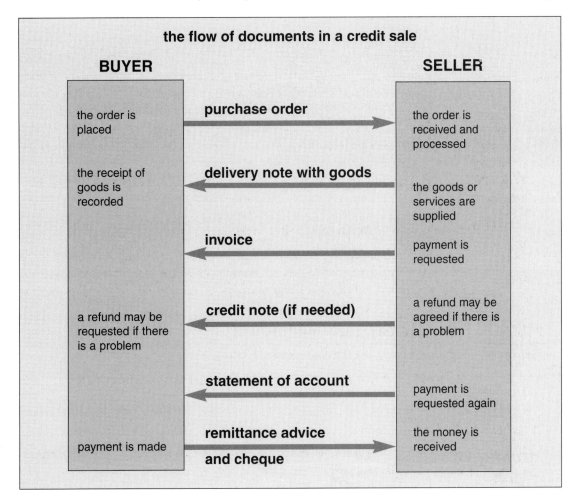

the flow of documents in a credit sale

BUYER		SELLER
the order is placed	**purchase order** →	the order is received and processed
the receipt of goods is recorded	← **delivery note with goods**	the goods or services are supplied
	← **invoice**	payment is requested
a refund may be requested if there is a problem	← **credit note (if needed)**	a refund may be agreed if there is a problem
	← **statement of account**	payment is requested again
payment is made	**remittance advice and cheque** →	the money is received

FINANCIAL DOCUMENTS

The documents shown on the diagram on the previous page are the:

* *purchase order* which the seller receives from the buyer
* *delivery note* which goes with the goods from the seller to the buyer
* *invoice* which lists the goods and tells the buyer what is owed
* *credit note* which is sent to the buyer if any refund is due
* *statement* sent by the seller to remind the buyer what is owed
* *cheque* sent by the buyer to settle up the account
* *remittance advice* sent by the buyer with the cheque

We will now illustrate these documents and explain them

PURCHASE ORDER

Wyvern Traders, a business, wants to buy some office furniture. They look at different supplier catalogues or website pages for prices. They might ask for a formal written **quotation**. A common way of placing an order is to complete a formal document known as a **purchase order**. Study the example below. Note the reference numbers used – the product code (which comes from the James & Sons Limited catalogue) and the purchase order number on the document itself.

Wyvern Traders   **PURCHASE ORDER**

Bell Lane
Wyvern
WY1 4DB
Tel 01907 761234 Fax 01907 761987
VAT REG GB 0745 8383 56

James & Sons Limited	purchase order no	47609
Wyvern Business Park	date	21 12 03
Wyvern		
WY1 8TQ		

product code	quantity	description
OC123	3	Office chairs
OD243	1	Office desk

AUTHORISED   signature........*R Singh*...date...*21/12/03*.....

DELIVERY AND INVOICING

delivery of the goods

When the purchase order is received by James and Sons Limited, the supplier, it will be checked to see if it is authorised (note the signature at the bottom of the purchase order) and if the goods are in stock. If all is in order, the goods will be despatched with a **delivery note,** prepared by James and Sons Limited. This document sets out the details of the goods and the order. A copy of the delivery note will be signed by the buyer and returned to the seller as proof of delivery. Study the delivery note shown below.

DELIVERY NOTE

James & Sons Limited

**Wyvern Business Park
Wyvern
WY1 8TQ**

Wyvern Traders Bell Lane Wyvern WY1 4DB	delivery note no	8123
	delivery method	Parcelswift
	your order	47609
	date	06 01 04

product code	quantity	description
OC123	3	Office chairs
OD243	1	Office desk

Received

signature................*V Williams*................name (capitals)...*V WILLIAMS*................date...*07/01/04*

---

the invoice

The seller of the goods, James & Sons Limited, will need to ensure that it receives payment for its goods by the due date. The seller will prepare and send to the buyer, Wyvern Traders, an **invoice** setting out:

- details of the goods that have been sold
- the price charged and the amount due after deduction of any discount
- any VAT (Value Added Tax) charged on the goods
- the date by which payment has to be made

Study the next few pages which explain the invoice in full and show some alternative formats.

the **name**, **address** and **contact details** of the **seller**, plus the VAT registration number of the buyer (please see page 18 for an explanation of VAT)

reference numbers include:
* the **invoice** number
* the reference number of the **purchase order** (so that the invoice can be 'tied up' with the order by the buyer)

the **name** and **address** of the **buyer**

the **date** of the **invo**ice – this is important for establishing when the invoice has to be paid by the buyer (see **terms** below)

columns for
* the **quantity** of the item required
* the **description** of the item (this might include a product code)
* the **unit price** – how much a single item costs
* the **total net** – this is the unit price multiplied by the quantity
* the **VAT rate*** is the percentage rate applied to the total net
* the **VAT amount*** is the total net multiplied by the VAT percentage
* the **TOTAL** is the total amount charged to the buyer for the items on the invoice (after deduction of any discounts*)

    * (please see page 18 for an explanation of VAT and the use of discounts)

column totals for
* the **total net** – this is the amount the seller charges for all the goods (or services) on an invoice **before VAT is added on**
* the **VAT amount** – this is the **total amount of VAT charged** on the invoice
* the **TOTAL** is the total amount of the invoice and is **the amount the buyer has to pay**

These totals are particularly important for the bookkeeper (see next chapter).

the **terms** of an invoice set out **when the invoice has to be paid** – for example 'net 30 days' means that the invoice has to be paid within 30 days of the invoice date printed on the invoice.

INVOICE

James & Sons Limited

Office furniture and stationery suppliers

Wyvern Business Park, Wyvern WY1 8TQ

Tel 01627 338877
Fax 01627 338878
email info@james&sonsltd.co.uk
VAT Reg 471 3245 84

to   Wyvern Traders
Bell Lane
Wyvern
WY1 4DB

invoice no.   5401

reference   47609

date   6 January 2004

quantity	description	unit price £	total net £	VAT rate %	VAT amount £	TOTAL £
3	Office chairs	85.15	255.45	17.5	44.70	300.15
1	Office desk	99.45	99.45	17.5	17.40	116.85
			354.90		62.10	417.00

terms: net 30 days

alternative invoice formats

There is no 'set' format for an invoice, and the bookkeeper encounters a number of different formats when dealing with documentation received from suppliers. Some invoices may be prepared by hand – in which case the arithmetic has to be checked carefully – or they may be produced by a computer accounting program, in which case the computer should produce the correct figures.

Other important details that should be checked by the bookkeeper when dealing with invoices received from suppliers include whether the right goods (or services) have been charged for, and whether the prices are right.

An alternative invoice format is shown on the next page. All the important details are there, but note how the columns are set out differently from the example on page 17, and there is trade discount deducted.

a note on discounts

A discount is 'money off' – a percentage reduction in the invoice total. The two main types of discount are:

- **cash discount** for early payment by the buyer
- **trade discount** given by the seller to regular customers

When writing up the accounts, you do not need to worry about trade discount because you will record the subtotal figure after trade discount has been deducted. You will need, however, to deal with cash discount in your studies. This is covered on pages 240-242.

Value Added Tax (VAT)

VAT is a Government tax charged on the selling price of goods and services. You see it added onto the selling price on invoices and other financial documents, such as receipts.

For example, office supplies costing £100 are currently charged VAT at 17.5%. The customer therefore pays in total:

$$£100 \text{ plus } \frac{£100 \times 17.5}{100} \text{ (the VAT)} = £100 + £17.50 = £117.50$$

Businesses with sales over a certain figure must by law register for VAT and are given a VAT registration number, which you see printed on invoices. Businesses charging VAT will receive the VAT amount from their customers and must then eventually pay it to the Government, at the same time deducting any VAT they themselves have to pay. This is one of the reasons why bookkeepers have to keep accurate records of VAT.

INVOICE

Osborne Fashion Limited

Unit 16 Millyard Estate
Fencote Road, Worcester WR2 6HY
Tel 01905 334482
Fax 01905 334493
email info@osbornefashion.co.uk
VAT Reg 987 544 21

to Gullwing Ltd	**invoice no.** 12313
Gullwing House	
Great West Road	
Hounslow	**date** 24 October 2004
Middlesex	
HO7 6GF	
	order no. 2740

quantity	description	cat. no.	unit price (£)	£
10	Large T shirts (black)	TS76	4.50	45.00
2	Sweatshirts (blue)	SS23	7.50	15.00
				60.00
		Less trade discount 10%		6.00
				54.00
		VAT at 17.5%		9.45
				63.45

terms: net 30 days

an alternative form of invoice

CREDIT NOTE

Another document which you will see in your exams is the **credit note**. A credit note is a 'refund' document. It reduces the amount owed by the buyer. The goods, remember, have not yet been paid for.

The credit note is prepared by the seller and sent to the buyer. Situations where this might happen include:

- the goods may have been damaged or faulty
- the goods may have been lost in transit
- incorrect goods may have been sent
- not enough goods have been sent
- the unit price on the invoice is too high

In the example transaction in this chapter, when the staff of Wyvern Traders unpack the furniture they find that one of the chair seats has been ripped. They telephone James & Sons Limited to report the problem and James & Sons Limited authorises the return of the chair 'for credit'. The chair is sent back to James & Sons Limited who then send the credit note for £100.05 (shown opposite) to Wyvern Traders.

As Wyvern Traders have not yet sent payment for the goods, the credit note reduces the amount they have to pay.

Note that:

- the reason for the issue of the credit note is stated at the bottom of the credit note – here 'damaged goods'
- the format of the document is very much the same as an invoice

Now study the credit note on the opposite page.

the business giving the credit (refund)

the business receiving the credit (refund)

the **reason for credit** is given

the amount refunded **includes the VAT** on the amount credited

the amount which will be deducted from the 'account' of the buyer of the goods

Credit Note

James & Sons Limited

Office furniture and stationery suppliers
Wyvern Business Park, Wyvern WY1 8TQ

Tel 01627 338877
Fax 01627 338878
email info@james&sonsltd.co.uk
VAT Reg 471 3245 84

to Wyvern Traders
Bell Lane
Wyvern
WY1 4DB

credit note no. 221

date 15 January 2004

quantity	description	unit price (£)	£ p
1	Office chair	85.15	85.15
		Total excluding VAT	85.15
		VAT at 17.5%	14.90
		Total credit	100.05

reason for credit:
Damaged goods

SENDING THE STATEMENT

The next step in the 'flow of documents' process is for the seller, James & Sons Limited, to send a **statement** to the buyer, Wyvern Traders.

A statement is a 'reminder' document, often sent at the end of each month, setting out details of:

- invoices due
- credit notes sent

The statement sent by James & Sons Limited to Wyvern Traders is shown below. Note that the invoice and credit note details shown are:

- date of the invoice and credit note
- document reference numbers
- the amounts of the invoice and credit note

Wyvern Traders are reminded by this statement that they owe £316.95 to James & Sons Limited.

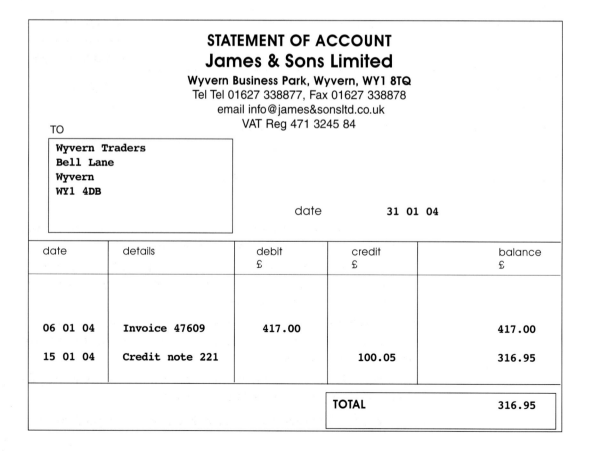

STATEMENT OF ACCOUNT
James & Sons Limited
Wyvern Business Park, Wyvern, WY1 8TQ
Tel Tel 01627 338877, Fax 01627 338878
email info@james&sonsltd.co.uk
VAT Reg 471 3245 84

TO

Wyvern Traders
Bell Lane
Wyvern
WY1 4DB

date   31 01 04

date	details	debit £	credit £	balance £
06 01 04	Invoice 47609	417.00		417.00
15 01 04	Credit note 221		100.05	316.95
			TOTAL	316.95

PAYING FOR THE GOODS

A common way of paying for goods is to use a cheque. There are other methods of payment available using the bank computer networks (see Chapter 13 later in this book) but we concentrate here on the cheque.

In the example transaction used in this chapter, Wyvern Traders owe £316.95 to James & Sons Limited. The bookkeeper writes out a cheque settling this amount on 5 February. The cheque is posted to James & Sons Limited with a slip known as a **remittance advice** which explains who the cheque is from and what it is for.

Study the cheque shown below and read the notes that follow.

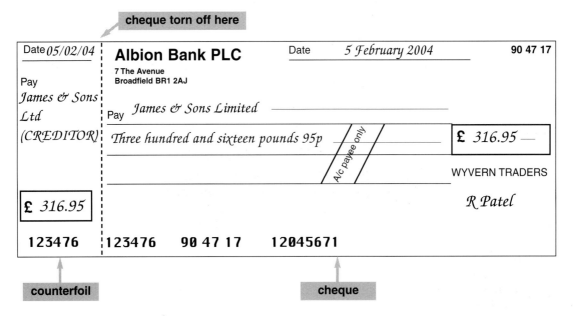

cheque torn off here

counterfoil

cheque

notes

- the cheque itself is on the right – the details (date, amount in words and figures, person being paid, signature) are written in full
- the details are summarised on the cheque stub (also known as a 'counterfoil') on the left – these details will be needed when the bookkeeper comes to write up the accounts
- when the cheque is torn out of the cheque book and sent off to James & Sons Limited, the stub remains to provide the business with the details of what the cheque was for
- the word 'CREDITOR' on the stub indicates that a supplier is being paid – a creditor is someone to whom you owe money

There is further information about cheques in Chapter 11 (pages 238-240).

the remittance advice

Wyvern Traders posts the cheque shown on the previous page with a slip known as a **remittance advice**. This document (shown below) explains to the accounts department at James & Sons Limited:

- the amount of the cheque
- the invoice(s) and credit note(s) covered by the cheque

Note the reference numbers of the seller's invoice and credit note and the reference number of the buyer's purchase order.

Wyvern Traders		**REMITTANCE ADVICE**	
Bell Lane			
Wyvern			
WY1 4DB			
Tel 01907 761234 Fax 01907 761987			
VAT REG GB 0745 8383 56			
James & Sons Limited Wyvern Business Park Wyvern WY1 8TQ		date	05 02 04
date	Your reference	our reference	payment amount
06 01 04	Invoice 5401	47609	417.00
15 01 04	Credit note 221	47609	(100.05)
		CHEQUE TOTAL	316.95

the flow of documents - a revision note

The documents involved in sales and purchases transactions are listed below. The documents important for your exam are shown with a grey background.

- **purchase order** which the seller receives from the buyer
- **delivery note** which goes with the goods from the seller to the buyer
- **invoice** which lists the goods and tells the buyer what is owed
- **credit note** which is sent to the buyer if any refund is due
- **statement** sent by the seller to remind the buyer what is owed
- **cheque** sent by the buyer to settle up the account
- **remittance advice** sent by the buyer with the cheque

CHAPTER SUMMARY

KEY TERMS

- Businesses commonly trade on credit, which means that payment is made at a later date.

- When a business buys or sells on credit, a number of different financial documents may be used in the process by the seller(supplier) and buyer.

- A purchase order may be used to place the order, after the price of the goods or services has been established.

- If goods are involved, the seller may send a delivery note with the goods. The buyer may be required to sign the delivery note as proof of receipt.

- The seller of the goods or service sends an invoice to the buyer, setting out the amount owing and the date by which it is due to be paid. The invoice includes details of VAT and any discounts.

- If there is any problem with the goods or service, such as faults or wrong quantities, a credit note is issued by the seller, giving a reduction in the amount owed by the buyer.

- The seller sends a statement to the buyer setting out details of invoices and credit notes, reminding the buyer what needs to be paid.

- Payment is often made by cheque, which is accompanied by a remittance advice explaining what the payment is for.

selling on credit	selling goods or services and agreeing to accept payment at a later date
purchase order	a document for ordering goods or services
delivery note	a document which goes with the goods from the seller to the buyer
invoice	issued by the seller, listing the goods or services and telling the buyer what is owed and the date by which payment is due
credit note	a document which is sent to the buyer if any refund is due
statement	sent by the seller to remind the buyer what is owed
cheque	a form of payment sent by the buyer to settle up what is owed
remittance advice	a document sent by the buyer with the cheque explaining what is being paid
Value Added Tax	a Government tax on sales of goods and services, added to invoices and credit notes
discount	an amount deducted by the seller from the selling price of goods and services, normally calculated as a percentage of the selling price

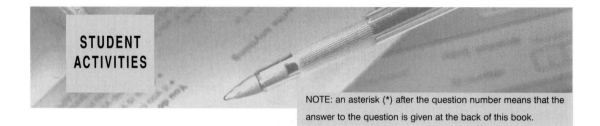

STUDENT
ACTIVITIES

NOTE: an asterisk (*) after the question number means that the
answer to the question is given at the back of this book.

2.1*   (a)   Explain what is meant by 'buying on credit terms'.

      (b)   What is the document issued by the seller which sets out what is owed by the buyer?

      (c)   What is the document issued by the seller if a reduction needs to be made in the amount owed by the buyer?

2.2*   Tania, a new trainee, is working alongside you in the Accounts Department at Gullwing Limited. You receive an invoice in the post:

INVOICE

Osborne Fashion Limited

Unit 16 Millyard Estate
Fencote Road, Worcester WR2 6HY
Tel 01905 334482
Fax 01905 334493
email info@osbornefashion.co.uk
VAT Reg 987 544 21

to Gullwing Ltd Gullwing House Great West Road Hounslow Middlesex HO7 6GF	**invoice no.** 12313 **date** 24 October 2004 **order no.** 2740

quantity	description	cat. no.	unit price (£)	£
10	Large T shirts (black)	TS76	4.50	45.00
2	Sweatshirts (blue)	SS23	7.50	15.00
				60.00
		Less trade discount 10%		6.00
				54.00
		VAT at 17.5%		9.45
				63.45

terms: net 30 days

Tania asks you a number of basic questions relating to the invoice. What would be your answers?

(a)   Who has sent the invoice?

(b)   What is the total amount that has to be paid?

(c)   When does it have to be paid?

(d)   What goods are being paid for?

(e)   Why has £6 been deducted from the total?

(f)   What is the amount owing before VAT is added on?

(g)   What is the VAT amount and why does Osborne Fashion Limited have to charge VAT?

2.3*   A week later (see Activity 2.2) Tania is still training alongside you in the Accounts Department at Gullwing Limited. You receive a credit note from Osborne Fashion Limited. It relates to the invoice in Activity 2.2.

Credit Note				
Osborne Fashion Limited				
Unit 16 Millyard Estate				
Fencote Road, Worcester WR2 6HY				
Tel 01905 334482				
Fax 01905 334493				
email info@osbornefashion.co.uk				
VAT Reg 987 544 21				

to Gullwing Ltd	**credit note no.** 456
Gullwing House	
Great West Road	
Hounslow	**date** 31 October 2004
Middlesex	
HO7 6GF	

quantity	description	unit price (£)	£ p
2	Sweatshirts (blue)	7.50	15.00
			15.00
	Less trade discount 10%		1.50
			13.50
reason for credit:	VAT at 17.5%		2.36
Incorrect goods supplied			15.86

Tania asks you some more questions – this time relating to the credit note. What would be your answers?

(a)   What is the purpose of the credit note?

(b)   Who is crediting whom?

(c)   Why is the credit being given?

(d)   How much will Gullwing Limited now owe Osborne Fashion Limited (see also Activity 2.2)?

(e)   Will Gullwing Limited receive any reminder of the amount owing from Osborne Fashion Limited – and if so, what form will the reminder take?

2.4* A month later Tania (see Activities 2.2 and 2.3) is now more confident in her work and has written out a cheque for settling the account of Carib Supplies Limited, a business that has supplied Gullwing Limited on credit terms. She has got the cheque signed ready for sending off.

Date 30/11/04		
Pay	**National Bank PLC**	Date 30 November 2004 73-10-06
Carib	75 Westway	
Supplies	Hounslow HO1 2AJ	
Limited	Pay Carib Supplies Limited	
(CREDITOR)	Two hundred and fifty pounds 50p A/c payee only	£ 250.50 —
		GULLWING LIMITED
£ 250.50		*G Holst*
896161	896161 73 10 06 98491087	

(a)   What details of the transaction are recorded on the cheque book counterfoil (stub) by the person completing the cheque?

(b)   Why are these details important to Gullwing Limited?

(c)   What does the word 'CREDITOR' mean?

(d)   What document is Gullwing Limited likely to send off to Carib Supplies Limited with the cheque?

2.5 You decide, after helping to train Tania (see previous Activities), that a short guide to financial documents would be useful in the Gullwing Limited accounts office.

Prepare an information sheet on the financial documents involved in credit sales and purchases.

This should include short definitions of the financial documents.

The definitions should be given in the order in which the documents are used.

Optional task

You can also prepare illustrations for the information sheet, for example:

• photocopies of sample documents

• a diagram to show the 'flow of documents'

2.6 Gullwing Limited receives the invoice shown below on November 5. Study the invoice and answer the questions that follow.

INVOICE

James & Sons Limited

Office furniture and stationery suppliers
Wyvern Business Park, Wyvern WY1 8TQ

Tel 01627 338877
Fax 01627 338878
email info@james&sonsltd.co.uk
VAT Reg 471 3245 84

| Gullwing Limited
Gullwing House
Great West Road
Hounslow
Middlesex
HO7 6GF | | **invoice no.** 7306

reference 2965

date 30 October 2004 |

quantity	description	unit price £	total net £	VAT rate %	VAT amount £	TOTAL £
5	Office chairs	85.15	425.75	17.5	74.50	500.25
			425.75		74.50	500.25

terms: net 30 days

(a) Which business is the seller of the goods?

(b) Which business is the buyer of the goods?

(c) What is the amount owing on the invoice?

(d) When is the amount payable?

(e) What is the VAT amount payable?

(f) What is the amount payable before VAT is added on?

(g) What document would have to be issued by the seller if two of the chairs were faulty?

(h) What money amount would be deducted for the two faulty chairs from the amount payable?

(i) What document would be issued by the seller reminding the buyer of the amount owing?

3 ACCOUNTS AND LEDGERS FOR CREDIT SALES AND RETURNS

this chapter covers . . .

In the last chapter we looked at various business documents, including invoices and credit notes. These are the main documents for credit sales and sales returns.

In this chapter we see how sales invoices and credit notes issued are recorded in the bookkeeping system. This is done by means of the double-entry bookkeeping system, which is used to keep up-to-date with the financial transactions of the business.

Firstly, though, we study the principles of double-entry bookkeeping as these form the basis of much of what we shall be doing in the rest of the book. Then we go on to see how credit sales and sales returns documents are recorded in the bookkeeping system.

OCR LEARNING OUTCOMES

unit 1: POSTING TO ACCOUNTS
Assessment objectives

2   *Maintain Sales Ledger*

   (a) Identify and open correct ledger account

   (b) Enter invoice into correct account

   (c) Enter returns into correct account

3   *Maintain Nominal Ledger*

   (a) Identify and open correct ledger account

   (b) Enter transactions into correct account

WHAT IS AN ACCOUNT?

The double-entry bookkeeping system uses a series of **accounts** to record financial transactions. Before we can study bookkeeping in detail we need to understand what is meant by the word 'account'.

An account is the place where financial transactions are recorded. For example, if you have a bank account, all the transactions that you carry out – money paid in, payments made – are recorded by the bank in an account in your name – the account keeps a note of the details and money amounts of all your transactions. In effect, the account provides a narrative of what you have paid in, what payments you have made, and how much money you have in your account at the bank.

In the same way, a business keeps accounts of its financial transactions so that it knows what it has bought, what it has sold, who owes it money, how much it owes, how much has been spent on expenses, how much money is in the bank, etc. To keep track of all these transactions requires quite a few accounts!

Think of an account as being like a file in a filing cabinet. Each file is an account into which transactions are placed, while the whole filing cabinet forms the entire bookkeeping system.

Accounts are prepared in two forms – those which are handwritten in a manual accounts system, and those which are computerised in a computer accounts system.

manual accounts systems

These are still widely used, especially by small businesses. Accounts are sorted into sections called 'ledgers'. A ledger was originally a leather bound book, neatly ruled into columns, into which the bookkeeper would enter each financial transaction in immaculate handwriting into individual accounts on each page of the book. Even today, the system of ledgers – containing the *books of account* – has changed surprisingly little, and most stationery shops stock paperback ledgers designed especially for the smaller business.

In this chapter – and in later chapters – we will be using a manual accounts system to record financial transactions.

computer accounts systems

Nowadays, computers are relatively cheap so that they can be afforded by all but the smallest business. With computer accounts systems, financial transactions are input into the computer using a bookkeeping program and are stored on disk. The major advantage of computer accounting is that it is a very accurate method of recording financial transactions; the disadvantage is that it may be time-consuming to set up, particularly for the smaller business. Interestingly, the word 'ledger' has survived into the computer age but, instead of being a bound volume, it is represented by data files held on a computer disk.

Whether financial transactions are recorded by hand, or by using a computer, the basic principles remain the same. This book concentrates on these basic principles, using a manual accounts system to demonstrate them. You may well be using a computer accounts system in other Units of the OCR Bookkeeping qualifications.

DOUBLE-ENTRY ACCOUNTS

Double-entry bookkeeping in a manual accounts system involves entries being made in accounts for each transaction – debit entries (on the left-hand side of the account) and credit entries (on the right-hand side of the account).

We will first look at the layout of a typical manual double-entry account. The illustration here shows sales account recording sales made on credit to Wyvern Traders for £354.90.

Debit			Sales Account		Credit
Date	Details	£	Date	Details	£
2004			2004 6 Jan ↑ date of the trans- action	Wyvern Traders ↑ name of the account in which the other entry is made	354.90 ↑ amount of the trans- action

Note the following from the layout of the account:
- the name of the account – Sales Account – is written at the top
- the account is divided into two identical halves, separated by a central double (or bold) vertical line: the left-hand side is called the 'Debit' side ('Debit' is abbreviated to 'Dr'), the right-hand side is called the 'Credit' (or 'Cr') side

   A note for UK drivers! – **Dr**ive on the left   **Cr**ash on the right

- the date, details and amount of the transaction are entered in the columns – in the 'Details' column is entered the name of the other account involved in the bookkeeping transaction – here it is the account of Wyvern Traders

In a manual accounts system each account occupies a whole page or more, but in textbooks it is usual to simplify the format to save space and to put several accounts on a single page. The Sales Account set out in this simplified format – often known as a 'T' account – is shown as follows:

Dr			**Sales Account**		Cr
2004		£	2004		£
			6 Jan	Wyvern Traders	354.90

You will see that the column divisions have gone and the account is all much simpler, with just a single vertical line dividing the debit and credit sides.

There are alternative formats for accounts which can be used. Other versions are shown on pages 47-48.

DEBITS AND CREDITS

The decisions faced by anyone operating the double-entry system are:
- deciding which two accounts should be used for each transaction, and more critically . . .
- deciding which entry is the debit and which is the credit

There are simple rules which guide you, but, as with learning to drive a car, the early stages require both thought and concentration!

dual aspect theory of double-entry

The principle of double-entry bookkeeping is that every business transaction has a dual aspect:
- one account receives value (the debit)
- the other account gives value (the credit)

Debit entries are on the left-hand side of the appropriate account, while credit entries are on the right. The rules for debits and credits are:
- **debit entry** – the account which gains value, or records an asset (something which is owned), or an expense
- **credit entry** – the account which gives value, or records a liability (something which is owed), or an income item

These are illustrated as follows:

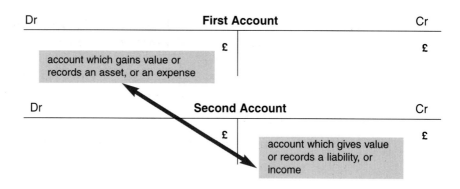

When one entry has been identified as a debit or credit, the other entry will be on the opposite side of the other account.

practical aspects of double-entry

If this sounds too theoretical, look at the practical aspects of the system. For each double-entry transaction (ignoring VAT for the moment):

- one account is debited (entry on the left of the account)
- another account is credited (entry on the right of the account)

The rules for debits and credits can be understood easily if you think in terms of assets (on the debit side) and liabilities (on the credit side). The four basic rules are:

- to increase an asset, make an entry on the debit side
- to decrease an asset, make an entry on the credit side
- to increase a liability, make an entry on the credit side
- to decrease a liability, make an entry on the debit side

To summarise:

debit entry	credit entry
• increase an asset	• decrease an asset
• decrease a liability	• increase a liability

Example 1

Sold goods on credit to Wyvern Traders for £354.90*

The double-entry bookkeeping for this transaction is:

debit: Wyvern Traders £354.90

credit: sales account £354.90

* for the moment we will ignore VAT on this transaction

The logic behind this is that the stock of goods held by a business for resale is an asset; the sale of the goods decreases the asset of stock and is recorded on the credit side of sales account. At the same time, Wyvern Traders owes the business £354.90 and this is recorded on the debit side of Wyvern Traders' account, ie the business has an asset in the form of a debtor.

Example 2

Goods returned by Wyvern Traders for £102.86*

The double-entry bookkeeping for this transaction is:

debit: sales returns account £102.86

credit: Wyvern Traders £102.86

* for the moment we will ignore VAT on this transaction

Here the asset of stock of goods held by the business increases because some goods have been returned. At the same time, Wyvern Traders owes the business less because of the returned goods, ie the asset in the form of a debtor is decreased.

Tutorial note

We will be dealing with the bookkeeping aspects of credit sales and sales returns – including VAT – in more detail later in this chapter. Nevertheless, it is a good starting point to think in terms of the changes to assets and liabilities which are caused by financial transactions.

DIVISION OF THE LEDGER

Most accounts systems use the ledger system to organise the accounts. The word 'ledger' means 'book', but is used freely by both manual and computer systems to represent a section or division of the accounts kept on paper or by the computer. The division of the ledger is summarised as follows:

- **sales ledger**

   the personal accounts of customers who have bought on credit (ie they have bought goods or services but will pay later) – these customers are known as 'debtors'

- **purchases ledger**

   the personal accounts of suppliers who have sold to the business on credit – these suppliers are known as 'creditors'

- **nominal (or general) ledger**

   all other accounts in the accounts system, the main ones being:

   – income from sales and other revenues

- purchases of materials and stock
- expenses, eg wages, rent, insurance, advertising
- assets (other than debtors) and liabilities (other than creditors)
- bank (money held by the business in its bank account)
- capital (the investment of the owners)
- VAT

The ledger system can be represented diagramatically:

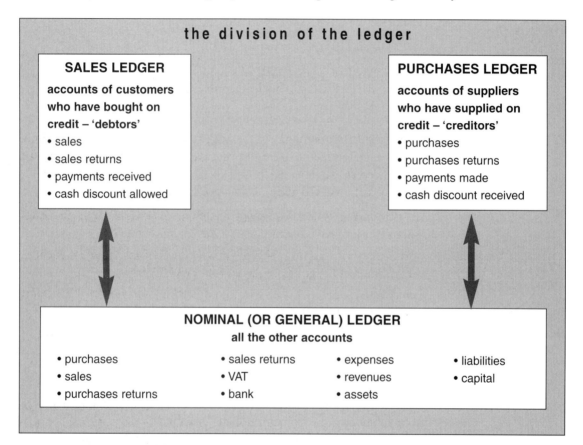

the division of the ledger

SALES LEDGER

accounts of customers who have bought on credit – 'debtors'
- sales
- sales returns
- payments received
- cash discount allowed

PURCHASES LEDGER

accounts of suppliers who have supplied on credit – 'creditors'
- purchases
- purchases returns
- payments made
- cash discount received

NOMINAL (OR GENERAL) LEDGER
all the other accounts

- purchases
- sales
- purchases returns
- sales returns
- VAT
- bank
- expenses
- revenues
- assets
- liabilities
- capital

CREDIT SALES – THE ACCOUNTS AND LEDGERS

In bookkeeping the term 'sales' has a specific meaning:

sales = the sale to a customer of goods or services in which the business trades

For example, an office stationery business selling goods to a customer records the transaction in *sales account*. The term *credit sales* means that payment for the products sold will be made by the customer at a later date.

The following ledgers and accounts are used in connection with credit sales:

nominal (or general) ledger

- *sales account* – to record the total of goods or services sold
- *Value Added Tax account* – to record the VAT amounts of sales

sales ledger

- separate accounts for each *debtor* – to record what each customer owes the business (this will be the price of the goods or service plus VAT – see the invoice on the next page)

DOUBLE-ENTRY BOOKKEEPING FOR CREDIT SALES

Invoices (see Chapter 2, pages 16 and 17), or copy invoices, issued by a business selling products on credit terms, are the documents used to write up the double-entry accounts. From the seller's viewpoint, the customer who is allowed to settle the account at a later date is a debtor.

The bookkeeping entries to record credit sales are made from the sales invoice (or copy invoice) issued:

- *debit:* debtor's (customer's) account with the total amount of the invoice, ie the price of the goods or service, plus VAT
- *credit:* sales account with the goods total of the invoice after trade discount (if any), but before VAT is added
- *credit:* Value Added Tax account with the VAT amount of the invoice

These entries are illustrated from the example invoice on the next page.

The logic behind the bookkeeping entries for credit sales is that the business has gained an asset in the form of a debtor's account, ie the customer owes the business an amount of money (which will be paid in due course).

At the same time the business has sold some goods and records the amount of income in sales account, while the VAT charged to the customer is recorded in VAT account.

Note that, with VAT charged on invoices, this does mean that there are three entries in the accounts for each invoice – despite this, the system is still called double-entry bookkeeping!

The accounting system for credit sales is summarised on page 39.

INVOICE

James & Sons Limited

Office furniture and stationery suppliers

Wyvern Business Park, Wyvern WY1 8TQ

Tel 01627 338877
Fax 01627 338878
email info@james&sonsltd.co.uk
VAT Reg 471 3245 84

to Wyvern Traders Bell Lane Wyvern WY1 4DB	**invoice no.**	5401
	date	6 January 2004
	order no.	2781

quantity	description	unit price £	total net £	VAT rate %	VAT amount £	TOTAL £
3	Office chairs	85.15	255.45	17.5	44.70	300.15
1	Office desk	99.45	99.45	17.5	17.40	116.85
			354.90		62.10	417.00

terms: net 30 days

Credit
sales account with goods
total of invoice after trade
discount (if any), but
before VAT is added

Credit
VAT account
with the VAT
amount of the
invoice

Debit
debtor's account
with total
amount of
invoice

These three entries are summarised in the diagram at the top of the next page.

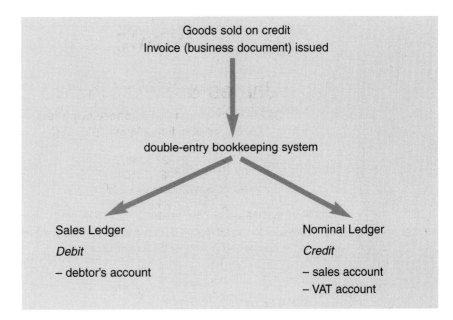

Goods sold on credit
Invoice (business document) issued

↓

double-entry bookkeeping system

Sales Ledger
Debit
– debtor's account

Nominal Ledger
Credit
– sales account
– VAT account

The Case Study which follows shows how credit sales transactions are recorded by means of double-entry bookkeeping in the nominal ledger and sales ledger. In this Case Study the invoice amounts are set out in a list.

CASE STUDY

JAMES & SONS LIMITED: DOUBLE-ENTRY FOR CREDIT SALES

situation

James & Sons Limited is a local office furniture and stationery supplier. It buys goods in bulk direct from the manufacturers and then sells smaller quantities on credit terms to businesses within the area.

The following are the credit sales transactions for January 2004:

6 January	Sold goods to Wyvern Traders for £354.90 + VAT £62.10, total invoice £417.00
8 January	Sold goods to A-Z Supplies Limited for £452.95 + VAT £79.26, total invoice £532.21
13 January	Sold goods to Doyle & Co for £154.29 + VAT £27.00, total invoice £181.29
16 January	Sold goods to Mereford Garden Centre for £485.38 + VAT £84.94, total invoice £570.32
21 January	Sold goods to A-Z Supplies Limited for £212.37 + VAT £37.16, total invoice £249.53
22 January	Sold goods to Doyle & Co for £876.23 + VAT £153.34, total invoice £1,029.57
27 January	Sold goods to Wyvern Traders for £643.14 + VAT £112.54, total invoice £755.68

The following accounts will be opened:

- nominal ledger
  - – sales
  - – Value Added Tax
- sales ledger
  - – Wyvern Traders
  - – A-Z Supplies Limited
  - – Doyle & Co
  - – Mereford Garden Centre

Note that the ledgers can be written up in any order – you can start with the nominal ledger or the sales ledger. It is best to be guided by the order of the transactions set out in the Student Activity or the Examination.

solution

These transactions are recorded in the nominal ledger and the sales ledger of the bookkeeping system of James & Sons Limited (assuming no opening balances – see next page) as follows:

NOMINAL LEDGER

Dr		Sales Account		Cr
2004	£	2004		£
		6 Jan	Wyvern Traders	354.90
		8 Jan	A-Z Supplies Ltd	452.95
		13 Jan	Doyle & Co	154.29
		16 Jan	Mereford Garden Centre	485.38
		21 Jan	A-Z Supplies Ltd	212.37
		22 Jan	Doyle & Co	876.23
		27 Jan	Wyvern Traders	643.14

Dr		Value Added Tax Account		Cr
2004	£	2004		£
		6 Jan	Wyvern Traders	62.10
		8 Jan	A-Z Supplies Ltd	79.26
		13 Jan	Doyle & Co	27.00
		16 Jan	Mereford Garden Centre	84.94
		21 Jan	A-Z Supplies Ltd	37.16
		22 Jan	Doyle & Co	153.34
		27 Jan	Wyvern Traders	112.54

SALES LEDGER

Dr			Wyvern Traders		Cr
2004		£	2004		£
6 Jan	Sales	417.00			
27 Jan	Sales	755.68			

Dr			A-Z Supplies Limited		Cr
2004		£	2004		£
8 Jan	Sales	532.21			
21 Jan	Sales	249.53			

Dr			Doyle & Co		Cr
2004		£	2004		£
13 Jan	Sales	181.29			
22 Jan	Sales	1,029.57			

Dr			Mereford Garden Centre		Cr
2004		£	2004		£
16 Jan	Sales	570.32			

Note to the accounts:

• the date of the transaction is used

• name of the other account involved in the double-entry is used in the details column as a description

• money amounts are recorded as follows:

  – amount of sales (excluding VAT) is credited to sales account

  – amount of VAT is credited to Value Added Tax account

  – invoice totals (ie sales, plus VAT) are debited to debtors' accounts

• double-entry accounts may be set out using different formats (see pages 47-48)

DEALING WITH OPENING BALANCES

In the Case Study above we assumed, for simplicity, that there were no balances (money amounts) recorded on any of the accounts at the beginning of the month. In practice, most accounts have an opening balance at the beginning of each week, month or year – if you have a bank account you will be familiar with the first line of your bank statement saying 'balance brought forward'. The same is true of the double-entry bookkeeping system (which, of course, banks use to keep their books). The opening balance is the total of the account to date (we will study the techniques of balancing accounts in Chapter 7). For the moment we need to know how to enter opening balances into accounts. Opening balances are described as being either 'debit' or 'credit', depending on which side of the account they appear. For example, with credit sales transactions, the accounts used have been sales account, VAT account and an account in the name of each debtor (customer); the balances on these are usually:

- Credit opening balances
  - sales account
  - VAT account
- Debit opening balances
  - debtors accounts

Note that VAT account usually has a credit balance but may, under certain circumstances, have a debit balance. Always follow the information given to you in the Student Activity or the Examination.

If the opening balances are given, then they need to be entered into the accounts – on the correct side – before recording any transactions. The usual way of entering them is to describe them as 'balance brought down' (or 'balance brought forward') – usually shortened to 'balance b/d' (or 'balance b/f') in the details column. These terms mean that the balance has been brought down from the previous month (or sometimes the previous week or year) and represent the total of the account to that date.

Suppose that in the Case Study on the previous few pages, we are told that the balances at 1 February 2004 are:

	DR	CR
	£	£
sales		3,179.26
Value Added Tax		556.34
Wyvern Traders	1,172.68	

These will be entered into the accounts as follows:

NOMINAL LEDGER

Dr		**Sales Account**		Cr
2004	£	2004		£
		1 Feb Balance b/d		3,179.26

Dr		**Value Added Tax Account**		Cr
2004	£	2004		£
		1 Feb Balance b/d		556.34

SALES LEDGER

Dr		Wyvern Traders		Cr
2004		£	2004	£
1 Feb	Balance b/d	1,172.68		

SALES RETURNS

Sales returns, in the case of goods, are items previously sold on credit being returned to the seller by its customers. This might be because items are incorrect or unsatisfactory. Where it is agreed to refund the customer for returned goods, the business document for sales returns is the **credit note** (see Chapter 2, pages 20 and 21) issued by the seller. Note that a credit note can also be issued if the product sold is a service and the service is found to be unsatisfactory or the buyer has been overcharged for the service.

The ledgers and accounts used for sales returns (also known as returns in) are:

nominal (or general) ledger
- *sales returns account* – to record the goods amount of credit notes issued
- *Value Added Tax account* – to record the VAT amounts of sales returns

sales ledger
- separate accounts for each debtor

Note that sales returns are kept in a separate account from sales – this enables the business to keep a check on the level of returns it is receiving.

DOUBLE-ENTRY BOOKKEEPING FOR SALES RETURNS

Credit notes or, more likely, copy credit notes, issued by a business are the business documents used to write up the double-entry accounts.

The bookkeeping entries to record sales returns are made from the credit note (or copy credit note) issued:

- *credit*: debtor's (customer's) account with the total amount of the credit note issued
- *debit*: sales returns account with the goods total of the credit note after trade discount (if any), but before VAT is added
- *debit*: Value Added Tax account with the VAT amount of the credit note

Note that, as VAT is involved, there are three entries to make, but the debits total will always equal the credit entry.

These entries are illustrated from the example credit note, on the next page.

Credit Note

James & Sons Limited

Office furniture and stationery suppliers
Wyvern Business Park, Wyvern WY1 8TQ

Tel 01627 338877
Fax 01627 338878
email info@james&sonsltd.co.uk
VAT Reg 471 3245 84

to Doyle & Co, Solicitors
Wyvern Chambers
Exchange Buildings
Wyvern
WY1 7TP

credit note no. 221

date 15 February 2004

quantity	description	unit price (£)	£ p
1	Office chair	85.15	85.15
			85.15
	Less trade discount		–
			85.15
	VAT at 17.5%		14.90
	Total credit		100.05

reason for credit:
Damaged in transit

Debit
sales returns account with the goods total of the credit note after trade discount (if any), but before VAT is added

Debit
VAT account with the VAT amount of the credit note

Credit
debtor's account with the total amount of the credit note

The logic behind the bookkeeping entries for sales returns is that the business has gained an asset in the form of the goods being returned, together with a reduction in the amount of VAT charged to the customer. At the same time the amount owed by the debtor is reduced. The accounting system for sales returns is summarised as follows:

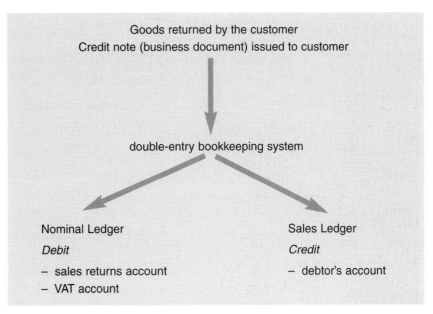

Goods returned by the customer
Credit note (business document) issued to customer

double-entry bookkeeping system

Nominal Ledger
Debit
– sales returns account
– VAT account

Sales Ledger
Credit
– debtor's account

The Case Study which follows shows how sales returns transactions are recorded by means of double-entry bookkeeping in the nominal ledger and sales ledger. As in the previous Case Study, the documents are listed rather than illustrated.

CASE STUDY

JAMES & SONS LIMITED: DOUBLE-ENTRY FOR SALES RETURNS

situation

James & Sons Limited (from the Case Study on page 39) has the following sales returns transactions for February 2004:

5 February	Goods returned by Doyle & Co for £85.15 + VAT £14.90, a credit note for £100.05 is issued
13 February	Goods returned by Wyvern Traders for £102.86 + VAT £18.00, a credit note for £120.86 is issued
19 February	Goods returned by Doyle & Co for £25.33 + VAT £4.43, a credit note for £29.76 is issued

At 1 February 2004, the relevant opening balances are as follows:

	DR	CR
sales returns	nil	nil
Value Added Tax		£556.34
Doyle & Co	£1,210.86	
Wyvern Traders	£1,172.68	

solution

These transactions are recorded in the nominal ledger and the sales ledger of the bookkeeping system of James & Sons Limited as follows:

NOMINAL LEDGER

Dr		Sales Returns Account		Cr
2004		£	2004	£
5 Feb	Doyle & Co	85.15		
13 Feb	Wyvern Traders	102.86		
19 Feb	Doyle & Co	25.33		

Dr		Value Added Tax Account		Cr
2004		£	2004	£
5 Feb	Doyle & Co	14.90	1 Feb Balance b/d	556.34
13 Feb	Wyvern Traders	18.00		
19 Feb	Doyle & Co	4.43		

SALES LEDGER

Dr		Doyle & Co		Cr
2004		£	2004	£
1 Feb	Balance b/d	1,210.86	5 Feb Sales returns	100.05
			19 Feb Sales returns	29.76

Dr		Wyvern Traders		Cr
2004		£	2004	£
1 Feb	Balance b/d	1,172.68	13 Feb Sales returns	120.86

Notes to the accounts:

- opening balances are entered as 'balance b/d' (or 'balance b/f')

- the name of the other account involved in the double-entry is used in the details column as a description

- money amounts are recorded as follows:

  - amount of sales returns (excluding VAT) is debited to sales returns account

  - amount of VAT is debited to Value Added Tax account

  - credit note totals (ie sales returns, plus VAT) are credited to debtors' accounts

- double-entry accounts may be set out using different formats (see next page)

OTHER FORMATS OF ACCOUNTS

The format of accounts that we have used in this chapter has a debit side and a credit side – often described as a 'T' account. To illustrate this format, the Value Added Tax account of James & Sons Limited (from the previous page) is shown as follows:

Dr			Value Added Tax Account			Cr
2004			£	2004		£
5 Feb	Doyle & Co		14.90	1 Feb Balance b/d		556.34
13 Feb	Wyvern Traders		18.00			
19 Feb	Doyle & Co		4.43			

Note that the account does not show a balance, and would need to be balanced (see Chapter 7).

Whilst the 'T' account format is very useful when learning the principles of bookkeeping, there are other versions of accounts which you may see, or wish to use.

two-column account

As its name implies, with this format there are two money columns – one for debit and one for credit. These money columns are set out on the right-hand side of the account. The Value Added Tax account, shown above, is set out in two-column format as follows:

Value Added Tax Account			
Date	**Details**	**Debit**	**Credit**
2004		£	£
1 Feb	Balance b/d		556.34
5 Feb	Doyle & Co	14.90	
13 Feb	Wyvern Traders	18.00	
19 Feb	Doyle & Co	4.43	

Note that the columns used are the same as a 'T' account – date, details, debit, credit – it is just that the money columns are set out on the right-hand side of the account. The account does not show a balance, and would need to be balanced (see Chapter 7).

three-column account

A common format of account has three money columns – debit, credit and balance. A familiar example of this type of account is a bank statement (see page 283). With a three-column format, the balance of the account is calculated after each transaction has been entered. Because of this, such a format is called a 'running balance account'.

Value Added Tax account (see the previous page), is set out in three-column format as follows:

Value Added Tax Account				
Date	Details	Debit	Credit	Balance
2004		£	£	£
1 Feb	Balance b/d		556.34	556.34 Cr
5 Feb	Doyle & Co	14.90		541.44 Cr
13 Feb	Wyvern Traders	18.00		523.44 Cr
19 Feb	Doyle & Co	4.43		519.01 Cr

With the three-column format, it is necessary to state after each transaction in the balance column whether the balance is debit (Dr) or credit (Cr).

CHAPTER SUMMARY

- Bookkeeping transactions are recorded in accounts using the double-entry system.
- The rules for debit and credit entries in accounts are:
  - debit entries: the account which gains value
  - credit entries: the account which gives value
- Division of the ledger divides the accounts contained in the double-entry system between three sections:
  - sales ledger: containing the accounts of debtors
  - purchases ledger: containing the accounts of creditors
  - nominal (or general) ledger: containing all other accounts
- Sales account is used to record the sale of goods or services in which the business trades.

- The sale of products on credit (credit sale) is recorded in the bookkeeping system as:
  - *debit* debtor's account with the total amount of the invoice
  - *credit* sales account with the goods total of the invoice
  - *credit* Value Added Tax account with the VAT amount of the invoice
- Sales returns are when products previously sold on credit are now being returned to the business by its customers.
- Sales returns are recorded in the bookkeeping system as:
  - *debit* sales returns account with the goods total of the credit note
  - *debit* Value Added Tax account with the VAT amount of the credit note
  - *credit* debtor's account with the total amount of the credit note

KEY TERMS

account	place where financial transactions are recorded
sales ledger	ledger section which contains the personal accounts of customers who have bought goods or services on credit and owe money – the debtors of the business
purchases ledger	ledger section which contains the personal accounts of suppliers who have sold goods or services to the business on credit and who are owed money – the creditors of the business
nominal (or general) ledger	ledger section which contains the remaining accounts of the business, such as income, expenses, assets, liabilities, bank, and capital (the investment of the owners)
sales	the sale to a customer of goods or services (products) in which the business trades
opening balances	totals of accounts at the beginning of each week, month or year – often described as 'balance brought down' (or 'balance brought forward')
sales returns	products previously sold by the business being returned by customers
'T' account	format of account with debit side on the left and credit side on the right
two-column account	format with two money columns – debit and credit – on right-hand side of the account
three-column account	format with three money columns – debit, credit and balance – on right-hand side of the account; described as a 'running balance account'

3.1* You are working for Wyvern Wholesalers and are required to enter the following credit sales transactions in the nominal ledger and the sales ledger of the bookkeeping system:

2004

2 Feb	Sold goods to Severn Supplies for £221.30 + VAT £38.72, total invoice £260.02
3 Feb	Sold goods to Malvern Stores for £173.35 + VAT £30.33, total invoice £203.68
6 Feb	Sold goods to A Cox Limited for £85.47 + VAT £14.95, total invoice £100.42
12 Feb	Sold goods to Roper & Sons for £196.33 + VAT £34.35, total invoice £230.68
16 Feb	Sold goods to A Cox Limited for £274.83 + VAT £48.09, total invoice £322.92
20 Feb	Sold goods to Malvern Stores for £362.13 + VAT £63.37, total invoice £425.50
24 Feb	Sold goods to Severn Supplies for £46.20 + VAT £8.08, total invoice £54.28
27 Feb	Sold goods to A Cox Limited for £169.30 + VAT £29.62, total invoice £198.92

Notes:

- None of the accounts has opening balances
- You need to open the following accounts:

  nominal ledger

  – sales

  – Value Added Tax

  sales ledger

  – Severn Supplies

  – Malvern Stores

  – A Cox Limited

  – Roper & Sons

Blank account layouts – which you can photocopy – are provided at the end of this chapter, either 'T' account format (page 70), or two-column format (page 71).

3.2* Wyvern Wholesalers (from the previous Activity) has the following sales returns transactions for March 2004:

3 Mar   Goods returned by A Cox Limited for £47.25 + VAT £8.26, a credit note for £55.51 is issued

11 Mar   Goods returned by Roper & Sons for £55.31 + VAT £9.67, a credit note for £64.98 is issued

16 Mar   Goods returned by A Cox Limited for £102.33 + VAT £17.90, a credit note for £120.23 is issued

You are to enter the sales returns transactions in the nominal ledger and the sales ledger of the bookkeeping system of Wyvern Wholesalers. You can either continue with the accounts already opened for Activity 3.1 (an account needs to be opened for sales returns), or you can use new accounts with opening balances at 1 March 2004 as follows:

	DR	CR
	£	£
sales returns	nil	nil
Value Added Tax		267.51
A Cox Limited	622.26	
Roper & Sons	230.68	

Blank account layouts – which you can photocopy – are provided at the end of this chapter, either 'T' account format (page 70), or two-column format (page 71).

3.3 You are the bookkeeper responsible for the sales ledger and nominal ledger of Alpha Furniture Limited. Open ledger accounts and enter the following balances at 1 April 2005:

	DR	CR
	£	£
sales		7,321.32
Value Added Tax		874.69
Wyvern Furniture Centre	338.96	
J & R Phillips Limited	701.15	
Thames Furnishing	1,204.13	

You are to enter the details of invoices sent to customers – on the next six pages – in the correct sales ledger accounts. Ensure that the nominal accounts are updated as appropriate.

Blank account layouts – which you can photocopy – are provided at the end of this chapter, either 'T' account format (page 70), or two-column format (page 71).

INVOICE

Alpha Furniture Limited

Unit 1, Ashtree Estate
Mereford MR3 7JG

Tel 01905 334482
Fax 01905 334493
VAT Reg 471 5732 84

to Wyvern Furniture Centre	**invoice no.**	2340
27 High Street		
Wyvern		
WV1 3PD	**date**	6 April 2005
	order no.	8460

quantity	description	unit price £	total net £	VAT rate %	VAT amount £	TOTAL £
3	Dining tables	120.00	360.00	17.5	63.00	423.00
12	Dining chairs	45.00	540.00	17.5	94.50	634.50
			900.00		157.50	1,057.50

terms: net 30 days

INVOICE

Alpha Furniture Limited

Unit 1, Ashtree Estate
Mereford MR3 7JG

Tel 01905 334482
Fax 01905 334493
VAT Reg 471 5732 84

to   J & R Phillips Limited
47-50 Merion Centre
Birmingham
B21 2LU

invoice no.   2341

date   12 April 2005

order no.   3364

quantity	description	unit price £	total net £	VAT rate %	VAT amount £	TOTAL £
3	3-seater settees	255.00	765.00	17.5	133.87	898.87
6	Side tables	33.50	201.00	17.5	35.17	236.17
			966.00		169.04	1,135.04

terms: net 30 days

INVOICE

Alpha Furniture Limited

Unit 1, Ashtree Estate
Mereford MR3 7JG

Tel 01905 334482
Fax 01905 334493
VAT Reg 471 5732 84

to   Thames Furnishing
Unit 18, River Court Centre
Reading
RG2 4LU

invoice no.   2342

date   16 April 2005

order no.   7384

quantity	description	unit price £	total net £	VAT rate %	VAT amount £	TOTAL £
4	Kitchen tables	35.00	140.00	17.5	24.50	164.50
16	Kitchen chairs	18.50	296.00	17.5	51.80	347.80
			436.00		76.30	512.30

terms: net 30 days

INVOICE

Alpha Furniture Limited

Unit 1, Ashtree Estate
Mereford MR3 7JG

Tel 01905 334482
Fax 01905 334493
VAT Reg 471 5732 84

to	Wyvern Furniture Centre	**invoice no.**	2343
	27 High Street		
	Wyvern		
	WV1 3PD	**date**	20 April 2005
		order no.	2214

quantity	description	unit price £	total net £	VAT rate %	VAT amount £	TOTAL £
2	2-seater settees	199.00	398.00	17.5	69.65	467.65
6	Armchairs	99.00	594.00	17.5	103.95	697.95
			992.00		173.60	1,165.60

terms: net 30 days

INVOICE

Alpha Furniture Limited

Unit 1, Ashtree Estate
Mereford MR3 7JG

Tel 01905 334482
Fax 01905 334493
VAT Reg 471 5732 84

to	Thames Furnishing		

to Thames Furnishing
Unit 18, River Court Centre
Reading
RG2 4LU

invoice no. 2344

date 22 April 2005

order no. 7404

quantity	description	unit price £	total net £	VAT rate %	VAT amount £	TOTAL £
3	2-seater settees	199.00	597.00	17.5	104.47	701.47
4	Side tables	33.50	134.00	17.5	23.45	157.45
			731.00		127.92	858.92

terms: net 30 days

INVOICE

Alpha Furniture Limited

Unit 1, Ashtree Estate
Mereford MR3 7JG

Tel 01905 334482
Fax 01905 334493
VAT Reg 471 5732 84

to J & R Phillips Limited 47-50 Merion Centre Birmingham B21 2LU	**invoice no.** 2345 **date** 26 April 2005 **order no.** 3391

quantity	description	unit price £	total net £	VAT rate %	VAT amount £	TOTAL £
2	Kitchen tables	35.00	70.00	17.5	12.25	82.25
6	Kitchen chairs	18.50	111.00	17.5	19.42	130.42
			181.00		31.67	212.67

terms: net 30 days

3.4 Alpha Furniture Limited (from the previous Activity) sends the credit notes shown on the next two pages to its customers. You are to enter the details from the credit notes in the correct sales ledger accounts. Ensure that the nominal accounts are updated as appropriate.

Note: you can either continue with the accounts already opened for Activity 3.3 (an account needs to be opened for sales returns), or you can use new accounts with opening balances at 1 May 2005 as follows:

	DR	CR
	£	£
sales returns	nil	nil
Value Added Tax		1,610.72
Wyvern Furniture Centre	2,562.06	
J & R Phillips Limited	2,048.86	

Blank account layouts – which you can photocopy – are provided at the end of this chapter, either 'T' account format (page 70), or two-column format (page 71).

CREDIT NOTE

Alpha Furniture Limited

Unit 1, Ashtree Estate
Mereford MR3 7JG

Tel 01905 334482
Fax 01905 334493
VAT Reg 471 5732 84

to   Wyvern Furniture Centre
27 High Street
Wyvern
WV1 3PD

credit note no.   261

date   4 May 2005

quantity	description	unit price (£)	£ p
1	Armchair	99.00	99.00
			99.00
		VAT at 17.5%	17.32
		Total credit	116.32

reason for credit:
Damaged in transit

CREDIT NOTE

Alpha Furniture Limited

Unit 1, Ashtree Estate
Mereford MR3 7JG

Tel 01905 334482
Fax 01905 334493
VAT Reg 471 5732 84

to J & R Phillips Limited 47-50 Merion Centre Birmingham B21 2LU	**credit note no.** 262 **date** 9 May 2005

quantity	description	unit price (£)	£ p
1	Side table	33.50	33.50
			33.50
		VAT at 17.5%	5.86
		Total credit	39.36

reason for credit:
Faulty hinge

3.5   You are the bookkeeper responsible for the sales ledger and nominal ledger of Cradley Computer Supplies.

(a)   Open ledger accounts and enter the following balances at 1 October 2006:

	DR	CR
	£	£
sales		55,107.22
sales returns	3,409.86	
Value Added Tax		2,315.22
Acorn Office Equipment	1,029.77	
AP Transport Limited	765.42	
Baxter Supermarkets plc	3,971.54	

(b)   Enter the details of invoices sent to customers on pages 62 to 67 in the correct sales ledger accounts. Ensure that nominal accounts are updated as appropriate.

(c)   Enter the details from credit notes sent to customers on pages 68 to 69 in the correct sales ledger accounts. Ensure that nominal accounts are updated as appropriate.

Blank account layouts – which you can photocopy – are provided at the end of this chapter, either 'T' account format (page 70), or two-column format (page 71).

Tutorial note: the invoices and credit notes in this Activity incorporate trade discount – the goods total of each document is the amount shown after trade discount has been deducted.

INVOICE

Cradley Computer Supplies

Mereford Drive
Cradley MR7 8ID

Tel 01745 553247
Fax 01745 553286
VAT Reg 497 3214 86

to	Acorn Office Equipment	**invoice no.**	2740
	Church Road		
	Mereford		
	MR1 2TP	**date**	3 October 2006
		order no.	4528

quantity	description	cat. no.	unit price (£)	£
4	Printers	P760	55.20	220.80
6	Scanners	S48	47.90	287.40
				508.20
		Less trade discount 15%		76.23
				431.97
		VAT at 17.5%		75.59
				507.56

terms: net monthly

INVOICE

Cradley Computer Supplies

Mereford Drive
Cradley MR7 8ID

Tel 01745 553247
Fax 01745 553286
VAT Reg 497 3214 86

to AP Transport Limited
Unit 4, Hop Pole Estate
Cradley
MR7 5JD

invoice no. 2741

date 9 October 2006

order no. 6391

quantity	description	cat. no.	unit price (£)	£
2	Computers	X100	799.99	1,599.98
2	Printers	P760	55.20	110.40
				1,710.38
		Less trade discount 10%		171.03
				1,539.35
		VAT at 17.5%		269.38
				1,808.73

terms: net monthly

INVOICE

Cradley Computer Supplies

Mereford Drive
Cradley MR7 8ID

Tel 01745 553247
Fax 01745 553286
VAT Reg 497 3214 86

to Baxter Supermarkets plc	**invoice no.** 2742
Saint Rose Lane	
Waitbury	
WY2 4QT	**date** 17 October 2006
	order no. 2232

quantity	description	cat. no.	unit price (£)	£
10	Computers	X200	899.99	8,999.90
15	Laser printers	LP10	289.50	4,342.50
10	Scanners	S48	47.90	479.00
				13,821.40
		Less trade discount 20%		2,764.28
				11,057.12
		VAT at 17.5%		1,934.99
				12,992.11

terms: net monthly

INVOICE

Cradley Computer Supplies

Mereford Drive
Cradley MR7 8ID

Tel 01745 553247
Fax 01745 553286
VAT Reg 497 3214 86

to Acorn Office Equipment
Church Road
Mereford
MR1 2TP

invoice no. 2743

date 20 October 2006

order no. 7684

quantity	description	cat. no.	unit price (£)	£
2	Computers	X100	799.99	1,599.98
1	Laser printer	LP10	289.50	289.50
				1,889.48
	Less trade discount 15%			283.42
				1,606.06
	VAT at 17.5%			281.06
				1,887.12

terms: net monthly

INVOICE

Cradley Computer Supplies

Mereford Drive
Cradley MR7 8ID

Tel 01745 553247
Fax 01745 553286
VAT Reg 497 3214 86

to	Baxter Supermarkets plc Saint Rose Lane Waitbury WY2 4QT	**invoice no.**	2744
		date	24 October 2006
		order no.	2410

quantity	description	cat. no.	unit price (£)	£
5	Computers	X200	899.99	4,499.95
6	Scanners	S48	47.90	287.40

	4,787.35
Less trade discount 20%	957.47
	3,829.88
VAT at 17.5%	670.22
	4,500.10

terms: net monthly

INVOICE

Cradley Computer Supplies

Mereford Drive
Cradley MR7 8ID

Tel 01745 553247
Fax 01745 553286
VAT Reg 497 3214 86

to AP Transport Limited
Unit 4, Hop Pole Estate
Cradley
MR7 5JD

invoice no. 2745

date 29 October 2006

order no. 6402

quantity	description	cat. no.	unit price (£)	£
2	Computers	X100	799.99	1,599.98
2	Scanners	S48	47.90	95.80

	£
	1,695.78
Less trade discount 10%	169.57
	1,526.21
VAT at 17.5%	267.08
	1,793.29

terms: net monthly

CREDIT NOTE

Cradley Computer Supplies

Mereford Drive
Cradley MR7 8ID

Tel 01745 553247
Fax 01745 553286
VAT Reg 497 3214 86

to   Acorn Office Equipment   **credit note no.**   141
Church Road
Mereford
MR1 2TP   **date**   6 October 2006

quantity	description	unit price (£)	£ p
1	Scanner	47.90	47.90

	47.90
Less trade discount 15%	7.18
	40.72
VAT at 17.5%	7.12
Total credit	47.84

reason for credit:
Faulty goods

CREDIT NOTE

Cradley Computer Supplies

Mereford Drive
Cradley MR7 8ID

Tel 01745 553247
Fax 01745 553286
VAT Reg 497 3214 86

to Baxter Supermarkets plc Saint Rose Lane Waitbury WY2 4QT	**credit note no.** 142 **date**	 20 October 2006

quantity	description	unit price (£)	£ p
1	Laser printer	289.50	289.50
			289.50
	Less trade discount 20%		57.90
			231.60
	VAT at 17.5%		40.53
	Total credit		272.13

reason for credit:
Damaged in transit

'T' account format

Account

Date	Details	£	p	Date	Details	£	p

Account

Date	Details	£	p	Date	Details	£	p

two-column account format

		Account			
Date	**Details**	**£**	**p**	**£**	**p**

		Account			
Date	**Details**	**£**	**p**	**£**	**p**

4 PAYMENTS FROM DEBTORS

this chapter covers . . .

In this chapter we look at the way in which payments received from debtors are recorded in the double-entry bookkeeping.

Bank account is an account in the double-entry system which is used to record receipts and payments made through the bank – the money side of bookkeeping transactions. Note that it is an account in the double-entry system – not to be confused with the records held at the bank branch where the business keeps its account.

In this chapter we see how bank account is used to record payments received from debtors in the form of cheques. We focus on the receipts (debit) side of bank account and see how the opposite (credit) entry is recorded in debtors' accounts.

OCR LEARNING OUTCOMES

unit 1: POSTING TO ACCOUNTS
Assessment objectives

2　**Maintain Sales Ledger**

　(d) Enter payments into correct account

3　**Maintain Nominal Ledger**

　(a) Identify and open correct ledger account

　(b) Enter transactions into correct account

RECEIVING PAYMENT FROM DEBTORS

In the previous chapter we recorded financial transactions for credit sales and sales returns in the bookkeeping system. The next step in the process is that the seller requests payment of the amount due. This is usually done by sending the debtor a statement of account (illustrated on page 22), which is a 'reminder' document setting out details of invoices and credit notes issued to the customer, and the amount owed for the period (eg month).

When the debtor makes payment, it will usually be by cheque, or other bank transfer (such as BACS). Cheques have already been described on page 23, while BACS transfers are discussed fully in Chapter 13, later in this book.

Payments received from debtors must be checked against documentation – such as the remittance advice (illustrated on page 24). Once payments have been checked and found to be in order they are recorded in the bookkeeping system using

- bank account, in the nominal ledger
- debtor's account, in the sales ledger

As bank account is an account which has not been used so far, we will take a detailed look at it before recording any bookkeeping transactions.

USING BANK ACCOUNT

Bank account is the double-entry bookkeeping account which records receipts and payments through the bank. It is held in the nominal ledger and uses the account format that we have seen earlier. In 'T' account format, bank account is set out as follows:

Dr			Bank Account		Cr
Date	**Details**	**£**	**Date**	**Details**	**£**

Other account formats – such as the two-column and three-column accounts – can be used. This chapter uses the 'T' account format and, as we did in the previous chapter, we will simplify the layout by omitting the column divisions to leave a single vertical line dividing the debit and credit sides.

Bank account is used to record the money side of bookkeeping transactions:

- all receipts by cheque and other bank transfers
- all payments by cheque and other bank transfers

Receipts are recorded on the debit side of bank account – this follows the principle that we saw in the previous chapter of the account gaining value when money is received. Payments are recorded on the credit side of bank account, ie the account gives value when money is paid out.

It is easy to make the correct entries in bank account – just think of the left-hand side of the account as being 'money in' and the right-hand side as being 'money out'. This chapter focuses on payments received from debtors, so we will be using the receipts (debit) side of bank account, and will also be recording the opposite (credit) entry in debtors' accounts.

Be careful not to confuse the bank account – which is the firm's *own* record of its bank transactions – with the records held at the bank branch where the business keeps its account.

Later in the book (Chapter 12) we will see how bank account can be incorporated into a firm's cash book, which brings together in one account bank transactions and cash transactions.

OPENING BALANCES FOR BANK ACCOUNT

You will often be required to enter an opening balance in bank account at the start of a month, just as you have entered opening balances in accounts in the previous chapter. Look at the following bank account where the balance at 1 March 2004 has been entered already:

Dr			Bank Account		Cr
2004		£	2004		£
1 Mar	Balance b/d	821.47			

This balance is recorded on the debit side – what do you think this means? A debit balance on bank account (remember that bank account is the firm's own record of its bank transactions) means that the business has money in the bank of £821.47, ie it has an asset. Don't be confused by the fact that it is a debit balance – this represents assets (think of debtors who owe money to the business). What the account tells us is that the bank owes £821.47 to this business, which can be drawn from the bank in cash or by cheque.

What about the following balance?

Dr			Bank Account		Cr
2004		£	2004		£
			1 Apr	Balance b/d	522.86

This is a credit balance which means that the business is overdrawn by £522.86. The balance is credit in the firm's own record of its bank transactions, ie it has a liability. As we will see in the next chapter, creditors are people that the business owes money to.

The important points to remember are:

• the balance of bank account can be either debit or credit (so check before you enter the balance!)

• a debit balance is an asset, and means that the business has money in the bank

• a credit balance is a liability, and means that the business is overdrawn at the bank

There is more on the use of bank account in Chapter 12, later in the book.

RECORDING PAYMENTS FROM DEBTORS

When customers (debtors) pay for goods or services that have been sold to them on credit, the payment is usually made by cheque or BACS transfer (described fully in Chapter 13, later in this book). The double-entry bookkeeping entries for payments received from debtors are:

nominal (or general) ledger

– *debit* bank account with the amount of the payment

sales ledger

– *credit* debtor's account with the amount of the payment

These are illustrated from the example cheque – received by James & Sons Limited from a debtor – which is shown on the next page.

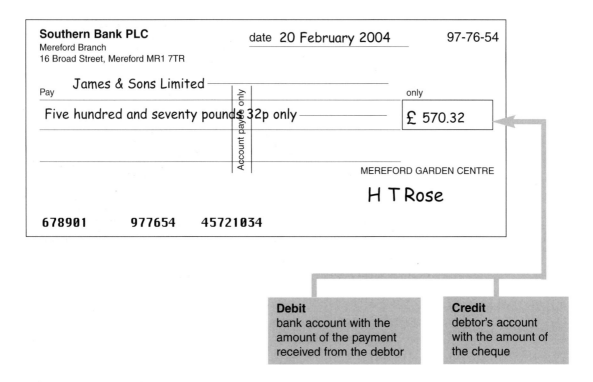

The details to be recorded in nominal ledger and sales ledger for the payment transaction are:

- **date** – often using the date of the cheque

- **narrative** – the name of the other account involved (eg in bank account the name of the debtor making the payment)

- **reference number** – not always required, this could be the invoice number being paid by the debtor

- **amount** of the cheque

On a practical note, take care to enter payments from debtors in the correct debtor's account in sales ledger – Jane Smith will not be too pleased if you, as the bookkeeper, credit in error the the debtor's account of John Smith with the payment that she has sent to you.

Always check that the payment received from a debtor is recorded in the correct account and on the credit side.

The accounting system for recording payments received from debtors is summarised at the top of the next page.

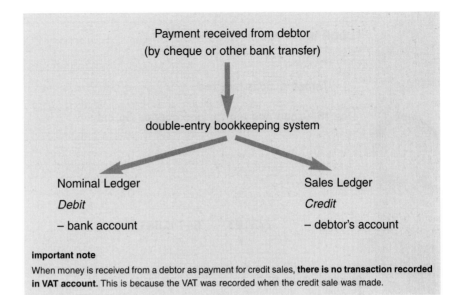

Payment received from debtor
(by cheque or other bank transfer)

↓

double-entry bookkeeping system

Nominal Ledger	Sales Ledger
Debit	*Credit*
– bank account	– debtor's account

important note

When money is received from a debtor as payment for credit sales, **there is no transaction recorded in VAT account.** This is because the VAT was recorded when the credit sale was made.

We will now see how these principles are put into practice in the Case Study which follows.

CASE STUDY

JAMES & SONS LIMITED: PAYMENTS RECEIVED FROM DEBTORS

situation

James & Sons Limited (see Case Study in Chapter 3, pages 39 and 45) has received the following payments from debtors. They are to be entered into the correct sales ledger accounts. The nominal ledger is to be updated as appropriate.

Southern Bank PLC
Mereford Branch
16 Broad Street, Mereford MR1 7TR

date 20 February 2004   97-76-54

Pay   James & Sons Limited ——————————————— only

Five hundred and seventy pounds 32p only ——————   £ 570.32

Account payee only

MEREFORD GARDEN CENTRE

H T Rose

678901   977654   45721034

TUDOR BANK PLC
Market Place
Crewe CW1 2TG

date 24 February 2004

72-31-03

Pay   James & Sons Limited ————————————————— only

One thousand and eighty-one pounds 5p only ————————   £ 1,081.05

DOYLE & CO

Arthur Doyle

745621   723103   84735684

Regency Bank PLC
Bridge Street
Nantwich CW3 4RF

date 26 February 2004

42-21-03

Pay   James & Sons Limited ————————————————— only

Five hundred pounds only ————————————————   £ 500.00

WYVERN TRADERS

W Wye   S Severn

875934   422103   24983564

---

solution

In nominal ledger, the cheques received are listed on the debit side of bank account, as follows:

NOMINAL LEDGER

Dr		Bank Account			Cr
2004			£	2004	£
20 Feb	Mereford Garden Centre		570.32		
24 Feb	Doyle & Co		1,081.05		
26 Feb	Wyvern Traders		500.00		

Notes to the account:

- the date of the cheque is used in the date column of bank account
- the name of the debtor is shown in the details column
- the amount of the cheque is recorded in the money column

The debit side of bank account is used to record payments received because the business is gaining an asset of money in the bank account. Remember that the bank account shown above is the firm's own record of how much it has in its bank account. The cheques will now be taken, or sent, to the bank and paid into the firm's account (see Chapter 13). In sales ledger the individual account of each debtor who has made payment is credited, as follows (balances b/d and sales returns transactions are taken from the Case Studies in Chapter 3 – see pages 39 and 45):

SALES LEDGER

Dr			**Mereford Garden Centre**			Cr
2004		£	2004			£
1 Feb	Balance b/d	570.32	20 Feb	Bank		570.32

Dr			**Doyle & Co**			Cr
2004		£	2004			£
1 Feb	Balance b/d	1,210.86	5 Feb	Sales returns		100.05
			19 Feb	Sales returns		29.76
			24 Feb	Bank		1,081.05

Dr			**Wyvern Traders**			Cr
2004		£	2004			£
1 Feb	Balance b/d	1,172.68	13 Feb	Sales returns		120.86
			26 Feb	Bank		500.00

Notes to the accounts:

- the credit side of debtors' accounts is used to record payments received; this is because the amounts owing by debtors (assets) are reduced by the payment
- the date of the cheque is used in the date column
- 'bank' is shown in the details column
- the amount of the cheque is recorded in the money column
- the double-entry accounts may be set out using different formats (see pages 47-48)

You may have noticed that the account of Mereford Garden Centre now has the same amount on both the debit and credit sides. This means that the account has a 'nil' balance, ie Mereford Garden Centre does not owe James & Sons Limited any more money – the balance brought down on 1 February has been paid for in full. We shall be looking in detail at balancing accounts in Chapter 7: for the moment you might like to add up the debit and credit sides of the other two debtors' accounts to see what has happened.

OTHER BANK TRANSFERS

This chapter has been concerned with payments from debtors in the form of cheques. There are a number of other ways for debtors to make payments by transfer through the banking system – most commonly by BACS transfers.

BACS stands for Bankers Automated Clearing Services, which is a computer transfer payment system owned by the banks. The system is described in detail in Chapter 13 (pages 286 and 289). In summary, instead of sending a cheque in payment, debtors set up a payment system with their bank and then tell the bank the amount to be paid and the date of the payment. The transfer is then made between the bank's computers, with the payment going direct from account to account.

The debtor sends an advice of the BACS payment to the person being paid, as illustrated below.

BACS REMITTANCE ADVICE			FROM: A-Z Supplies Limited The Broadway Porthperran TR8 9UP
TO James & Sons Limited Wyvern Business Park, Wyvern, WY1 8TQ			28 02 04
Your ref	Our ref		Amount
12345	67890	BACS TRANSFER	781.74
			TOTAL 781.74

THIS HAS BEEN PAID BY BACS CREDIT TRANSFER DIRECTLY INTO YOUR BANK ACCOUNT AT NATIONAL BANK NO 47369784 SORT CODE 89 18 34

This shows that A-Z Supplies Limited, a debtor, has made a payment to James & Sons Limited by BACS transfer for £781.74. The amount will be received direct by James & Sons Limited's bank. After checking carefully the amount of the payment, it is entered into the double-entry bookkeeping system of James & Sons Limited in the same way as receiving payment from debtors by cheque:

– *debit* bank account with the amount of the BACS transfer

– *credit* debtor's account

Continuing with bank account from the Case Study on page 77, the payment from A-Z Supplies Limited is recorded as follows:

NOMINAL LEDGER

Dr	Bank Account			Cr
2004		£	2004	£
20 Feb Mereford Garden Centre		570.32		
24 Feb Doyle & Co		1,081.05		
26 Feb Wyvern Traders		500.00		
28 Feb A-Z Supplies Limited		781.74		

SALES LEDGER

Dr	A-Z Supplies Limited			Cr
2004		£	2004	£
1 Feb Balance b/d		781.74	28 Feb Bank	781.74

CHAPTER SUMMARY

- Bank account, in the nominal ledger, is used to record:
  - all receipts by cheque and other bank transfers
  - all payments by cheque and other bank transfers
- In bank account, receipts are recorded on the debit side (which gains value), payments are recorded on the credit side (which gives value)
- Payments from debtors are recorded in the accounts as:
  - *debit* bank account with the amount of the payment
  - *credit* debtor's account with the amount of the payment
- Details to be recorded in the nominal ledger and sales ledger include:
  - date of the cheque
  - narrative
  - reference number (if any)
  - the amount of the cheque

- Take care to enter payments from debtors in the correct debtor's account in the sales ledger.
- Other ways of making payment through the banking system include BACS transfers.

KEY TERMS

bank account	double-entry bookkeeping account used to record receipts and payments through the bank
receipts	money received, recorded on the debit side of bank account
payments	money paid out, recorded on the credit side of bank account
debit side of bank account	records payments received (bank account gains value)
credit side of bank account	records payments made (bank account gives value)
BACS	Bankers Automated Clearing Services, a computer transfer system owned by the banks

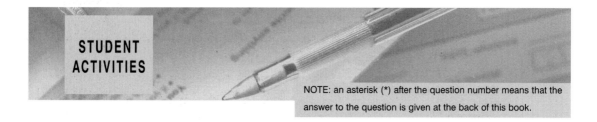

STUDENT ACTIVITIES

NOTE: an asterisk (*) after the question number means that the answer to the question is given at the back of this book.

4.1* The following debtors' accounts are taken from the sales ledger of Wyvern Wholesalers:

SALES LEDGER

Dr			Severn Supplies		Cr
2004		£	2004		£
1 Mar	Balance b/d	314.30			

Dr			A Cox Limited		Cr
2004		£	2004		£
1 Mar	Balance b/d	622.26	3 Mar	Sales returns	55.51
			16 Mar	Sales returns	120.23

Dr			Roper & Sons		Cr
2004		£	2004		£
1 Mar	Balance b/d	230.68	11 Mar	Sales returns	64.98

Copy out these accounts in either 'T' account format (as above) or in two-column format. Blank account layouts – which you can photocopy – are provided on pages 88 and 89.

Open a bank account in nominal ledger with a balance of £1,022.48 debit at 1 March 2004. The following payments have been received from debtors. They are to be entered in the correct sales ledger accounts. The nominal ledger is to be updated as appropriate.

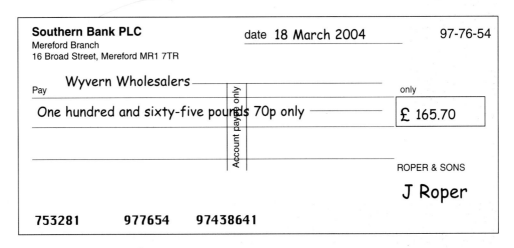

Southern Bank PLC
Mereford Branch
16 Broad Street, Mereford MR1 7TR

date 18 March 2004   97-76-54

Pay   Wyvern Wholesalers   only

One hundred and sixty-five pounds 70p only   £ 165.70

Account payee only

ROPER & SONS

J Roper

753281   977654   97438641

TUDOR BANK PLC
Market Place
Crewe CW1 2TG

date 24 March 2004   72-31-03

Pay   Wyvern Wholesalers   only

Three hundred pounds only   £ 300.00

Account payee only

A COX LIMITED

Andrew Cox

246812   723103   49635714

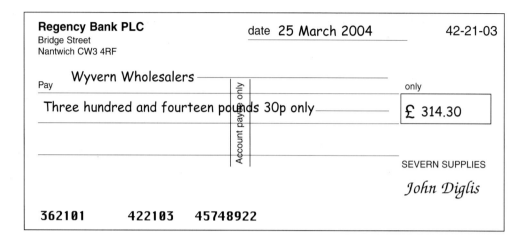

4.2 The following debtors' accounts are taken from the sales ledger of Alpha Furniture Limited:

SALES LEDGER

Dr		**Wyvern Furniture Centre**			Cr
2005		£	2005		£
1 May	Balance b/d	2,562.06	4 May	Sales returns	116.32

Dr		**J & R Phillips Limited**			Cr
2005		£	2005		£
1 May	Balance b/d	2,048.86	9 May	Sales returns	39.36

Dr		**Thames Furnishing**			Cr
2005		£	2005		£
1 May	Balance b/d	2,575.35			

Copy out these accounts in either 'T' account format (as above) or in two-column format. Blank account layouts – which you can photocopy – are provided on pages 88 and 89.

Open a bank account in nominal ledger with a balance of £2,364.97 debit at 1 May 2005. The following payments have been received from debtors. They are to be entered in the correct sales ledger accounts. The nominal ledger is to be updated as appropriate.

Southern Bank PLC
Wyvern Branch
10 Bridge Street, Wyvern WY1 4JB

date 6 May 2005

97-48-20

Pay Alpha Furniture Limited

Three hundred and thirty-eight pounds 96p only

only

£ 338.96

Account payee only

WYVERN FURNITURE CENTRE

J Carver

547123   974820   24679384

TUDOR BANK PLC
Market Place
Reading RG1 3BT

date 15 May 2005

72-26-19

Pay Alpha Furniture Limited

Two thousand, five hundred and seventy-five pounds

35p only

only

£ 2,575.35

Account payee only

THAMES FURNISHING

A Khan

462147   722619   98734521

Regency Bank PLC
Bridge Street
Nantwich CW3 4RF

date 22 May 2005

42-21-03

Pay Alpha Furniture Limited

Seven hundred and one pounds 15p only

only

£ 701.15

Account payee only

J & R PHILLIPS LTD

R Phillips

832246   422103   49732761

4.3   The following debtors' accounts are taken from the sales ledger of Cradley Computer Supplies:

SALES LEDGER

Dr		**Acorn Office Equipment**		Cr
2006		£	2006	£
1 Nov	Balance b/d	3,376.61		

Dr		**AP Transport Limited**		Cr
2006		£	2006	£
1 Nov	Balance b/d	4,367.44		

Dr		**Baxter Supermarkets plc**		Cr
2006		£	2006	£
1 Nov	Balance b/d	21,191.62		

Copy out these accounts in either 'T' account format (as above) or in two-column format. Blank account layouts – which you can photocopy – are provided on pages 88 and 89.

Open a bank account in nominal ledger with a balance of £4,326.33 credit at 1 November 2006. The following payments have been received from debtors. They are to be entered in the correct sales ledger accounts. The nominal ledger is to be updated as appropriate.

Southern Bank PLC
Mereford Branch
16 Broad Street, Mereford MR1 7TR

date 6 November 2006   97-76-54

Pay   *Cradley Computer Supplies*   only

One thousand and twenty-nine pounds 77p only   £ 1,029.77

Account payee only

ACORN OFFICE EQUIPMENT

Tom Oak

721342   977654   56459739

TUDOR BANK PLC
Market Place
Crewe CW1 2TG

date 15 November 2006

72-31-03

Pay   _Cradley Computer Supplies_

Ten thousand pounds only

only

£ 10,000.00

Account payee only

BAXTER SUPERMARKETS PLC

J Baxter   _T Baxter_

684951   723103   20043478

Regency Bank PLC
Bridge Street
Nantwich CW3 4RF

date 24 November 2006

42-21-03

Pay   _Cradley Computer Supplies_

Seven hundred and sixty-five pounds 42p only

only

£ 765.42

Account payee only

AP TRANSPORT LIMITED

A Patel

762391   422103   74879521

'T' account format

Account

Date	Details	£	p	Date	Details	£	p

Account

Date	Details	£	p	Date	Details	£	p

two-column account format

Date	Details	£	p	£	p
	— Account				

Date	Details	£	p	£	p
	— Account				

5 ACCOUNTS AND LEDGERS FOR CREDIT PURCHASES AND RETURNS

this chapter covers . . .

In Chapters 3 and 4 we looked at how the double-entry bookkeeping transactions are made for credit sales to customers, sales returns, and payments received from debtors.

In this chapter we focus on the 'other side of the coin' – that is a business buying goods from suppliers. The business documents are purchases invoices and credit notes received (described in Chapter 2). These are the main documents for credit purchases and purchases returns.

They are recorded in the accounts system, which is used to keep up-to-date with the financial transactions of the business.

We will be following the principles of double-entry bookkeeping that we have seen in the previous two chapters.

OCR LEARNING OUTCOMES

unit 1: POSTING TO ACCOUNTS
Assessment objectives

1   *Maintain Purchase Ledger*

(a) Identify and open correct ledger

(b) Enter invoice into correct account

(c) Enter returns into correct account

3   *Maintain Nominal Ledger*

(a) Identify and open correct ledger account

(b) Enter transactions into correct account

A RECAP ON THE RULES OF DOUBLE-ENTRY

This chapter focuses on the accounts system for credit purchases and purchases returns. Before we look at the double-entry transactions, it is worth recapping on the rules for debits and credits. Remember that assets are shown on the debit side of accounts, and liabilities are shown on the credit side. The four basic rules are:

- to increase an asset, make an entry on the debit side
- to decrease an asset, make an entry on the credit side
- to increase a liability, make an entry on the credit side
- to decrease a liability, make an entry on the debit side

To summarise:

debit entry	credit entry
• increase an asset	• decrease an asset
• decrease a liability	• increase a liability

Example 1

Bought goods on credit from Osborne Fashion Limited for £1,305.00*

The double-entry bookkeeping for this transaction is:

debit: purchases account £1,305.00

credit: Osborne Fashion Limited £1,305.00

The logic behind this is that the stock of goods held by a business for resale is an asset; the purchase of the goods increases the asset of stock and is recorded on the debit side of purchases account. At the same time, the business owes Osborne Fashion Limited £1,305.00 and this is recorded on the credit side of Osborne Fashion's account, ie the business has a liability in the form of a creditor.

Example 2

Goods returned to Osborne Fashion Limited for £66.00*

The double-entry bookkeeping for this transaction is:

debit: Osborne Fashion Limited £66.00

credit: purchases returns account £66.00

* for the moment we will ignore VAT on these transactions

Here the asset of stock of goods held by the business decreases because some goods have been returned. At the same time, the business owes Osborne Fashion less because of the returned goods, ie the liability in the form of a creditor is decreased.

Tutorial note

We will be dealing with the bookkeeping aspects of credit purchases and purchases returns – including VAT – very soon. Nevertheless, it is a good starting point to think in terms of the changes to assets and liabilities for purchases and returns transactions.

CREDIT PURCHASES – THE ACCOUNTS AND LEDGERS

In bookkeeping the term 'purchases' has a specific meaning:

purchases = the purchase from a supplier of goods or services in which the business trades.

For example, an office stationery business buying goods from suppliers, which it intends to sell to its customers, records the transaction in *purchases account*. The term *credit purchases* means that payment for the products bought will be made to the supplier at a later date. When a business buys products for use by the business rather than for resale – for example, the office stationery business buys a van so that it can make deliveries to customers – this 'purchase' is treated differently in the accounts. Instead of using purchases account, this transaction will be recorded in a separate account for motor vehicles – see pages 133-134.

In this chapter we concern ourselves with recording purchases and purchases returns transactions relating to the products in which the business trades.

As we have already seen in Chapter 3, most accounts systems use the ledger system to organise the accounts. For credit purchases transactions, the following ledgers and accounts are used:

nominal (or general ledger)

- purchases account – to record the price charged for products purchased
- Value Added Tax account – to record the VAT amounts of purchases

purchases ledger

- separate accounts for each *creditor* – to record the amount owed to each supplier (this will be the price of the goods or service plus VAT – see the invoice on page 94)

DOUBLE-ENTRY BOOKKEEPING FOR CREDIT PURCHASES

Invoices (see Chapter 2, pages 16 and 17) received from suppliers who sell products on credit terms are the documents used to write up the double-entry accounts. From the buyer's viewpoint, the supplier who allows settlement of the account at a later date is a creditor.

The bookkeeping entries to record credit purchases are made from the purchases invoice received:

– *debit:* purchases account with the goods total of the invoice after trade discount (if any), but before VAT is added

– *debit:* Value Added Tax account with the VAT amount of the invoice

– *credit:* creditor's (supplier's) account with the total amount of the invoice, ie the price of the product plus VAT

These entries are illustrated from the example invoice, on the next page.

The logic behind the bookkeeping entries for credit purchases is that the business has gained an asset in the form of a stock of goods for resale – the goods total of the invoice is debited to purchases account, while the VAT amount is debited to VAT account. At the same time the business has gained a liability in the form of a creditor's account, ie the business owes the supplier an amount of money (which will be paid in due course).

As we have seen before, with VAT charged on invoices, it does mean that there are three entries for each invoice.

The accounting system for credit purchases is summarised as follows:

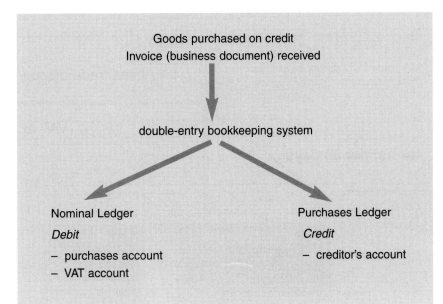

Goods purchased on credit
Invoice (business document) received

double-entry bookkeeping system

Nominal Ledger

Debit

– purchases account
– VAT account

Purchases Ledger

Credit

– creditor's account

INVOICE

Osborne Fashion Limited

Unit 16 Millyard Estate
Fencote Road, Worcester WR2 6HY
Tel 01905 334482
Fax 01905 334493
email info@osbornefashion.co.uk
VAT Reg 987 544 21

to Arona Limited 18-24 Friar Street Wyvern WY1 8TQ	**invoice no.** 14512 **date** 8 January 2004 **order no.** 4107

quantity	description	cat. no.	unit price (£)	£
50	Dresses	D45	22.00	1,100.00
10	Jackets	J65	35.00	350.00

	1,450.00
Less trade discount 10%	145.00
	1,305.00
VAT at 17.5%	228.37
	1,533.37

terms: net 30 days

Debit
purchases account with
goods total of invoice after
trade discount (if any), but
before VAT is added

Debit
VAT account
with the VAT
amount of the
invoice

Credit
creditor's
account with
total amount of
invoice

The Case Study which follows shows how credit purchases transactions are recorded by means of double-entry bookkeeping in the nominal ledger and purchases ledger. As with previous Case Studies, the transactions are listed.

CASE STUDY

ARONA LIMITED: DOUBLE-ENTRY FOR CREDIT PURCHASES

situation

Arona Limited is a local clothing store which sells the latest fashions to its customers. It buys goods on credit from manufacturers and suppliers.

The following are the credit purchases transactions for January 2004:

8 January	Bought goods from Osborne Fashion Limited for £1,305.00 + VAT £228.37, total invoice £1,533.37
11 January	Bought goods from Morretti & Co for £1,081.10 + VAT £189.19, total invoice £1,270.29
12 January	Bought goods from First Style Limited for £364.94 + VAT £63.86, total invoice £428.80
17 January	Bought goods from Osborne Fashion Limited for £539.64 + VAT £94.43, total invoice £634.07
20 January	Bought goods from First Style Limited for £1,502.38 + VAT £262.91, total invoice £1,765.29
24 January	Bought goods from Morretti & Co for £636.81 + VAT £111.44, total invoice £748.25
26 January	Bought goods from First Style Limited for £597.86 + VAT £104.62, total invoice £702.48

The following accounts will be opened:

- nominal ledger
  - purchases
  - Value Added Tax
- purchases ledger
  - Osborne Fashion Limited
  - Morretti & Co
  - First Style Limited

Note that the ledgers can be written up in any order – you can start with the nominal ledger or the purchases ledger. It is best to be guided by the order of the transactions set out in the Student Activity or the Examination.

solution

These transactions are recorded in the nominal ledger and the purchases ledger of the bookkeeping system of Arona Limited (assuming no opening balances – see page 97) as shown on the next page:

NOMINAL LEDGER

Dr			Purchases Account		Cr
2004		£	2004		£
8 Jan	Osborne Fashion Ltd	1,305.00			
11 Jan	Morretti & Co	1,081.10			
12 Jan	First Style Ltd	364.94			
17 Jan	Osborne Fashion Ltd	539.64			
20 Jan	First Style Ltd	1,502.38			
24 Jan	Morretti & Co	636.81			
26 Jan	First Style Ltd	597.86			

Dr			Value Added Tax Account		Cr
2004		£	2004		£
8 Jan	Osborne Fashion Ltd	228.37			
11 Jan	Morretti & Co	189.19			
12 Jan	First Style Ltd	63.86			
17 Jan	Osborne Fashion Ltd	94.43			
20 Jan	First Style Ltd	262.91			
24 Jan	Morretti & Co	111.44			
26 Jan	First Style Ltd	104.62			

PURCHASES LEDGER

Dr		Osborne Fashion Limited			Cr
2004		£	2004		£
			8 Jan	Purchases	1,533.37
			17 Jan	Purchases	634.07

Dr		Morretti & Co			Cr
2004		£	2004		£
			11 Jan	Purchases	1,270.29
			24 Jan	Purchases	748.25

Dr		First Style Limited			Cr
2004		£	2004		£
			12 Jan	Purchases	428.80
			20 Jan	Purchases	1,765.29
			26 Jan	Purchases	702.48

Note to the accounts:

- the date of the transaction is used
- the name of the other account involved in the double-entry is used in the details column as a description
- money amounts are recorded as follows:
  - amount of purchases (excluding VAT) is debited to purchases account
  - amount of VAT is debited to Value Added Tax account
  - invoice totals (ie purchases, plus VAT) are credited to creditors' accounts
- double-entry accounts may be set out using different formats, eg two-column

DEALING WITH OPENING BALANCES

In the Case Study above we assumed, for simplicity, that there were no balances on any of the accounts at the beginning of the month. In practice, most accounts have an opening balance at the beginning of each week, month or year – if you have a bank account you will be familiar with the first line of your bank statement saying 'balance brought forward'. The same is true of the double-entry bookkeeping system (which, of course, banks use to keep their books). The opening balance is the total of the account to date (we will study the techniques of balancing accounts in Chapter 7). For the moment we need to know how to enter opening balances into accounts.

Opening balances are described as being either 'debit' or 'credit', depending on which side of the account they appear. For example, with credit purchases transactions, the accounts used have been purchases account, VAT account and an account in the name of each creditor (supplier); the balances on these are usually:

- Debit opening balances
  - purchases account
- Credit opening balances
  - creditors' accounts

Note that VAT account can have either a debit or a credit balance, depending on the circumstances of the business. Always follow the information given to you in the Student Activity or the Examination.

If the opening balances are given, then they need to be entered into the accounts – on the correct side – before recording any transactions. The usual way of entering them is to describe them as 'balance brought down' (or 'balance brought forward') – usually shortened to 'balance b/d' (or 'balance b/f') in the details column. These terms mean that the balance has been brought down from the previous month (or sometimes the previous week or year) and represent the total of the account to that date.

For example, using the data from the last Case Study, suppose we are told that the balances at 1 February 2004 are:

	DR	CR
	£	£
purchases	6,027.73	
Value Added Tax	1,054.82	
Osborne Fashion Limited		2,167.44

These will be entered into the accounts as follows:

NOMINAL LEDGER

Dr		**Purchases Account**			Cr
2004		£	2004		£
1 Feb	Balance b/d	6,027.73			

Dr		**Value Added Tax Account**			Cr
2004		£	2004		£
1 Feb	Balance b/d	1,054.82			

PURCHASES LEDGER

Dr	**Osborne Fashion Limited**			Cr
2004	£	2004		£
		1 Feb	Balance b/d	2,167.44

PURCHASES RETURNS

Purchases returns are products previously bought on credit being returned by the business to the supplier. A credit note (see Chapter 2, pages 20 and 21) is requested and, when received, it is entered in the accounts system to reduce the amount owing to the creditor.

The ledgers and accounts used for purchases returns (also known as returns out) are:

nominal (or general) ledger

- *purchases returns account* – to record the goods amount of credit notes received
- *Value Added Tax account* – to record the VAT amounts of purchases returns

purchases ledger

- separate accounts for each creditor

Note that purchases returns are kept separate from purchases, ie they are entered in a purchases returns account. This enables the business to keep a check on the level of returns the business is making in relation to its purchases.

DOUBLE-ENTRY BOOKKEEPING FOR PURCHASES RETURNS

Credit notes issued by the supplier are the business documents used to write up the double-entry accounts.

The bookkeeping entries to record purchases returns are made from the credit note received:

- *debit*: creditor's (supplier's) account with the total amount of the credit note
- *credit*: purchases returns account with the goods total of the credit note after trade discount (if any), but before VAT is added
- *credit*: Value Added Tax account with the VAT amount of the credit note

Note that, as VAT is involved, there are three entries to make, but the debit entry will always equal the credits total.

These entries are illustrated from the example credit note received, on the next page.

The logic behind the bookkeeping entries for purchases returns is that when the credit note is issued:

- the supplier of goods or services is owed less
- the amount of VAT that needs to be charged is less

Note that if the transaction involves stock – ie stock is sent back – then the stock of goods held by the purchaser decreases.

The accounting entries are shown on the credit note on the next page and are summarised on the page that follows.

CREDIT NOTE

Osborne Fashion Limited

Unit 16 Millyard Estate
Fencote Road, Worcester WR2 6HY
Tel 01905 334482
Fax 01905 334493
email info@osbornefashion.co.uk
VAT Reg 987 544 21

to   Arona Limited
18-24 Friar Street
Wyvern
WY1 8TQ

credit note no.   954

date   3 February 2004

quantity	description	cat. no.	unit price (£)	£
3	Dresses	D45	22.00	66.00

	66.00
Less trade discount 10%	6.60
	59.40
VAT at 17.5%	10.39
	69.79

reason for credit:
Faulty goods

Credit
purchases returns account
with goods total of credit note
after trade discount (if any),
but before VAT is added

Credit
VAT account
with the VAT
amount of the
credit note

Debit
creditor's
account with
total amount of
credit note

The accounting system for purchases returns can be summarised as follows:

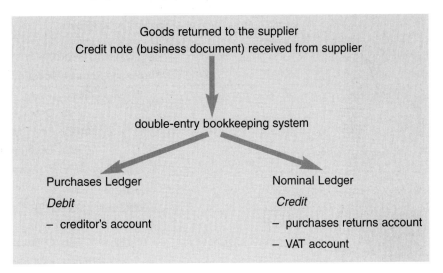

Goods returned to the supplier
Credit note (business document) received from supplier

double-entry bookkeeping system

Purchases Ledger
Debit
– creditor's account

Nominal Ledger
Credit
– purchases returns account
– VAT account

The Case Study which follows shows how purchases returns transactions are recorded by means of double-entry bookkeeping in the nominal ledger and purchases ledger. As with previous Case Studies, the transactions are listed.

CASE STUDY

ARONA LIMITED: DOUBLE-ENTRY FOR PURCHASES RETURNS

situation

Arona Limited (from the Case Study on page 95) has the following purchases returns transactions for February 2004:

3 February	Goods returned to Osborne Fashion Limited for £59.40 + VAT £10.39, a credit note for £69.79 is received
10 February	Goods returned to First Style Limited for £85.60 + VAT £14.98, a credit note for £100.58 is received
16 February	Goods returned to Osborne Fashion Limited for £40.32 + VAT £7.05, a credit note for £47.37 is received

At 1 February 2004, the relevant opening balances are as follows:

	DR	CR
purchases returns	nil	nil
Value Added Tax	£1,054.82	
Osborne Fashion Limited		£2,167.44
First Style Limited		£2,896.57

102 Level 1 Bookkeeping

solution

These transactions are recorded in the nominal ledger and the purchases ledger of the bookkeeping system of Arona Limited as follows:

NOMINAL LEDGER

Dr 2004		£	Cr 2004		£
			3 Feb	Osborne Fashion Ltd	59.40
			10 Feb	First Style Ltd	85.60
			16 Feb	Osborne Fashion Ltd	40.32

Purchases Returns Account

Dr 2004		£	Cr 2004		£
1 Feb	Balance b/d	1,054.82	3 Feb	Osborne Fashion Ltd	10.39
			10 Feb	First Style Ltd	14.98
			16 Feb	Osborne Fashion Ltd	7.05

Value Added Tax Account

PURCHASES LEDGER

Osborne Fashion Limited

Dr 2004		£	Cr 2004		£
3 Feb	Purchases returns	69.79	1 Feb	Balance b/d	2,167.44
16 Feb	Purchases returns	47.37			

First Style Limited

Dr 2004		£	Cr 2004		£
10 Feb	Purchases returns	100.58	1 Feb	Balance b/d	2,896.57

Notes to the accounts:

• opening balances are entered as 'balance b/d' (or 'balance b/f')

• the name of the other account involved in the double-entry is used in the details column as a description

• money amounts are recorded as follows:

– amount of purchases returns (excluding VAT) is credited to purchases returns account

– amount of VAT is credited to Value Added Tax account

– credit note totals (ie purchases returns, plus VAT) are debited to creditors' accounts

• double-entry accounts may be set out using different formats, eg two-column

- Purchases account is used to record the purchase of products in which the business trades.

- Other items bought by the business are recorded in separate accounts, eg motor vehicles account.

- The purchase of products on credit (credit purchase) is recorded in the bookkeeping system as:
  - *debit* purchases account with the goods total of the invoice
  - *debit* Value Added Tax account with the VAT amount of the invoice
  - *credit* creditor's account with the total amount of the invoice

- Purchases returns are when products previously bought on credit are returned by the business to the supplier.

- Purchases returns are recorded in the bookkeeping system as:
  - *debit* creditor's account with the total amount of the credit note
  - *credit* purchases returns account with the goods total of the credit note
  - *credit* Value Added Tax account with the VAT amount of the credit note

purchases ledger	ledger section which contains the personal accounts of suppliers who have sold goods or services to the business on credit and who are owed money – the creditors of the business
purchases	the purchase from a supplier of goods or services in which the business trades
opening balances	totals of accounts at the beginning of each week, month or year – often described as 'balance brought down' (or 'balance brought forward')
purchases returns	products previously bought on credit are returned by the business to the supplier

STUDENT ACTIVITIES

NOTE: an asterisk (*) after the question number means that the answer to the question is given at the back of this book.

5.1* You are working for Trevaunance Limited and are required to enter the following credit purchases transactions in the nominal ledger and the purchases ledger of the bookkeeping system:

2004

3 Feb	Bought goods from Perran & Sons for £305.47 + VAT £53.45, total invoice £358.92
5 Feb	Bought goods from Durning Supplies for £247.80 + VAT £43.36, total invoice £291.16
7 Feb	Bought goods from Zelah Trading Company for £110.54 + VAT £19.34, total invoice £129.88
10 Feb	Bought goods from Bissoe Limited for £278.11 + VAT £48.66, total invoice £326.77
14 Feb	Bought goods from Zelah Trading Company for £358.15 + VAT £62.67, total invoice £420.82
18 Feb	Bought goods from Durning Supplies for £122.19 + VAT £21.38, total invoice £143.57
23 Feb	Bought goods from Perran & Sons for £162.48 + VAT £28.43, total invoice £190.91
26 Feb	Bought goods from Zelah Trading Company for £87.40 + VAT £15.29, total invoice £102.69

Notes:

• None of the accounts has opening balances

• You need to open the following accounts:

nominal ledger

– purchases

– Value Added Tax

purchases ledger

– Perran & Sons

– Durning Supplies

– Zelah Trading Company

– Bissoe Limited

Blank account layouts – which you can photocopy – are provided at the end of this chapter, either 'T' account format (page 124), or two-column format (page 125).

5.2*   Trevaunance Limited (from the previous Activity) has the following purchases returns transactions for March 2004.

5 Mar	Goods returned to Durning Supplies for £25.46 + VAT £4.45, a credit note for £29.91 is received
10 Mar	Goods returned to Zelah Trading Company for £53.80 + VAT £9.41, a credit note for £63.21 is received
14 Mar	Goods returned to Durning Supplies for £15.62 + VAT £2.73, a credit note for £18.35 is received

You are to enter the purchases returns transactions in the nominal ledger and the purchases ledger of the bookkeeping system of Trevaunance Limited. You can either continue with the accounts already opened for Activity 5.1 (an account needs to be opened for purchases returns), or you can use new accounts with opening balances at 1 March 2004 as follows:

	DR	CR
	£	£
purchases returns	nil	nil
Value Added Tax	292.58	
Durning Supplies		434.73
Zelah Trading Company		653.39

Blank account layouts – which you can photocopy – are provided at the end of this chapter, either 'T' account format (page 124), or two-column format (page 125).

5.3   You are the bookkeeper responsible for the purchases ledger and nominal ledger of Beacon Surf Limited. Open ledger accounts and enter the following balances at 1 April 2005:

	DR	CR
	£	£
purchases	15,842.64	
Value Added Tax		1,360.45
Performance Clothing Limited		890.45
Boards 'R Us		1,210.28
Surf Supplies Limited		546.93

You are to enter the details of invoices received from suppliers – on the next six pages – in the correct purchases ledger accounts. Ensure that the nominal accounts are updated as appropriate.

Blank account layouts – which you can photocopy – are provided at the end of this chapter, either 'T' account format (page 124), or two-column format (page 125).

INVOICE

PERFORMANCE CLOTHING LIMITED

28-30 Commercial Road
Leeds LS5 4JP

Tel 01702 876543
Fax 01702 987654
email info@performance_clothing.co.uk
VAT Reg 264 871 94

to	Beacon Surf Ltd	**invoice no.**	3241
	Towan House		
	22 Beach Road		
	Porthperran	**date**	6 April 2005
	Cornwall		
	TR7 0UX		
		order no.	4455

quantity	description	unit price £	total net £	VAT rate %	VAT amount £	TOTAL £
10	'Orca' wetsuits WS10	55.00	550.00	17.5	96.25	646.25
5	'Minke' wetsuits WS5	35.00	175.00	17.5	30.62	205.62
			725.00		126.87	851.87

terms: net 30 days

Invoice

Boards 'R Us

Unit 10 Seaview Estate
Truro Road, Penpol TR10 2ZP
Tel 01782 884884
Fax 01782 884885

VAT Reg 231 681 20

to	Beacon Surf Ltd	**invoice no.**	4579
	Towan House		
	22 Beach Road		
	Porthperran	**date**	10 April 2005
	Cornwall		
	TR7 0UX		
		order no.	4460

quantity	description	cat. no.	unit price (£)	£
8	'Tasman' bodyboards	BB21	35.00	280.00
5	'Bondi' bodyboards	BB14	22.00	110.00
				390.00
		Less trade discount 15%		58.50
				331.50
		VAT at 17.5%		58.01
				389.51

terms: net monthly

INVOICE

Surf Supplies Limited

Unit 10, Cradley Estate
Mereford MR10 3TD

Tel 01745 384123
Fax 01745 384227
email info@surfsupplies.co.uk
VAT Reg 274 8431 28

to Beacon Surf Ltd
Towan House
22 Beach Road
Porthperran
Cornwall
TR7 0UX

invoice no. 34041

date 15 April 2005

order no. 4457

quantity	description	unit price £	total net £	VAT rate %	VAT amount £	TOTAL £
10 pairs	Boots B10	15.00	150.00	17.5	26.25	176.25
5 pairs	Socks S15	5.00	25.00	17.5	4.37	29.37
			175.00		30.62	205.62

terms: net 30 days

Invoice

Boards 'R Us

Unit 10 Seaview Estate
Truro Road, Penpol TR10 2ZP
Tel 01782 884884
Fax 01782 884885

VAT Reg 231 681 20

to Beacon Surf Ltd		**invoice no.** 4612	
Towan House			
22 Beach Road			
Porthperran		**date** 20 April 2005	
Cornwall			
TR7 0UX			
		order no. 4465	

quantity	description	cat. no.	unit price (£)	£
10	'Tasman' bodyboards	BB21	35.00	350.00
2	'Bondi' bodyboards	BB14	22.00	44.00

	394.00
Less trade discount 15%	59.10
	334.90
VAT at 17.5%	58.60
	393.50

terms: net monthly

INVOICE

Surf Supplies Limited

Unit 10, Cradley Estate
Mereford MR10 3TD

Tel 01745 384123
Fax 01745 384227
email info@surfsupplies.co.uk
VAT Reg 274 8431 28

to Beacon Surf Ltd
Towan House
22 Beach Road
Porthperran
Cornwall
TR7 0UX

invoice no.   34103

date   23 April 2005

order no.   4467

quantity	description	unit price £	total net £	VAT rate %	VAT amount £	TOTAL £
6 pairs	Boots B10	15.00	90.00	17.5	15.75	105.75
8 pairs	Socks S15	5.00	40.00	17.5	7.00	47.00
			130.00		22.75	152.75

terms: net 30 days

INVOICE

PERFORMANCE CLOTHING LIMITED

28-30 Commercial Road
Leeds LS5 4JP

Tel 01702 876543
Fax 01702 987654
email info@performance_clothing.co.uk
VAT Reg 264 871 94

to   Beacon Surf Ltd
Towan House
22 Beach Road
Porthperran
Cornwall
TR7 0UX

invoice no.   3322

date   28 April 2005

order no.   4466

quantity	description	unit price £	total net £	VAT rate %	VAT amount £	TOTAL £
5	'Orca' wetsuits WS10	55.00	275.00	17.5	48.12	323.12
3	'Minke' wetsuits WS5	35.00	105.00	17.5	18.37	123.37
			380.00		66.49	446.49

terms: net 30 days

5.4   Beacon Surf Limited (from the previous Activity) receives the credit notes shown on the next two pages from its suppliers. You are to enter the details from the credit notes in the correct purchases ledger accounts. Ensure that the nominal accounts are updated as appropriate.

Note: you can either continue with the accounts already opened for Activity 5.3 (an account needs to be opened for purchases returns), or you can use new accounts with opening balances at 1 May 2005 as follows:

	DR £	CR £
purchases returns	nil	nil
Value Added Tax		997.11
Performance Clothing Limited		2,188.81
Boards 'R Us		1,993.29

Blank account layouts – which you can photocopy – are provided at the end of this chapter, either 'T' account format (page 124), or two-column format (page 125).

CREDIT NOTE

PERFORMANCE CLOTHING LIMITED

28-30 Commercial Road
Leeds LS5 4JP

Tel 01702 876543
Fax 01702 987654
email info@performance_clothing.co.uk
VAT Reg 264 871 94

to Beacon Surf Ltd
Towan House
22 Beach Road
Porthperran
Cornwall
TR7 0UX

credit note no. 4590

date 4 May 2005

quantity	description	unit price £	total net £	VAT rate %	VAT amount £	TOTAL £
1	'Minke' wetsuit WS5	35.00	35.00	17.5	6.12	41.12
			35.00		6.12	41.12

reason for credit:
Faulty goods

Credit Note

Boards 'R Us

Unit 10 Seaview Estate
Truro Road, Penpol TR10 2ZP
Tel 01782 884884
Fax 01782 884885

VAT Reg 231 681 20

to Beacon Surf Ltd	**credit note no.** 5917
Towan House	
22 Beach Road	
Porthperran	**date** 6 May 2005
Cornwall	
TR7 0UX	

quantity	description	unit price (£)	£ p
2	'Bondi' bodyboards	22.00	44.00

	44.00
Less trade discount 15%	6.60
	37.40
VAT at 17.5%	6.54
Total credit	43.94

reason for credit:
Damaged goods

5.5   You are the bookkeeper responsible for the purchases ledger and nominal ledger of Sesame Shoes Limited.

(a)   Open ledger accounts and enter the following balances at 1 October 2006:

	DR	CR
	£	£
purchases	15,271.84	
purchases returns		2,931.80
Value Added Tax		1,087.29
Parks Limited		1,086.21
Rocco Shoes plc		984.15
Mova Shoe Company		2,369.10

(b)   Enter the details of invoices received from suppliers on pages 116 to 121 in the correct purchases ledger accounts. Ensure that nominal accounts are updated as appropriate.

(c)   Enter the details from credit notes received from suppliers on pages 122 to 123 in the correct purchases ledger accounts. Ensure that nominal accounts are updated as appropriate.

Blank account layouts – which you can photocopy – are provided at the end of this chapter, either 'T' account format (page 124), or two-column format (page 125).

INVOICE

Parks Limited

The Shoe Factory
Station Road
Streetingly SR5 0JG
Tel 01230 456789
Fax 01230 456790

VAT Reg 234 855 62

to	Sesame Shoes Ltd Unit 14 Kingsway Shopping Centre Mereford MR1 1TK	**invoice no.**	12345
		date	5 October 2006
		order no.	6490

quantity	description	cat. no.	unit price (£)	£
10 pairs	Boots (black), size 38	B41	40.00	400.00
2 pairs	Shoes (blue), size 40	S30	30.00	60.00

	£
	460.00
Less trade discount 20%	92.00
	368.00
VAT at 17.5%	64.40
	432.40

terms: net monthly

INVOICE

ROCCO SHOES LIMITED

Unit 10, Lowlands Estate
Bath Road, Shepley Morton BA13 3BY

Tel 01430 678876
Fax 01430 678870
email info@roccoshoes.co.uk
VAT Reg 924 361 84

to Sesame Shoes Ltd
Unit 14
Kingsway Shopping Centre
Mereford
MR1 1TK

invoice no.   3749

date   10 October 2006

order no.   6485

quantity	description	unit price £	total net £	VAT rate %	VAT amount £	TOTAL £
8 pairs	Trainers T15, size 43	25.00	200.00	17.5	35.00	235.00
4 pairs	Slippers SL4, size 38	20.00	80.00	17.5	14.00	94.00
			280.00		49.00	329.00

terms: net 30 days

Invoice

Mova Shoe Company

26-30 Queensway
Longton, Birmingham B15 8TD
Tel 0121 876 5432
Fax 0121 876 5433
email info@movashoe.co.uk
VAT Reg 763 291 33

to   Sesame Shoes Ltd
Unit 14
Kingsway Shopping Centre
Mereford
MR1 1TK

invoice no.   74621

date   14 October 2006

order no.   6488

quantity	description	cat. no.	unit price (£)	£
6 pairs	Walkers (brown), size 38	W47	45.00	270.00
4 pairs	Walkers (black), size 41	W58	45.00	180.00
				450.00
		Less trade discount 15%		67.50
				382.50
		VAT at 17.5%		66.93
				449.43

terms: net monthly

INVOICE

Parks Limited

The Shoe Factory
Station Road
Streetingly SR5 0JG
Tel 01230 456789
Fax 01230 456790

VAT Reg 234 855 62

to	Sesame Shoes Ltd	**invoice no.**	12451
	Unit 14		
	Kingsway Shopping Centre		
	Mereford	**date**	18 October 2006
	MR1 1TK		
		order no.	6491

quantity	description	cat. no.	unit price (£)	£
5 pairs	Boots (blue), size 40	B66	40.00	200.00
4 pairs	Shoes (black), size 43	S85	30.00	120.00
				320.00
		Less trade discount 20%		64.00
				256.00
		VAT at 17.5%		44.80
				300.80

terms: net monthly

INVOICE

ROCCO SHOES LIMITED

Unit 10, Lowlands Estate
Bath Road, Shepley Morton BA13 3BY

Tel 01430 678876
Fax 01430 678870
email info@roccoshoes.co.uk
VAT Reg 924 361 84

to Sesame Shoes Ltd Unit 14 Kingsway Shopping Centre Mereford MR1 1TK	**invoice no.** 3933 **date** 22 October 2006 **order no.** 6487

quantity	description	unit price £	total net £	VAT rate %	VAT amount £	TOTAL £
8 pairs	Trainers T15, size 38	25.00	200.00	17.5	35.00	235.00
2 pairs	Trainers T15, size 41	25.00	50.00	17.5	8.75	58.75
			250.00		43.75	293.75

terms: net 30 days

Invoice

Mova Shoe Company

26-30 Queensway
Longton, Birmingham B15 8TD
Tel 0121 876 5432
Fax 0121 876 5433
email info@movashoe.co.uk
VAT Reg 763 291 33

| **to** | Sesame Shoes Ltd | **invoice no.** | 74933 |

to Sesame Shoes Ltd
Unit 14
Kingsway Shopping Centre
Mereford
MR1 1TK

invoice no. 74933

date 24 October 2006

order no. 6486

quantity	description	cat. no.	unit price (£)	£
4 pairs	Walkers (brown), size 41	W47	45.00	180.00
3 pairs	Walkers (black), size 45	W58	45.00	135.00
				315.00
	Less trade discount 15%			47.25
				267.75
	VAT at 17.5%			46.85
				314.60

terms: net monthly

CREDIT NOTE

ROCCO SHOES LIMITED

Unit 10, Lowlands Estate
Bath Road, Shepley Morton BA13 3BY

Tel 01430 678876
Fax 01430 678870
email info@roccoshoes.co.uk
VAT Reg 924 361 84

to Sesame Shoes Ltd
Unit 14
Kingsway Shopping Centre
Mereford
MR1 1TK

credit note no. 591

date 23 October 2006

quantity	description	unit price £	total net £	VAT rate %	VAT amount £	TOTAL £
1 pair	Trainers T15, size 43	25.00	25.00	17.5	4.37	29.37
			25.00		4.37	29.37

reason for credit:
Faulty manufacture

Credit Note

Mova Shoe Company

26-30 Queensway
Longton, Birmingham B15 8TD
Tel 0121 876 5432
Fax 0121 876 5433
email info@movashoe.co.uk
VAT Reg 763 291 33

to Sesame Shoes Ltd		**credit note no.**	884
Unit 14			
Kingsway Shopping Centre			
Mereford		**date**	30 October 2006
MR1 1TK			

quantity	description	cat. no.	unit price (£)	£ p
1 pair	Walkers (black), size 41	W58	45.00	45.00

	45.00
Less trade discount 15%	6.75
	38.25
VAT at 17.5%	6.69
Total credit	44.94

reason for credit:
Faulty manufacture

'T' account format

Account

Date	Details	£	p	Date	Details	£	p

Account

Date	Details	£	p	Date	Details	£	p

two-column account format

Date	Details	£	p	£	p

———————————————— Account

Date	Details	£	p	£	p

———————————————— Account

6 PAYMENTS FOR PURCHASES AND EXPENSES

this chapter covers ...

In this chapter we look at the way in which payments made to creditors for purchases and payments for expenses, are recorded in the double-entry bookkeeping.

Bank account – in the double-entry system – is used to record the money side of bookkeeping transactions.

We see how bank account is used to record payments made to creditors for purchases in the form of cheques. We focus on the payments (credit) side of bank account and see how the opposite (debit) entry is recorded in creditors' accounts.

As well as payments to creditors for purchases, this chapter also looks at payments for expenses, assets and liabilities. These payments include:

– expenses of running the business, such as business rates, general (or 'sundry') expenses

– purchase of assets for use in the business, such as furniture and fittings, office equipment, motor vehicles

– payment of business liabilities, such as VAT due

OCR LEARNING OUTCOMES

unit 1: POSTING TO ACCOUNTS
Assessment objectives

1   Maintain Purchase Ledger

(d) Enter payments into correct account

3   Maintain Nominal Ledger

(a) Identify and open correct ledger account

(b) Enter transactions into correct account

MAKING PAYMENT TO CREDITORS

In the previous chapter we recorded financial transactions for credit purchases and purchases returns in the bookkeeping system. The next step in the process is to make payment to the creditor – often following receipt of a statement of account (illustrated on page 22). The statement is a 'reminder' document sent to the buyer, which sets out details of invoices and credit notes issued by the supplier, and shows the total amount due for the period.

Payments to creditors are usually made by cheque, or other bank transfer (such as BACS). Cheques have already been described on page 23, while BACS transfers are discussed fully in Chapter 13, later in this book. In this chapter we focus on recording cheque payments in the accounts system.

Before making payments to creditors it is important to check against documentation – such as invoices, credit notes and statements of account. The amount to be paid varies according to business policy (and also how much money is in the bank!). Some businesses will pay the entire balance due on the statement received from the supplier; others will take advantage of credit terms offered by the supplier – eg 30 days – and will pay for only those invoices which are close to their payment date. Once payments due to creditors have been authorised and the cheques written out, they are recorded in the bookkeeping system using:

- bank account, in the nominal ledger
- the creditor's account, in the purchases ledger

USING BANK ACCOUNT

We have used bank account already (in Chapter 4) for payments received from debtors. The account, which is held in the nominal ledger, takes the account format that has been used previously – either 'T' account, or two-column/three-column account format. This chapter uses 'T' accounts, with a single vertical line dividing the debit and credit sides.

In Chapter 4 we saw how receipts are recorded on the debit side of bank account. This chapter focuses on payments made to creditors, so we will be using the payments (credit) side of bank account, and will also be recording the opposite (debit) entry in creditors' accounts. Later in the chapter we look at the entries to be made in the accounts system to record payments for expenses, assets and liabilities.

Remember not to confuse the bank account – which is the firm's *own* record of its bank transactions – with the records held at the bank branch where the business keeps its account.

Later in the book (Chapter 12) we will see how bank account can be incorporated into a firm's cash book, which brings together in one account bank transactions and cash transactions.

OPENING BALANCES FOR BANK ACCOUNT

You will often be required to enter an opening balance in bank account at the start of the month. As we have seen already in Chapter 4, bank account is an account where the opening balance could be on either side, depending on the financial circumstances of the firm:

- an opening debit balance is an asset, and means that the business has money in the bank
- an opening credit balance is a liability, and means that the business is overdrawn at the bank

This is shown in the account below:

Dr	Bank Account	Cr
£		£
an opening balance on the debit side means that, according to the accounts system, the business has an *asset* of money in the bank		an opening balance on the credit side means that, according to the accounts system, the business has the *liability* of a bank overdraft

Remember that the balance of bank account – whether debit or credit – is the balance shown by the firm's accounts system. When the bank statement is received, it may well show a different balance – the reasons for this are explained in Chapter 14. However, in this chapter we are concerned solely with recording payments for purchases, expenses, assets and liabilities.

RECORDING PAYMENTS TO CREDITORS

When paying creditors who have supplied goods or services on credit, the payment is usually made by cheque (or BACS transfer – described fully in Chapter 13, later in this book).

The double-entry bookkeeping entries for payments made to creditors are:

purchases ledger

– *debit* creditor's account with the amount of the payment

nominal (or general) ledger

– *credit* bank account with the amount of the payment

These are illustrated from the example cheque which follows. Note that the cheque itself is sent to the creditor, while the bookkeeping entries are made from the details of the cheque which are recorded on the counterfoil (or cheque 'stub').

25 Feb 2004		
To		
Osborne		
Fashion Ltd		
(CREDITOR)		
£ 2,050.28		
540123		

Southern Bank PLC
Wyvern Branch
10 High Street, Wyvern WY1 7TR

date 25 February 2004 97-77-05

Pay Osborne Fashion Limited ———— only

Two thousand and fifty pounds, 28p only ———— £ 2,050.28

Account payee only

ARONA LIMITED

T Shah I Williams

540123 977705 45732941

counterfoil

cheque sent to creditor

Debit
creditor's account with the amount of the cheque

Credit
bank account with amount of payment made to the creditor

The details to be recorded in nominal ledger and purchases ledger for the payment transaction are:

• date, using the date of the cheque (ie the date the payment is made)

• narrative, being the name of the other account involved (eg in bank account the name of the creditor to whom payment is made)

• reference number (not always required, this could be the number of the cheque which is being sent to the creditor, here 540123)

• amount of the cheque

All of these details are shown on the counterfoil of the cheque, from which the bookkeeping entries are made. Note that the word 'CREDITOR' is written on the counterfoil to remind the bookkeeper that the payment relates to purchases, rather than to expenses or assets or liabilities (see page 133).

On a practical note, take care to enter payments made to creditors in the correct creditor's account in purchases ledger. The accounts supervisor will not be too pleased if you, as the bookkeeper, debit payments made to the wrong creditors' accounts – the business will not know how much it owes and to whom. Always check that payments made to creditors are recorded in the correct accounts and on the debit side.

The accounting system for recording payments made to creditors is summarised as follows:

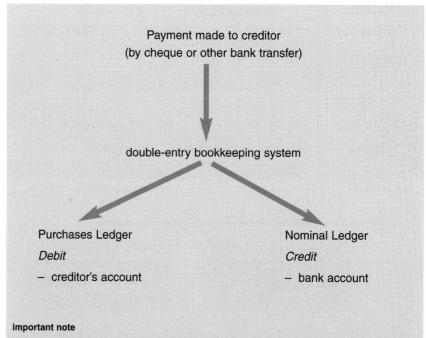

Payment made to creditor
(by cheque or other bank transfer)

double-entry bookkeeping system

Purchases Ledger

Debit

– creditor's account

Nominal Ledger

Credit

– bank account

important note
When money is paid to a creditor as payment for credit purchases, **there is no transaction recorded in VAT account.** This is because the VAT was recorded when the credit purchase was made.

We will now see how these principles are put into practice in the Case Study which follows.

CASE STUDY

ARONA LIMITED: PAYMENTS MADE TO CREDITORS

situation

The bookkeeper of Arona Limited (see Case Study in Chapter 5, pages 95 and 101) has made a number of payments by cheque to creditors for purchases. The cheque counterfoils are given below and are to be entered in the correct purchases ledger accounts. The nominal ledger is to be updated as appropriate.

25 Feb 2004	25 Feb 2004	25 Feb 2004
To	To	To
Osborne	Morretti &	First Style
Fashion Ltd	Co	Ltd
(CREDITOR)	(CREDITOR)	(CREDITOR)
£ 2,050.28	£ 1,270.29	£ 2,194.09
540123	540124	540125

Note: At 1 February 2004, bank account has an opening balance of £10,764.09 debit

solution

In nominal ledger, the cheques paid to creditors are listed on the credit side of bank account, as follows:

NOMINAL LEDGER

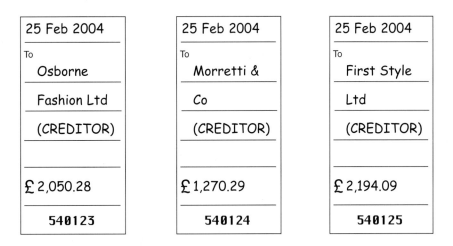

Dr		Bank Account		Cr
2004	£	2004		£
1 Feb Balance b/d	10,764.09	25 Feb Osborne Fashion Ltd		2,050.28
		25 Feb Morretti & Co		1,270.29
		25 Feb First Style Ltd		2,194.09

Notes to the account:

- the details needed to write up bank account are taken from the cheque counterfoils
- the date of the cheque is used in the date column of bank account
- the name of the creditor is shown in the details column
- the amount of the cheque is recorded in the money column

The credit side of bank account is used to record payments made because the business is reducing the asset of money in bank account. Remember that the bank account shown on the previous page is the firm's own record of how much it has in its bank account. The cheques are sent to the creditors, who will pay them in to their own bank accounts.

In purchases ledger the individual account of each creditor who has been paid is debited, as follows (balances b/d and purchases returns transactions are taken from the Case Studies in Chapter 5 – see pages 95 and 101):

PURCHASES LEDGER

Dr			Osborne Fashion Limited			Cr
2004		£	2004			£
3 Feb	Purchases returns	69.79	1 Feb	Balance b/d		2,167.44
16 Feb	Purchases returns	47.37				
25 Feb	Bank	2,050.28				

Dr			Morretti & Co			Cr
2004		£	2004			£
25 Feb	Bank	1,270.29	1 Feb	Balance b/d		2,018.54

Dr			First Style Limited			Cr
2004		£	2004			£
10 Feb	Purchases returns	100.58	1 Feb	Balance b/d		2,896.57
25 Feb	Bank	2,194.09				

Notes to the accounts:

• the debit side of creditors' accounts is used to record payments made; this is because the amounts owed to creditors (liabilities) are reduced by the payment

• the date of the cheque is used in the date column

• 'Bank' is shown in the details column

• the amount of the cheque is recorded in the money column

• the double-entry accounts may be set out using different formats, eg two-column

If you add up the money amounts on both sides of Osborne Fashion's account you will find that there is the same amount on both the debit and credit sides. This means that the account has a 'nil' balance, ie Arona Limited does not owe Osborne Fashion any more money – the balance brought down on 1 February is cleared by the purchases returns transactions and the payment by cheque. We shall be looking in detail at balancing accounts in Chapter 7: for the moment you might like to add up the debit and credit sides of the other two creditors' accounts to see what has happened.

PAYMENT FOR EXPENSES, ASSETS AND LIABILITIES

As well as making payment to creditors for purchases, businesses also make other payments, including:

- expenses of running the business, such as business rates, general (or 'sundry') expenses
- purchase of assets for use in the business, such as furniture and fittings, office equipment, motor vehicles
- payment of business liabilities, such as VAT due

Remember that an asset is something which is owned, while a liability is something which is owed.

The way in which these payments are recorded in the bookkeeping system is similar to that for paying creditors. Bank account, in the nominal ledger, records the payment; however, instead of using accounts in the names of creditors, an account is used for each type of payment, eg

- business rates account, general expenses account
- furniture and fittings account, office equipment account
- VAT account

Note that all of these accounts are in nominal ledger.

Example 1 – paying expenses

Sundry expenses* of £68.25 + VAT £11.94, paid by cheque for £80.19

The double-entry bookkeeping for this transaction is:

– *debit* sundry expenses* account £68.25

– *debit* VAT account £11.94

– *credit* bank account £80.19

* 'Sundry expenses' is the term used to describe a variety of expenses incurred when running a business.

The logic behind this is that the business has received the value of the expense – eg postage stamps have been bought, telephone calls have been made, spare parts have been supplied – therefore the expense is recorded on the debit side of the appropriate expense account, here sundry expenses account, while the VAT amount is debited to VAT account. At the same time, the business has paid for the expense by cheque, which is recorded on the credit side of bank account, ie the asset of bank is reduced by the amount of the payment.

Example 2 – buying an asset

Bought office equipment for £500.00 + VAT £87.50, paid by cheque for £587.50.

The double-entry bookkeeping for this transaction is:

– *debit* office equipment account £500.00

– *debit* VAT account £87.50

– *credit* bank account £587.50

Here the business gains an asset in the form of office equipment – the goods total is debited to office equipment account, while the VAT amount is debited to VAT account. At the same time, the business has paid for the cost (equipment + VAT) by cheque, which is recorded on the credit side of bank account, ie the asset of bank is reduced by the amount of the payment.

payment for expenses and the purchase of assets

The bookkeeping entries for payments for expenses are:

nominal (or general ledger)

– *debit* appropriate expense account with cost before VAT (if any) is added

– *debit* VAT account with the amount of tax (if any)

– *credit* bank account with the amount of the payment

Notes:

• the accounts involved in paying for expenses are all contained in nominal ledger

• details of the amount paid, together with VAT (if any), is given on the cheque counterfoil, for example:

14 May 2004
To Western
Telecom (Sundry expenses
£68.25 + VAT £11.94)
£ 80.19
680269

• the cheque counterfoil indicates clearly the name of the expense account that is to be debited – for the above, it is sundry expenses account

Payments for the purchase of assets are dealt with in the same way in the accounts system. The only difference is that the debit entry, instead of being to an expense account, is to an account in the name of the asset being purchased, eg office equipment account – see Example 2 on the previous page, and the Case Study on page 137.

The accounting system for payment of expenses and the purchase of assets is summarised as follows:

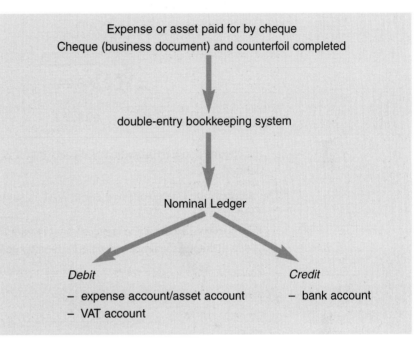

payment for liabilities, such as VAT

As well as payments to creditors, businesses make payment for other liabilities. A regular payment for most businesses is the amount of Value Added Tax that they have collected. This is paid to HM Customs & Excise, which is the VAT authority. The amount to be paid is indicated by a credit balance on VAT account and is usually the balance of the account at the end of the VAT period – commonly every three months.

The bookkeeping entries for the payment of VAT are:

nominal (or general ledger)

– *debit* VAT account with the amount due

– *credit* bank account with the amount of the payment

Notes:

• both accounts involved in paying the VAT due are contained in nominal ledger

- details of the amount paid is given on the cheque counterfoil, for example:

8 May 2004

To

HM Customs

& Excise

(VAT)

£ 2,648.24

680267

- the cheque counterfoil indicates clearly that it is VAT account that is to be debited

The accounting system for payment of VAT is summarised as follows:

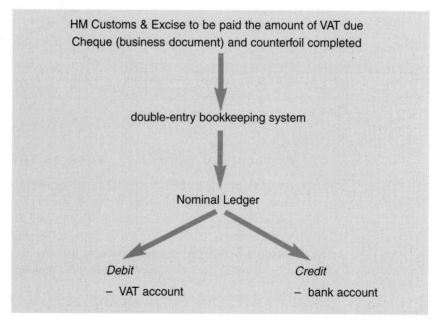

HM Customs & Excise to be paid the amount of VAT due
Cheque (business document) and counterfoil completed

double-entry bookkeeping system

Nominal Ledger

Debit
– VAT account

Credit
– bank account

Payments for any other liabilities – eg a loan repayment (see page 155) – are dealt with in the same way in the accounts system. The only difference is that the debit entry, instead of being to VAT account, is to an account in the name of the liability being paid, eg loan account.

CASE STUDY	MARTLEY FURNITURE LIMITED: PAYMENT FOR EXPENSES, ASSETS AND LIABILITIES

situation

Martley Furniture Limited is a specialist manufacturer of dining tables and chairs. The bookkeeper has made a number of payments by cheque for expenses, assets and liabilities. The cheque counterfoils are given below and are to be entered in the correct ledger accounts. The nominal ledger is to be updated as appropriate.

3 May 2004	8 May 2004	10 May 2004	14 May 2004
To	To	To	To
Wyvern Office Supplies Ltd (Office equipment £500.00 + VAT £87.50)	HM Customs & Excise (VAT)	Martley City Council (Business rates: no VAT)	Western Telecom (Sundry expenses £68.25 + VAT £11.94)
£ 587.50	£ 2,648.24	£ 902.55	£ 80.19
680266	680267	680268	680269

There were the following account balances at 1 May 2004:

	DR £	CR £
Office equipment	3,250.00	
Value Added Tax		2,648.24
Business rates	1,320.86	
Sundry expenses	627.33	
Bank	5,257.19	

solution

All of these payments are recorded in nominal ledger. Taking the details from the cheque counterfoils, the amounts of the payments are listed on the credit side of bank account.

NOMINAL LEDGER

Dr			Bank Account		Cr
2004		£	2004		£
1 May	Balance b/d	5,257.19	3 May	Office equipment	587.50
			8 May	HM Customs & Excise	2,648.24
			10 May	Business rates	902.55
			14 May	Sundry expenses	80.19

Notes to the account:

- the date of the cheque is used in the date column of bank account
- the expense, asset, or liability being paid is shown in the details column
- the amount of the cheque is recorded in the money column

In the appropriate expense, asset, or liability accounts, the amounts are recorded on the debit side.

NOMINAL LEDGER

Dr			Office Equipment Account			Cr
2004			£	2004		£
1 May	Balance b/d		3,250.00			
3 May	Bank		500.00			

Dr			Value Added Tax Account			Cr
2004			£	2004		£
3 May	Office equipment		87.50	1 May Balance b/d		2,648.24
8 May	Bank	2,648.24				
14 May	Sundry expenses	11.94				

Dr			Business Rates Account			Cr
2004			£	2004		£
1 May	Balance b/d		1,320.86			
10 May	Bank		902.55			

Dr			Sundry Expenses Account			Cr
2004			£	2004		£
1 May	Balance b/d		627.33			
14 May	Bank		68.25			

Notes to the accounts:

- the date of the cheque is used in the date column
- 'bank' is shown in the details column
- the amount of the cheque is recorded in the money column
- the double-entry accounts may be set out using different formats, eg two-column

- Bank account, in nominal ledger, is used to record payments by cheque and other bank transfers (such as BACS) for:
  - payment to creditors for purchases
  - payment for expenses, assets and liabilities

- In bank account, payments are recorded on the credit side (which gives value).

- Payments made to creditors are recorded in the accounts as:
  - *debit* creditor's account with the amount of the payment
  - *credit* bank account with the amount of the payment

- Details to be recorded in nominal ledger and purchases ledger include:
  - date of the cheque
  - narrative
  - reference number (eg the cheque number)
  - the amount of the cheque

- Take care to enter payments made to creditors in the correct creditor's account in the purchases ledger.

- Payments for expenses and assets are recorded in the accounts as:
  - *debit* expense account or asset account with the payment amount before VAT
  - *debit* Value Added Tax account with the VAT amount
  - *credit* bank account with the total amount of the payment (expense or asset + VAT)

- Payment for VAT due to HM Customs & Excise, the VAT authority, is recorded in the accounts as:
  - *debit* VAT account with the amount due
  - *credit* bank account with the amount of the payment

bank account	double-entry bookkeeping account used to record receipts and payments through the bank
cheque counterfoil	cheque 'stub' which records details of the payment, and whether for purchases, expenses, assets or liabilities
payments for purchases	amounts paid to creditors for credit purchases
payments for expenses	amounts paid for expenses of running the business
payments for assets	amounts paid for the purchase of assets used in the business
payments for liabilities	amounts paid for business liabilities, such as VAT due

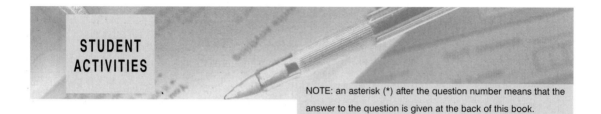

NOTE: an asterisk (*) after the question number means that the
answer to the question is given at the back of this book.

6.1* The following creditors' accounts are taken from the purchases ledger of Trevaunance Limited:

PURCHASES LEDGER

Dr			Perran & Sons			Cr
2004			£	2004		£
				1 Mar	Balance b/d	549.83

Dr			Durning Supplies			Cr
2004			£	2004		£
5 Mar	Purchases returns		29.91	1 Mar	Balance b/d	434.73
14 Mar	Purchases returns		18.35			

Dr			Zelah Trading Company			Cr
2004			£	2004		£
10 Mar	Purchases returns		63.21	1 Mar	Balance b/d	653.39

Dr			Bissoe Limited			Cr
2004			£	2004		£
				1 Mar	Balance b/d	326.77

Copy out these accounts in either 'T' account format (as above) or in two-column format. Blank account layouts – which you can photocopy – are provided on pages 146 and 147.

Open a bank account in nominal ledger with a balance of £2,386.45 debit at 1 March 2004. A number of payments have been made to creditors for purchases. The cheque counterfoils are given on the next page and are to be entered in the correct purchases ledger accounts. The nominal ledger is to be updated as appropriate.

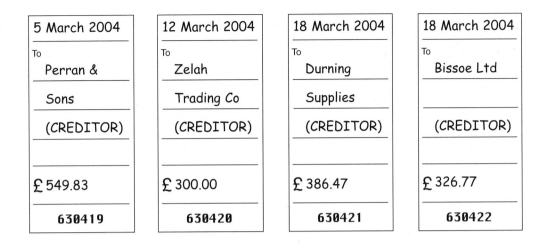

5 March 2004	12 March 2004	18 March 2004	18 March 2004
To	To	To	To
Perran &	Zelah	Durning	Bissoe Ltd
Sons	Trading Co	Supplies	
(CREDITOR)	(CREDITOR)	(CREDITOR)	(CREDITOR)
£ 549.83	£ 300.00	£ 386.47	£ 326.77
630419	630420	630421	630422

6.2   The following creditors' accounts are taken from the purchases ledger of Beacon Surf Limited:

PURCHASES LEDGER

Dr		Performance Clothing Limited			Cr
2005		£	2005		£
4 May	Purchases returns	41.12	1 May	Balance b/d	2,188.81

Dr		Boards 'R Us			Cr
2005		£	2005		£
6 May	Purchases returns	43.94	1 May	Balance b/d	1,993.29

Dr		Surf Supplies Limited			Cr
2005		£	2005		£
			1 May	Balance b/d	905.30

Copy out these accounts in either 'T' account format (as above) or in two-column format. Blank account layouts – which you can photocopy – are provided on pages 146 and 147.

Open a bank account in nominal ledger with a balance of £6,368.27 debit at 1 May 2005. A number of payments have been made to creditors for purchases. The cheque counterfoils are given on the next page and are to be entered in the correct purchases ledger accounts. The nominal ledger is to be updated as appropriate.

7 May 2005	10 May 2005	16 May 2005
To	To	To
Performance Clothing Ltd	Surf Supplies Ltd	Boards 'R Us
(CREDITOR)	(CREDITOR)	(CREDITOR)
£1,000.00	£905.30	£1,949.35
545870	545871	545872

6.3   The following creditors' accounts are taken from the purchases ledger of Sesame Shoes Limited:

PURCHASES LEDGER

Dr			Parks Limited		Cr
2006		£	2006		£
			1 Nov	Balance b/d	1,819.41

Dr			Rocco Shoes plc		Cr
2006		£	2006		£
			1 Nov	Balance b/d	1,577.53

Dr			Mova Shoe Company		Cr
2006		£	2006		£
			1 Nov	Balance b/d	3,088.19

Copy out these accounts in either 'T' account format (as above) or in two-column format. Blank account layouts – which you can photocopy – are provided on pages 146 and 147.

Open a bank account in the nominal ledger with a balance of £1,324.68 credit at 1 November 2006. A number of payments have been made to creditors for purchases. The cheque counterfoils are given on the next page and are to be entered in the correct purchases ledger accounts. The nominal ledger is to be updated as appropriate.

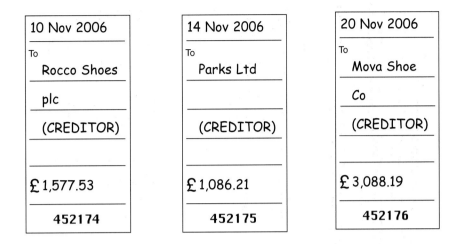

10 Nov 2006	14 Nov 2006	20 Nov 2006
To Rocco Shoes plc (CREDITOR)	To Parks Ltd (CREDITOR)	To Mova Shoe Co (CREDITOR)
£1,577.53	£1,086.21	£3,088.19
452174	452175	452176

6.4* You are the bookkeeper responsible for the purchases ledger and nominal ledger of Galaxy Media.

(a) Open ledger accounts and enter the following balances at 1 August 2004:

	DR	CR
	£	£
Stardust & Company		1,328.43
Nova Limited		851.24
General expenses	638.49	
Furniture and fittings	3,295.00	
Value Added Tax		564.97
Bank	3,628.98	

(b) Enter the details of the payments shown below and on the next page in the correct ledger accounts. Update nominal accounts as appropriate.

5 Aug 2004	9 Aug 2004	12 Aug 2004
To Stardust & Co (CREDITOR)	To HM Customs & Excise (VAT)	To Style Furnishings New desk (Furniture & fittings) £210.30 + VAT £36.80)
£654.91	£564.97	£247.10
176543	176544	176545

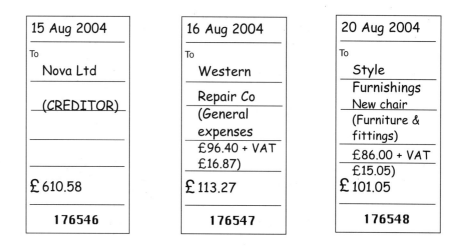

15 Aug 2004	16 Aug 2004	20 Aug 2004
To Nova Ltd (CREDITOR) £ 610.58 176546	To Western Repair Co (General expenses £96.40 + VAT £16.87) £ 113.27 176547	To Style Furnishings New chair (Furniture & fittings) £86.00 + VAT £15.05) £ 101.05 176548

Note: Blank account layouts – which you can photocopy – are provided at the end of this chapter, either 'T' account format (page 146) or two-column format (page 147).

6.5 You are the bookkeeper responsible for the purchases ledger and nominal ledger of Metro Trading Company.

(a) Open ledger accounts and enter the following balances at 1 September 2005:

	DR	CR
	£	£
City Supplies Limited		1,597.62
Aziz & Company		1,108.04
Sundry expenses	954.84	
Office equipment	5,186.50	
Value Added Tax		848.31
Bank		1,023.94

(b) Enter the details of the payments shown on the next page in the correct ledger accounts. Update nominal accounts as appropriate.

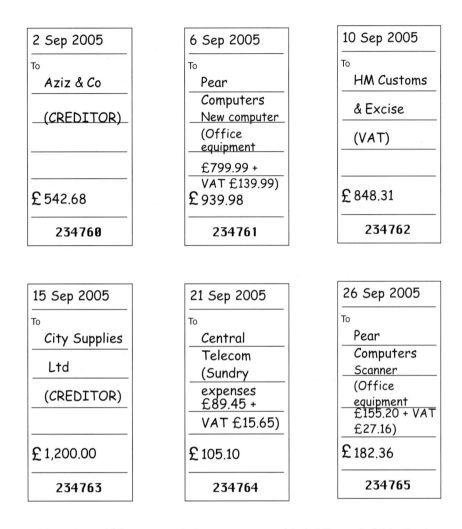

2 Sep 2005
To
Aziz & Co
(CREDITOR)
£ 542.68
234760

6 Sep 2005
To
Pear Computers
New computer (Office equipment £799.99 + VAT £139.99)
£ 939.98
234761

10 Sep 2005
To
HM Customs & Excise
(VAT)
£ 848.31
234762

15 Sep 2005
To
City Supplies Ltd
(CREDITOR)
£ 1,200.00
234763

21 Sep 2005
To
Central Telecom (Sundry expenses £89.45 + VAT £15.65)
£ 105.10
234764

26 Sep 2005
To
Pear Computers
Scanner (Office equipment £155.20 + VAT £27.16)
£ 182.36
234765

Note: Blank account layouts – which you can photocopy – are provided at the end of this chapter, either 'T' account format (page 146) or two-column format (page 147).

'T' account format

Account

Date	Details	£	p	Date	Details	£	p

Account

Date	Details	£	p	Date	Details	£	p

two-column account format

Date	Details	£	p	£	p
	——————————————— Account				

Date	Details	£	p	£	p
	——————————————— Account				

7 BALANCING ACCOUNTS

this chapter covers . . .

In previous chapters we have seen how to record transactions for sales and purchases, and receipts and payments in the accounts system. When we use 'T' accounts and two-column accounts, it is necessary to calculate the balance of each account from time-to-time, according to the needs of the business. The balance of an account is the running total of that account to date, eg the amount of sales made, the amount due for VAT, the amount of money in the bank. In this chapter we see how the process of balancing of accounts is carried out.

The chapter also covers recording of capital account and loan account, and their significance in the accounts system.

Towards the end of the chapter is a fully-worked Case Study which brings together much of the material which has been covered in the book so far, and presents the types of task which could appear in your Examination. The Case Study incorporates purchases ledger, sales ledger and nominal ledger.

OCR LEARNING OUTCOMES

unit 1: POSTING TO ACCOUNTS
Assessment objectives

1   *Maintain Purchase Ledger*

    (e) Balance accounts

2   *Maintain Sales Ledger*

    (e) Balance accounts

3   *Maintain Nominal Ledger*

    (c) Balance accounts

Note: In addition to the requirement to 'balance accounts', the Case Study on pages 156-163 covers the other Assessment Objectives of Unit 1, 'Posting to Accounts'

BALANCING ACCOUNTS

At regular intervals, often at the end of each month, accounts in 'T' account and two-column formats are balanced in order to calculate the running total of the account to date. This provides the owner of the business with valuable information, such as:

- the amount of sales and purchases made
- the amount owing by each debtor and to each creditor
- expenses to date
- whether bank account shows money in the bank or an overdraft
- the amount of VAT due to, or from, HM Customs & Excise

When using three-column accounts – or a computer accounting system – there is no need to balance each account. This is because, with such running balance accounts, the balance is calculated automatically and shown in the third column (after debit and credit). An example of a three-column account is given on page 48.

METHOD OF BALANCING 'T' ACCOUNTS

The mechanics of balancing accounts are straightforward, but care is needed to ensure that the principles of double-entry are followed. Set out below is an example of a debtor's account which has been balanced at the month-end:

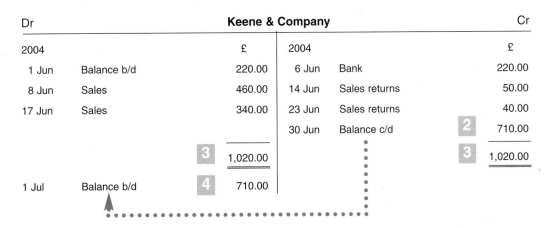

Dr			Keene & Company			Cr
2004		£	2004			£
1 Jun	Balance b/d	220.00	6 Jun	Bank		220.00
8 Jun	Sales	460.00	14 Jun	Sales returns		50.00
17 Jun	Sales	340.00	23 Jun	Sales returns		40.00
			30 Jun	Balance c/d	2	710.00
		3 1,020.00			3	1,020.00
1 Jul	Balance b/d	4 710.00				

When balancing the account, the bookkeeper takes the following steps, indicated (except for the first step) by the numbers in the boxes on the account above.

1 The debit and the credit columns are separately added up and the totals noted in pencil. It is important to appreciate that nothing is entered in the account at this stage.

2 The difference between the two totals (the balance of the account) is entered in the account

- on the side of the smaller total
- on the next available line
- with the date of the balancing
- with the words 'Balance c/d', an abbreviation of 'Balance carried down'

The balance carried down on the above account is shown to be £710.00.

3 Both sides of the account are now added up and the totals (which should be identical, and the higher of the two totals calculated in Step 1) are entered on the same line in the appropriate column, with a single line above and double underlined. The double underlining indicates that the account is ruled off and the figures above the underlining should not be added to the figures below.

4 As we are dealing with double-entry bookkeeping, the bookkeeper must now complete the transaction of entering the difference (see Step 2) and enter the same amount on the other side of the account, below the totals entered in Step 3. In doing this, the bookkeeper will have completed both a debit and a credit entry. The entry in this example reads '1 Jul Balance b/d £710.00'. This means that this is the amount owed by Keene and Company to the business on 1 July. The date here is not the month-end date (30 June) but the first day of the following month. The abbreviation 'b/d' stands for 'brought down'; alternatively 'b/f' can be used, which stands for 'brought forward'.

FURTHER EXAMPLES OF BALANCING 'T' ACCOUNTS

Dr			Purchases Account		Cr
2004		£	2004		£
1 Feb	Balance b/d	3,560.50	29 Feb	Balance c/d	4,311.00
7 Feb	Jarvis Ltd	300.00			
10 Feb	Nazir & Co	200.50			
20 Feb	T Pembridge	250.00			
		4,311.00			4,311.00
1 Mar	Balance b/d	4,311.00			

The above purchases account has transactions on one side only, but is still balanced in the same way. The account has a debit balance at 1 March of £4,311.00, which is the figure for total purchases to the end of February.

Dr			**Sales Account**		Cr
2004		£	2004		£
31 Oct	Balance c/d	16,410.50	1 Oct	Balance b/d	15,280.00
			10 Oct	Pete Singh Ltd	550.50
			12 Oct	Otley & Co	280.00
			20 Oct	J Anzar	300.00
		16,410.50			16,410.50
			1 Nov	Balance b/d	16,410.50

This sales account, like purchases account above, has transactions on one side only. The account has a credit balance at 1 November of £16,410.50, which is the figure for total sales to the end of October.

Dr			**B Lewis Limited**		Cr
2004		£	2004		£
10 Apr	Purchases returns	41.00	1 Apr	Balance b/d	240.50
28 Apr	Bank	300.00	6 Apr	Purchases	100.50
		341.00			341.00

This account in the name of a creditor has a 'nil' balance after the transactions for April have taken place. The two sides of the account are totalled and, as both debit side and credit side are the same amount, there is nothing further to do, apart from entering the double underlined total. There is no opening balance on this account for the next month.

Dr			**Furniture Account**		Cr
2004		£	2004		£
10 Jul	Bank	500.00			

This account has just the one transaction and, in practice, there is no need to balance it. It should be clear that the account has a debit balance of £500.00, which is represented by the asset of furniture.

Dr		Malvern Retail Limited			Cr
2004		£	2004		£
1 Aug	Balance b/d	308.45	20 Aug	Bank	308.45

This debtor's account has a 'nil' balance, with just one transaction on each side. All that is needed here is to double underline the amount on both sides.

METHOD OF BALANCING TWO-COLUMN ACCOUNTS

The following is an example of a debtor's account, set out in two-column format, which has been balanced at the month-end.

Keene & Company				Account		
Date	**Details**	**£**	**p**	**£**	**p**
2004					
1 Jun	Balance b/d	220	00		
6 Jun	Bank			220	00
8 Jun	Sales	460	00		
14 Jun	Sales returns			50	00
17 Jun	Sales	340	00		
23 Jun	Sales returns			40	00
		1 1,020	00	310	00
1 Jul	Balance b/d	**2** 710	00		

To balance the account, the bookkeeper takes the following steps indicated by the numbers in the boxes on the account above.

 The debit and credit columns are added up separately and the totals written in ink on the account.

2 The difference between the two totals (the balance of the account) is entered in the account

- on the side of the larger total
- on the next available line
- with the date of the first day of the following month
- with the words 'Balance b/d' or 'Balance b/f'

The balance brought down on the above account is shown to be £710.00.

Tutorial note

An alternative to this method of balancing two-column accounts is to balance them in the same way as you would a 'T' account, with

– balance carried down (on the date of balancing)
– the debit and credit money columns totalled to the same figure
– balance brought down (on the first day of the following month)

The following are further examples of balancing two-column format accounts.

Purchases						Account
Date	**Details**	**£**	**p**		**£**	**p**
2004						
1 Feb	Balance b/d	3,560	50			
7 Feb	Jarvis Ltd	300	00			
10 Feb	Nazir & Co	200	50			
20 Feb	T Pembridge	250	00			
		4,311	00			
1 Mar	Balance b/d	4,311	00			

The debit balance of this account at 1 March is £4,311.00

Sales		Account				
Date	**Details**	**£**	**p**	**£**	**p**
2004					
1 Oct	Balance b/d			15,280	00
10 Oct	Pete Singh Ltd			550	50
12 Oct	Otley & Co			280	00
20 Oct	J Anzar			300	00
				16,410	50
1 Nov	Balance b/d			16,410	50

The credit balance of this account at 1 November is £16,410.50.

B Lewis Limited		Account				
Date	**Details**	**£**	**p**	**£**	**p**
2004					
1 Apr	Balance b/d			240	50
6 Apr	Purchases			100	50
10 Apr	Purchases returns	41	00		
28 Apr	Bank	300	00		
		341	00	341	00

This account has a 'nil' balance at the end of April.

CAPITAL ACCOUNT AND LOAN ACCOUNT

Capital account and loan account are both liability accounts and, therefore, have credit balances. The significance of these accounts needs a short explanation.

capital account

Capital, as already mentioned in Chapter 1 (page 3), is the amount of money put in by the owner (or owners) of the business, ie it is the owner's investment – or stake – in the business. Capital account records the amount of this investment and almost always has a credit balance. When studying bookkeeping, it can be a puzzle to understand why capital account has a credit balance, ie is shown as a liability. It is easy to say that 'as capital is the owner's investment <u>in</u> the business, then it ought to be shown as an asset.' This is incorrect because the business is separate from the owner. What the accounts system records is that the business owes the amount of capital back to the owner, ie capital is a liability of the business. In practice, the business is unlikely to have sufficient money to be able to repay the owner in full, as otherwise the business could cease to exist. Sometimes partial repayments of capital might be made; however the most usual transaction is for the owner to increase the amount of capital invested in the business.

The bookkeeping entries for an increase in capital made by cheque are:

nominal (or general) ledger

– *debit* bank account with the amount of money received

– *credit* capital account with the amount of the increase in capital

For a partial repayment of capital made by cheque, the bookkeeping entries are:

nominal (or general) ledger

– *debit* capital account with the amount of the decrease in capital

– *credit* bank account with the amount of money repaid

loan account

When starting up a business, or running an existing business, it is quite common to raise money which can be invested in business assets. Whilst the owner's capital is one way of raising money, another way is by means of a loan from a bank, or from a friend or relative. In Chapter 1 (page 3), we saw how Ronaldo Antoni raised sufficient money to start his pizza business by means of:

– capital (his own investment)

– a bank loan

– a loan from his brother, Carlo

As we have seen above, capital is a liability of a business – so too are bank loans and loans from friends or relatives. In fact any form of lending to the business is a liability. The main difference between capital and loans is that, with loans, the lender expects to be repaid within an agreed time, but, as noted above, capital is unlikely to be repaid in full. Also, a lender will normally expect to be paid interest during the period of the loan.

The bookkeeping entries when a loan is first raised, or for an increase, are:

nominal (or general) ledger

– *debit* bank account with the amount of money received

– *credit* loan account with the amount of the loan raised, or the increase

For a repayment – or partial repayment – of a loan, the bookkeeping entries are:

nominal (or general) ledger

– *debit* loan account with the amount of the repayment

– *credit* bank account with the amount of money repaid

See also payment for liabilities, which were discussed earlier (page 135).

As well as loans – which are often raised to cover a long time period – many businesses are allowed by the bank to have a bank overdraft as a way of providing finance in the shorter term.

As we have seen already (pages 74-75), the balance of bank account can be either debit or credit:

• a **debit** balance is an **asset**, and means that the business has money in the bank

• a **credit** balance is a **liability**, and means that the business is overdrawn at the bank

CASE STUDY

PEMBRIDGE LIMITED: EXTENDED CASE STUDY

Tutorial notes

• This Case Study brings together the material that has been covered in the first seven chapters of this book. As such it provides a consolidating exercise for Unit 1, 'Posting to Accounts' and will help with preparation for the Examination.

- The main difference between this Case Study and the Examination for Unit 1 is that full documents – invoices, credit notes, cheques – are not provided here. The reason for this is that documents have been covered extensively in earlier chapters – also the focus here is on recording transactions in the accounts and then balancing the accounts at the month-end.

  Practice Examinations and Assignments – with documents – are contained in the Osborne Books 'Tutor Pack' (please refer to your Tutor or call 01905 748071).

situation

You are the bookkeeper responsible for keeping the purchase, sales and nominal ledgers of Pembridge Limited.

Task 1

Open ledger accounts and enter the following balances as at 1 November 2004.

	DR £	CR £
Wyvern Supplies	730.25	
Harry's Stores	1,028.54	
Aziz & Co		696.38
Hepworth Ltd		1,204.16
Durning & Co		709.56
Bank	3,026.15 ·	
Capital		3,216.27
Furniture	3,650.00	
General expenses	2,394.17	
Purchases	11,681.59	
Purchase returns		543.87
Sales		16,243.27
Sales returns	498.01	
VAT		395.20

Task 2

Enter the details below, taken from invoices received from suppliers, in the correct purchase ledger accounts. Update nominal accounts as appropriate.

3 Nov	Bought goods from Aziz & Co for £298.64 + VAT £52.26, total invoice £350.90
7 Nov	Bought goods from Hepworth Ltd for £515.64 + VAT £90.23, total invoice £605.87
11 Nov	Bought goods from Durning & Co for £211.18 + VAT £36.95, total invoice £248.13
16 Nov	Bought goods from Hepworth Ltd for £364.15 + VAT £63.72, total invoice £427.87
17 Nov	Bought goods from Durning & Co for £307.68 + VAT £53.84, total invoice £361.52

| 25 Nov | Bought goods from Aziz & Co for £496.84 + VAT £86.94, total invoice £583.78 |

Task 3

Enter the details below, taken from credit notes received from suppliers, in the correct purchase ledger accounts. Update nominal accounts as appropriate.

| 15 Nov | Credit note received from Aziz & Co for £58.34 + VAT £10.20, total £68.54 |
| 24 Nov | Credit note received from Durning & Co for £102.26 + VAT £17.89, total £120.15 |

Task 4

Enter the details below of payments made in the correct ledger accounts. Update ledger accounts as appropriate.

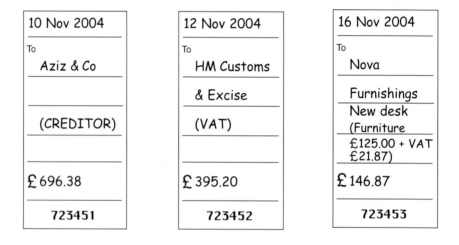

10 Nov 2004	12 Nov 2004	16 Nov 2004
To	To	To
Aziz & Co	HM Customs & Excise	Nova Furnishings New desk (Furniture £125.00 + VAT £21.87)
(CREDITOR)	(VAT)	
£ 696.38	£ 395.20	£ 146.87
723451	723452	723453

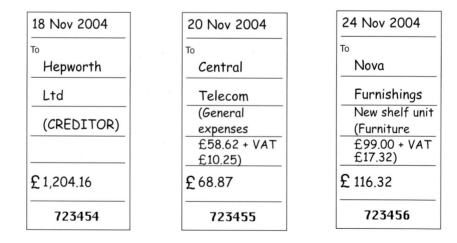

18 Nov 2004	20 Nov 2004	24 Nov 2004
To	To	To
Hepworth Ltd	Central Telecom (General expenses £58.62 + VAT £10.25)	Nova Furnishings New shelf unit (Furniture £99.00 + VAT £17.32)
(CREDITOR)		
£ 1,204.16	£ 68.87	£ 116.32
723454	723455	723456

Task 5

Enter the details below, taken from invoices sent to customers, in the correct sales ledger accounts. Update nominal accounts as appropriate.

6 Nov	Sold goods to Wyvern Supplies for £210.84 + VAT £36.89, total invoice £247.73
10 Nov	Sold goods to Harry's Stores for £315.26 + VAT £55.17, total invoice £370.43
18 Nov	Sold goods to Wyvern Supplies for £168.45 + VAT £29.47, total invoice £197.92
25 Nov	Sold goods to Harry's Stores for £189.47 + VAT £33.15, total invoice £222.62

Task 6

Enter the details below, taken from credit notes sent to customers, in the correct sales ledger accounts. Update nominal accounts as appropriate.

13 Nov	Credit note sent to Wyvern Supplies for £33.30 + VAT £5.82, total £39.12
20 Nov	Credit note sent to Harry's Stores for £45.62 + VAT £7.98, total £53.60

Task 7

Enter the details below, of payments received from debtors, in the correct sales ledger accounts. Update nominal accounts as appropriate.

7 Nov	Cheque received from Harry's Stores for £1,028.54
10 Nov	Cheque received from Wyvern Supplies for £977.98

Task 8

Balance all ledger accounts at the end of the month, 30 November 2004.

s o l u t i o n

SALES LEDGER

Dr			**Wyvern Supplies**			Cr
2004		£	2004			£
1 Nov	Balance b/d	730.25	13 Nov	Sales returns		39.12
6 Nov	Sales	247.73	10 Nov	Bank		977.98
18 Nov	Sales	197.92	30 Nov	Balance c/d		158.80
		1,175.90				1,175.90
1 Dec	Balance b/d	158.80				

Dr	Harry's Stores					Cr
2004		£	2004			£
1 Nov	Balance b/d	1,028.54	20 Nov	Sales returns		53.60
10 Nov	Sales	370.43	7 Nov	Bank		1,028.54
25 Nov	Sales	222.62	30 Nov	Balance c/d		539.45
		1,621.59				1,621.59
1 Dec	Balance b/d	539.45				

PURCHASES LEDGER

Dr	Aziz & Company					Cr
2004		£	2004			£
15 Nov	Purchases returns	68.54	1 Nov	Balance b/d		696.38
10 Nov	Bank	696.38	3 Nov	Purchases		350.90
30 Nov	Balance c/d	866.14	25 Nov	Purchases		583.78
		1,631.06				1,631.06
			1 Dec	Balance b/d		866.14

Dr	Hepworth Limited					Cr
2004		£	2004			£
18 Nov	Bank	1,204.16	1 Nov	Balance b/d		1,204.16
30 Nov	Balance c/d	1,033.74	7 Nov	Purchases		605.87
			16 Nov	Purchases		427.87
		2,237.90				2,237.90
			1 Dec	Balance b/d		1,033.74

Dr	Durning & Company					Cr
2004		£	2004			£
24 Nov	Purchases returns	120.15	1 Nov	Balance b/d		709.56
30 Nov	Balance c/d	1,199.06	11 Nov	Purchases		248.13
			17 Nov	Purchases		361.52
		1,319.21				1,319.21
			1 Dec	Balance b/d		1,199.06

NOMINAL LEDGER

Bank Account

Dr			£	Cr			£
2004				2004			
1 Nov	Balance b/d		3,026.15	10 Nov	Aziz & Co		696.38
7 Nov	Harry's Stores		1,028.54	12 Nov	HM Customs & Excise		395.20
10 Nov	Wyvern Supplies		977.98	16 Nov	Furniture		146.87
				18 Nov	Hepworth Ltd		1,204.16
				20 Nov	General expenses		68.87
				24 Nov	Furniture		116.32
				30 Nov	Balance c/d		2,404.87
			5,032.67				5,032.67
1 Dec	Balance b/d		2,404.87				

Capital Account

Dr		£	Cr		£
2004			2004		
			1 Nov	Balance b/d	3,216.27

Furniture Account

Dr		£	Cr		£
2004			2004		
1 Nov	Balance b/d	3,650.00	30 Nov	Balance c/d	3,874.00
16 Nov	Bank	125.00			
24 Nov	Bank	99.00			
		3,874.00			3,874.00
1 Dec	Balance b/d	3,874.00			

General Expenses Account

Dr		£	Cr		£
2004			2004		
1 Nov	Balance b/d	2,394.17	30 Nov	Balance c/d	2,452.79
20 Nov	Bank	58.62			
		2,452.79			2,452.79
1 Dec	Balance b/d	2,452.79			

Dr		Purchases Account			Cr
2004		£	2004		£
1 Nov	Balance b/d	11,681.59	30 Nov	Balance c/d	13,875.72
3 Nov	Aziz & Co	298.64			
7 Nov	Hepworth Ltd	515.64			
11 Nov	Durning & Co	211.18			
16 Nov	Hepworth Ltd	364.15			
17 Nov	Durning & Co	307.68			
25 Nov	Aziz & Co	496.84			
		13,875.72			13,875.72
1 Dec	Balance b/d	13,875.72			

Dr		Purchases Returns Account			Cr
2004		£	2004		£
30 Nov	Balance c/d	704.47	1 Nov	Balance b/d	543.87
			15 Nov	Aziz & Co	58.34
			24 Nov	Durning & Co	102.26
		704.47			704.47
			1 Dec	Balance b/d	704.47

Dr		Sales Account			Cr
2004		£	2004		£
30 Nov	Balance c/d	17,127.29	1 Nov	Balance b/d	16,243.27
			6 Nov	Wyvern Supplies	210.84
			10 Nov	Harry's Stores	315.26
			18 Nov	Wyvern Supplies	168.45
			25 Nov	Harry's Stores	189.47
		17,127.29			17,127.29
			1 Dec	Balance b/d	17,127.29

Dr		Sales Returns Account			Cr
2004		£	2004		£
1 Nov	Balance b/d	498.01	30 Nov	Balance c/d	576.93
13 Nov	Wyvern Supplies	33.30			
20 Nov	Harry's Stores	45.62			
		576.93			576.93
1 Dec	Balance b/d	576.93			

Dr	Value Added Tax Account				Cr
2004		£	**2004**		£
3 Nov	Aziz & Co	52.26	1 Nov	Balance b/d	395.20
7 Nov	Hepworth Ltd	90.23	15 Nov	Aziz & Co	10.20
11 Nov	Durning & Co	36.95	24 Nov	Durning & Co	17.89
16 Nov	Hepworth Ltd	63.72	6 Nov	Wyvern Supplies	36.89
17 Nov	Durning & Co	53.84	10 Nov	Harry's Stores	55.17
25 Nov	Aziz & Co	86.94	18 Nov	Wyvern Supplies	29.47
12 Nov	Bank	395.20	25 Nov	Harry's Stores	33.15
16 Nov	Furniture	21.87	30 Nov	Balance c/d	264.41
20 Nov	General expenses	10.25			
24 Nov	Furniture	17.32			
13 Nov	Wyvern Supplies	5.82			
20 Nov	Harry's Stores	7.98			
		842.38			842.38
1 Dec	Balance b/d	264.41			

Notes to the accounts:

- 'T' accounts are used here; the accounts may also be set out using different formats, eg two-column.
- Transactions have been entered to the accounts in the order of the tasks from the Case Study – this does mean that, from time-to-time, the date order of accounts is not consecutive, eg VAT account.

CHAPTER SUMMARY

- 'T' accounts and two-column accounts are balanced at regular intervals – often the month-end
- The 'balance b/d' (or 'balance b/f') is the account balance at the start of the next period
- Capital account is a liability of the business which is unlikely to be repaid in full as the business could then cease to exist
- All forms of loans – bank loan, loan from a friend or relative, etc – are liabilities of the business
- The balance of bank account can be either debit (money in the bank) or credit (an overdraft)

KEY TERMS

balance of account	the running total of the account to date
capital account	the amount of money put in by the owner (or owners) of the business
loans	bank loans, and loans from friends or relatives – often raised to cover a long time period
bank overdraft	a way of financing a business in the shorter term by borrowing on the bank account

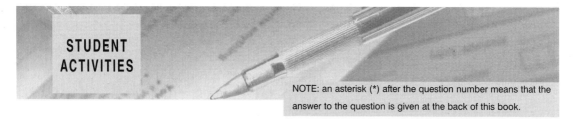

STUDENT ACTIVITIES

NOTE: an asterisk (*) after the question number means that the answer to the question is given at the back of this book.

7.1* The following accounts are taken from the bookkeeping system of Premier Traders Limited:

Dr		**Sales Account**		Cr
2005	£	2005		£
		1 Apr	Balance b/d	2,468.30
		5 Apr	Perran Stores	532.18
		11 Apr	L Johnson	386.97
		20 Apr	Doyle & Co	1,246.15

Dr		**Purchases Account**		Cr
2005	£	2005		£
1 Apr Balance b/d	1,524.92			
7 Apr Shah & Co	345.99			
18 Apr P Devoran	211.63			
27 Apr Bissoe Ltd	509.38			

Dr		**Perran Stores**		Cr
2005	£	2005		£
1 Apr Balance b/d	826.91	12 Apr Sales returns		86.24
5 Apr Sales	532.18	20 Apr Bank		826.91

Dr		Shah & Company				Cr
2005		£	2005			£
14 Apr	Purchases returns	96.45	1 Apr		Balance b/d	826.15
28 Apr	Bank	1,075.69	7 Apr		Purchases	345.99

As bookkeeper to Premier Traders Limited you are to copy out these accounts in either 'T' account format (as above) or in two-column format. You are then to balance each account at 30 April 2005, bringing down the balances on 1 May.

Blank account layouts – which you can photocopy – are provided on pages 168 and 169.

7.2   You are the bookkeeper responsible for keeping the purchase, sales and nominal ledgers of Hassan & Company.

Task 1

Open ledger accounts and enter the following balances as at 1 September 2005.

	DR	CR
	£	£
Ghuman Ltd		506.21
Nova Supplies		394.87
Mithian Stores	711.33	
Hawke Ltd	548.62	
Singh & Co	397.46	
Bank	1,502.47	
Capital		6,391.68
Office equipment	6,390.65	
Sundry expenses	2,610.55	
Purchases	6,405.91	
Purchase returns		496.21
Sales		11,095.68
Sales returns	851.28	
VAT		533.62

Use either 'T' accounts or two-column accounts; blank layouts – which you can photocopy – are provided on pages 168 and 169.

Task 2

Enter the details below, taken from invoices received from suppliers, in the correct purchase ledger accounts. Update nominal accounts as appropriate.

5 Sep	Bought goods from Ghuman Ltd for £210.31 + VAT £36.80, total invoice £247.11
12 Sep	Bought goods from Nova Supplies for £359.64 + VAT £62.93, total invoice £422.57
19 Sep	Bought goods from Ghuman Ltd for £397.84 + VAT £69.62, total invoice £467.46
26 Sep	Bought goods from Nova Supplies for £186.24 + VAT £32.59, total invoice £218.83

Task 3

Enter the details below, taken from credit notes received from suppliers, in the correct purchase ledger accounts. Update nominal accounts as appropriate.

14 Sep   Credit note received from Ghuman Ltd for £28.47 + VAT £4.98, total £33.45

23 Sep   Credit note received from Nova Supplies for £86.24 + VAT £15.09, total £101.33

Task 4

Enter the details below of payments made in the correct ledger accounts. Update ledger accounts as appropriate.

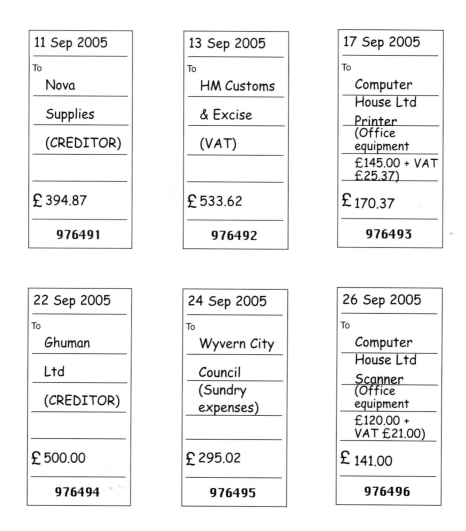

| 11 Sep 2005 |
| To |
| Nova |
| Supplies |
| (CREDITOR) |
| £ 394.87 |
| 976491 |

| 13 Sep 2005 |
| To |
| HM Customs |
| & Excise |
| (VAT) |
| £ 533.62 |
| 976492 |

| 17 Sep 2005 |
| To |
| Computer |
| House Ltd |
| Printer |
| (Office equipment £145.00 + VAT £25.37) |
| £ 170.37 |
| 976493 |

| 22 Sep 2005 |
| To |
| Ghuman |
| Ltd |
| (CREDITOR) |
| £ 500.00 |
| 976494 |

| 24 Sep 2005 |
| To |
| Wyvern City |
| Council |
| (Sundry expenses) |
| £ 295.02 |
| 976495 |

| 26 Sep 2005 |
| To |
| Computer |
| House Ltd |
| Scanner |
| (Office equipment £120.00 + VAT £21.00) |
| £ 141.00 |
| 976496 |

Task 5

Enter details below, taken from invoices sent to customers, in the correct sales ledger accounts. Update nominal accounts as appropriate.

2 Sep	Sold goods to Mithian Stores for £190.33 + VAT £33.30, total invoice £223.63
5 Sep	Sold goods to Singh & Co for £215.49 + VAT £37.71, total invoice £253.20
11 Sep	Sold goods to Hawke Ltd for £255.62 + VAT £44.73, total invoice £300.35
16 Sep	Sold goods to Singh & Co for £107.43 + VAT £18.80, total invoice £126.23
22 Sep	Sold goods to Mithian Stores for £395.27 + VAT £69.17, total invoice £464.44
28 Sep	Sold goods to Hawke Ltd for £212.39 + VAT £37.16, total invoice £249.55

Task 6

Enter details below, taken from credit notes sent to customers, in the correct sales ledger accounts. Update nominal accounts as appropriate.

13 Sep	Credit note sent to Singh & Co for £40.85 + VAT £7.14, total £47.99
25 Sep	Credit note sent to Hawke Ltd for £53.97 + VAT £9.44, total £63.41

Task 7

Enter details below, of payments received from debtors, in the correct sales ledger accounts. Update nominal accounts as appropriate.

6 Sep	Cheque received from Hawke Ltd for £548.62
15 Sep	Cheque received from Mithian Stores for £934.96

Task 8

Balance all ledger accounts at the end of the month, 30 September 2005.

'T' account format

Account

Date	Details	£	p	Date	Details	£	p

Account

Date	Details	£	p	Date	Details	£	p

two-column account format

		_____ Account			
Date	Details	£	p	£	p
	`				

		_____ Account			
Date	Details	£	p	£	p

8 PRINCIPLES OF PETTY CASH

this chapter covers . . .

A petty cash book is used to record low-value cash payments for various small purchases and expenses incurred by a business or other organisation. This chapter covers the areas of:

- the principles of maintaining a petty cash system using either the imprest or non-imprest system

- the completion of the petty cash vouchers for both payments and receipts

- the importance of checking details on the vouchers, including amounts claimed

- the authorisation of vouchers including signatures

- the principles and procedures of VAT

- the importance of accuracy

- the importance of keeping the petty cash safe and secure

OCR LEARNING OUTCOMES

unit 2: MAINTAINING PETTY CASH

Assessment objectives

1   **Analysed Petty Cash Books**

   (b)   Restore imprest

2   **Enter Petty Cash Vouchers for Payments and Receipts into Petty Cash Book**

   (a)   Enter correct date

   (b)   Enter correct folio reference

   (c)   Enter correct description

   (d)   Enter correct total

   (e)   Calculate VAT accurately

   (f)   Enter correct VAT amount

   (h)   Enter all entries legibly

INTRODUCTION TO PETTY CASH

All businesses and organisations regularly incur small items of expenditure. Often these expenses are paid for by cash since the amount required may be too small for the payment to be made by cheque. Such examples of this type of expense could be payment of postage stamps, travelling expenses, small items of stationery, and so on. Such small items of expenses are usually recorded in the petty cash book that is designed specifically for this purpose. Other expenditure incurring larger amounts of money is recorded in the cash book and this is dealt with in Unit 3 (Chapters 11 - 14).

THE PETTY CASH PROCEDURE

The business will appoint a petty cashier, often a junior member of staff, who is responsible for looking after the petty cash on behalf of the main cashier. The main cashier will provide the petty cashier with a sum of money, called a 'float'. The petty cashier is then responsible for this money, making payments to members of staff to repay them for expenses incurred on behalf of the business and keeping records of payments made, amounts received and balancing the petty cash book at regular intervals.

The petty cashier will need the following to carry out this task:

*   a petty cash book in which to record transactions
*   a lockable petty cash box to hold the money
*   a stock of blank petty cash vouchers (see page 175) for claims on petty cash to be made
*   a lockable desk drawer in which to keep these items

making a claim

Before studying the form-filling procedures we will look at how a claim for petty cash is made by an employee with the following example:

John works for Harpers Estate Agents as an office junior. His supervisor, Mrs May, asks John to go to the post office and buy postage stamps for the office. John carries out this request as follows:

*   John goes to the post office and buys the postage stamps for the office. He pays for them in cash £4.20 and asks for a receipt.
*   On his return to the office John gives the stamps and receipt to Mrs May.
*   Mrs May authorises a petty cash voucher that details the purchase of the postage stamps made by John and attaches the receipt to the voucher.

- The petty cashier gives John £4.20 in cash.
- The petty cashier enters the details in the petty cash book.

items claimed for by petty cash

As already mentioned, petty cash is used to make small cash payments for purchases and expenses incurred by the business. Examples of the type of payments made from petty cash include:

- postage
- small items of stationery
- casual labour
- window cleaning
- travel expenses such as bus and rail fares incurred on behalf of the business
- donations

Note, however, that petty cash should not be used to pay for private expenses of employees, eg tea, coffee and milk, unless the business has agreed these in advance. Usually there will be a list of approved expenses that can be reimbursed from petty cash.

The business will also decide on the maximum value for any transaction that can be paid out of petty cash; for example, £25 is a common figure.

CASE STUDY

PETTY CASH EXPENSES

situation

You are employed as an accounts assistant for Astley Controls Limited. One of your duties is that of petty cashier. Which of the following expenses would you allow to be paid out of the petty cash? The upper limit for petty cash transactions is £25.

- Postage stamps, £6.50
- Window cleaning, £8.00
- Envelopes for office use, £3.20
- Computer disks, £38.50
- Coffee and milk for the office, £5.76
- Donation to the local church, £10.00
- Train fare to work £4.60 claimed by the office assistant
- Car mileage to work of Manager who was called in on Sunday morning following a break-in of the premises

solution

Postage	pay from petty cash
Window cleaning	pay from petty cash
Envelopes	pay from petty cash
Computer disks	this is a business expense but, since the amount is £38.50 it is too large to be paid out of petty cash, instead it should be paid by cheque
Coffee and milk	this payment can only be made out of petty cash if the items were used for the use of official visitors and customers and not for use by the employees
Donation	pay from petty cash
Train fare	this is a personal expense and cannot be paid for out of petty cash
Car mileage	travel to work is a personal expense, as seen from the previous item; however, as this expense was a special journey on a Sunday following a break-in to the premises, it can be paid from petty cash

Notes on the case study

- If the petty cashier cannot decide whether or not an item of expense can be paid from petty cash, the item should be referred to the accounts supervisor for a decision.

- Before payments can be made for petty cash expenses they must be supported by documentary evidence and be properly authorised (see below).

THE IMPREST SYSTEM

As mentioned above, the petty cashier is given a 'float' of money at the beginning of the period to enable payments to be made for expenses incurred during the period. At the end of the period the amount spent is added up, this amount is then reclaimed from the cashier to restore the money to the original float. It is the same principle as filling up the tank of your car each week. The amount of fuel you put in is the same as the amount you have used. The following example illustrates the procedure:

		£
January 1	Float received from cashier	100.00
January 31	Amount spent during month	70.00
	Balance of cash in hand	30.00
February 1	Amount received from cashier to restore float to original amount	70.00
	Cash at start of next month ie imprest	100.00

If, during the period, all the cash is used up then it is possible to obtain further amounts of money from the cashier to top up the float. It is also possible to increase the float from time to time if extra money is required for additional expenditure, for example; at Christmas when cards and calendars are purchased and extra postage stamps are required.

advantages of using the imprest system

One advantage of using the imprest system is that it is possible to check the cash at any time since the total of expenditure incurred during a period together with the cash in hand should always equal the original float. Another advantage is that small items of expenditure can be recorded separately in the petty cash book thereby eliminating such items from the main cash book. Since this task can be carried out by a junior member of staff it saves the cashier valuable time that can then be spent in other areas of work.

NON-IMPREST SYSTEM

Most businesses use the imprest system, as described above, otherwise they obtain an amount of money from the cashier, when this has been used up they simply go to the main cashier and obtain more money. This is known as the non-imprest system. Therefore, unlike the imprest system, which is replenished at the end of the period be it a week or a month, a non-imprest system is only "topped" up as and when required.

PETTY CASH VOUCHER

When an employee incurs expenditure on behalf of the business and then wishes to get the money back he/she will have to complete a petty cash voucher and provide documentary evidence such as a receipt if possible. Petty cash vouchers contain the following details:

- details of expenditure together with a receipt for money spent (if possible)

- amount spent, including VAT, if applicable

- signature of person making the claim and to whom the money will be paid

- signature of person authorising the payment, usually the petty cashier for amounts within the authorisation limit, larger amounts will be authorised by the accounts supervisor or manager

- the petty cash voucher will then be numbered to enable the documentation to be filed correctly and easily identified in the petty cash book

An example of a petty cash voucher is shown below.

petty cash voucher			No. 83
		date	6 December 2004
description			amount
		£	p
Train fare (no VAT)		5	83
		5	83
signature	*S J Worrall*		
authorised	*J K Blake*		

Petty cash vouchers are the *prime documents* for the petty cash book.

authorisation of petty cash vouchers

When the petty cashier receives a completed petty cash voucher from a member of staff it is important to check that the voucher has been completed correctly, signed by the person making the claim and has been properly authorised. It is important to check that the amount claimed for is within the authorised limit. For example, the organisation may allow payments to be made by petty cash up to £25 as already mentioned above. The petty cashier should also check the voucher for accuracy in the calculations and wherever possible ensure that a receipt is attached to the voucher.

The petty cash voucher details are then entered in the petty cash book and the voucher filed away in numerical order so that it may be easily located if necessary.

Note: in the next chapter details of entering the petty cash voucher will be covered (see pages 190-193).

RECEIPTS

Occasionally the petty cashier may receive money from a member of staff for goods sold to them, for example, the sale of postage stamps for personal use. When this happens the petty cashier completes a receipt, usually in duplicate, one copy is given to the person buying the postage stamps and a copy is retained for the petty cashier's records.

The following is an example of a receipt used for this purpose:

RECEIPT		No. 3
	date	23 October 2004

received from	Susan Adams
the sum of	Two pounds ten pence
for	postage stamps
cheque	———
cash	2.10
discount	———
total	2.10
signature	James Barker

The petty cashier will enter the receipt of the money, ie £2.10 in the petty cash book under the column headed 'Receipts' (see page 177).

PETTY CASH BOOK

A petty cash book is shown on the next page. Note the analysis columns that enable the transaction to be recorded and analysed at the same time, according to the type of expenditure incurred. We will look in detail at the entries that are made in the petty cash book in the next chapter.

PETTY CASH AND VAT

Value Added Tax is charged by VAT-registered businesses on their taxable supplies as we have seen in Chapter 2 (page 18). Consequently, there may often be VAT included as part of an expense paid out of petty cash. However, not all expenses will have been subject to VAT, such as supplies that are exempt (eg financial services, postal services). Perhaps the supplier is not VAT-registered or the goods supplied are zero-rated such as food and drink, books, newspapers and transport. (Note, however, that meals supplied in a restaurant are standard-rated, as are taxi fares and car hire.)

In order to reclaim the VAT charged by a supplier, a receipt or invoice must

Petty Cash Book

Receipts		Date	Details	Voucher Number	Total			VAT			Postage			Cleaning			Motor Expenses			Stationery			Refresh-ments		
£	p				£	p		£	p		£	p		£	p		£	p		£	p		£	p	

be obtained for the expense incurred. The document must contain the suppliers name, address and most importantly their VAT registration number. Such a receipt or invoice usually identifies the cost of the item purchased together with the VAT charged to give a total amount, as shown below:

INVOICE

Business Products & Co
Unit 3 Wellington Industrial Estate
Burton-upon-Trent
BV1 7TS

Vat Registration No. 501 2764 72

to Kerr and Partners High Street Burton-upon-Trent BT1 6FG	**invoice no.** K 4621/03 **date** 18 August 2004 **order no.** 04/9848

quantity	description	cat. no.	unit price (£)	£
4 reams	A4 photocopier paper	PP639T	3.00	12.00
	Less trade discount %			–
		VAT at 17.5%		2.10
				14.10

terms: net monthly

To prepare a petty cash voucher from this invoice and enter the details in the petty cash book is straightforward because all the figures are there: the £2.10 will be entered in the VAT column of the petty cash book, the £12.00 in the appropriate expense column and the total amount paid £14.10 will be entered in the total column.

documents not showing VAT

Sometimes, however, receipts are issued showing the total amount paid but not indicating the amount of VAT incurred. This is quite normal practice for smaller amounts. An example of a receipt that does not identify the amount of VAT separately is shown below:

RECEIPT

Logan Labels & Co., Dunwoody Lane, Derby, DA8 6HJ

Tel: 01332 280421

Vat Registration No. 488 2720 76

No.123

date 23 Sept 2004

received with thanks from   R Dudek

the sum of   seven pounds and five pence

for   1 pack adhesive labels

cheque	—
cash	7.05
discount	—
total	7.05

signature   J Murphy

In the above case it will be necessary to calculate the amount of VAT included in the total price of the adhesive labels of £7.05. This is calculated as follows:

The formula, with VAT at 17.5% is:

price including VAT divided by 1.175 = price before VAT is added on...

in this case...

      £7.05 divided by 1.175 = £6.00 = price before VAT is added on

the VAT content is therefore

      £7.05 less £6.00 = £1.05

Here the £1.05 will be entered in the VAT column in the petty cash book, £6.00 in the appropriate expense column, and the full £7.05 in the total payment column.

Note that when calculating VAT amounts, fractions of a penny are ignored, ie the tax is rounded down to a whole penny.

SECURITY

It is important that the petty cash book and the money are kept in a safe and secure place. Ideally the money should be kept in a lockable cash box. The petty cashier should keep the key to the petty cash box in a safe place with a duplicate key being kept by the main cashier or accountant. The box together with the petty cash book should ideally be kept in a fireproof safe or cabinet. Only the petty cashier or main cashier should be authorised to make payments of petty cash and they should obtain a signature from the person receiving the money.

As mentioned above, one of the advantages of using the imprest system is that it is easy to check the petty cash at any time. This enables checks to be made on the petty cashier at various intervals to ensure that he or she is honest and the money is secure.

CHAPTER SUMMARY

- The petty cash book is used to record small items of cash expenditure incurred by a business and an occasional cash receipt.

- The person responsible for maintaining the petty cash book is called the petty cashier, and he or she is responsible for security.

- Most businesses operate petty cash using the imprest system. Initially a cash 'float' of a fixed amount of money is given to the petty cashier for a specific time period. During the period payment is made against the correct documentation – usually a petty cash voucher – which must be signed and authorised for payment. At the end of the period, any cash paid out is restored to the same amount for the beginning of the next week or month.

- The advantage of using the imprest system is the ability to check the cash at any time since the total amount spent together with the cash in hand should always equal the original float. It also minimises the number of entries made in the main cash book.

- Petty cash can also be carried out using a non-imprest system, which involves 'top ups' of cash as and when it is required.

- Petty cash vouchers are entered in the petty cash book and are analysed according to the type of expenditure incurred.

- If VAT has been paid it is important to analyse the relevant amount separately in the VAT column. If VAT is not shown separately on a receipt or petty cash voucher it may be necessary to calculate this figure to enable the VAT to be recorded in the appropriate column.

- It is important that the money is kept in a lockable box and – together with the petty cash book – kept in a secure place.

KEY TERMS

cash float	an amount of money given to the petty cashier at the beginning of a period to enable them to make payments
imprest system	where money held in the petty cash float is restored to the original amount for the beginning of the next period
non-imprest system	where the petty cashier obtains a amount of money from the cashier and when this is used up they go to the cashier and obtain some more money
petty cash book	a subsidiary book used for recording small items of cash expenditure and occasional cash receipts which are usually analysed as they are entered
petty cashier	person responsible for the petty cash system
petty cash voucher	the form used to claim amounts from petty cash, which must be properly completed, signed and authorised

STUDENT ACTIVITIES

NOTE: an asterisk (*) after the question number means that the answer to the question is given at the back of this book.

8.1 * You are employed as petty cashier for a small advertising agency. The agency operates the petty cash imprest system in which small items of expenditure incurred by staff members up to £25.00 are paid by you, any item of expense above £25.00 is paid by cheque. The accountant asks you to look through a list of expenditure incurred by employees and to state which items should be paid by you out of petty cash, paid by the accountant by cheque and those items which you consider not to be business expenses.

(a)   Photo-copier paper £12.60

(b)   Office cleaner £26.75

(c)   Postage on parcel to Hong Kong £3.74

(d)   Secretary's weekly train ticket to work £44.00

(e)   Tea, sugar and milk £4.92 for the office (given to visitors)

(f)   Coffee £5.20 for staff

(g)   Postage stamps £8.00

(h)   Card, fabric and staples for client's display £83.50

(i)   Advertisement in local press for new cleaner £21.70

(j)   Flowers for reception area £7.00

8.2 * Morgan's Garage Limited employs several staff including James Dean, the accounts assistant, who unfortunately has to go into hospital for treatment and will be absent from work for the next four weeks. The garage operates their petty cash using the imprest system and one of James's tasks is that of petty cashier. James has a float of £200.00 that he uses to operate the imprest system on a monthly basis.

Whilst James is absent from work the owner of the garage, John Morgan, has asked Louise, the secretary, to look after the petty cash. To enable Louise to carry out this task John Morgan asks James to write some instructions on how the imprest system is used to operate the business's petty cash.

Task

Assume you are James and write brief notes on the operation of the petty cash using the imprest system. Ensure the instructions are clear and easy to follow.

8.3* As petty cashier you have been asked to prepare the petty cash vouchers, shown below, for signature by the person making the claim. You are to use today's date and are able to authorise payments up to £20.00; any amount above that is to be authorised by the cashier, Bob Allen. You are to assume that Bob Allen duly authorises any payment above £20.00.

- Louise Carter posted a special delivery package to the bank and incurred postage charges of £18.30 (no VAT).

- Martin Gould purchased two packets of computer discs from Baxter's Stationers at a cost of £4.70 each, including VAT totalling £1.40.

- The office manager, Chris Edge, recently attended a training conference and wishes to be reimbursed for his train fare to London of £35.00 (no VAT).

State what other documentation would also be required besides the completed petty cash vouchers in each of the above.

Blank petty cash vouchers are reproduced on the pages that follow. You may photocopy them. Blank vouchers are also available for download from the resources sections of www.osbornebooks.co.uk

petty cash voucher		No. 22
	date	
description		amount
	£	p
signature		
authorised		

petty cash voucher		No. 23
	date	
description		amount
	£	p
signature		
authorised		

petty cash voucher		No. 24
	date	
description		amount
	£	p
signature		
authorised		

8.4 Star Secretarial Agency has an office in Leeds and due to an increase in business has recently employed a new junior accounts assistant, Fred Grainger, who likes to be called Freddy. One of Freddy's duties is that of petty cashier and during Freddy's initial training he is shown the following instructions that must be followed when paying petty cash expenses to members of staff:

- All requests for payment of petty cash expenses must be made on petty cash vouchers showing full details of the expense, the date and if possible a receipt must be attached.

- Vouchers must be signed by the person claiming the money.

- Vouchers must be authorised for payment by the company secretary, Nick Burns.

- The petty cashier is authorised to pay claims up to £25.00, any item above that must be made by cheque.

- The agency uses the imprest system with a float of £100.00 for a two week period.

As petty cashier, Freddy, is asked to complete petty cash vouchers for any of the items shown below in accordance with the agency's instructions shown above.

STAR SECRETARIAL AGENCY

Details of transactions for 9 September 2004 are listed below. The last voucher used was No. 82.

- Stationery for use in the accounts department costing £15.20, including VAT of £2.26. This was bought by Joe Simpson, the assistant accountant, and a receipted invoice is attached.

- Nick Burns, the company secretary, gives you a receipt for the cost incurred in taking clients out for lunch, the bill totalled £56.40 including VAT of £8.40.

- Donation to the local church fete £25.00, this was paid by Joe Simpson on behalf of the agency and a receipt obtained. No VAT.

- Postage stamps £9.00 paid for by Jane Adams the office administrator. No VAT.

- Train fare for employee, Alice Gee, to work £5.50. No VAT.

- Office window cleaning £18.00 paid by Nick Burns, no receipt available. No VAT involved.

- Office milk, tea and coffee paid for by Jane Adams £12.30 (no VAT). The agency pays for these items for staff use.

Task

Assume you are Freddy. Complete, where appropriate, the petty cash vouchers. If, for any reason you are unable to pay a particular item you are to state why.

petty cash voucher		No.
	date	
description		amount
	£	p
signature		
authorised		

petty cash voucher		No.
	date	
description		amount
	£	p
signature		
authorised		

petty cash voucher

No.

date

description		amount
	£	p

signature ....

authorised ....

petty cash voucher

No.

date

description		amount
	£	p

signature ....

authorised ....

petty cash voucher

No.

date

description		amount
	£	p

signature ....

authorised ....

8.5* You are the petty cashier for Bode Manufacturers Ltd and have been given the following petty cash vouchers all of which include VAT at 17.5%. You have been asked to calculate the amount of VAT that will be shown in the VAT column of the petty cash book and the amount that will appear in the appropriate expense column

Note that VAT amounts should always be rounded <u>down</u> to the nearest penny.

(a)	£21.30		(f)	£ 3.30
(b)	£ 2.35		(g)	90p
(c)	£ 8.40		(h)	£ 7.75
(d)	£ 1.41		(i)	£10.10
(e)	£15.60		(j)	£14.10

8.6 As petty cashier of The Holly Hotel you have been given the following petty cash vouchers, all of which include VAT at 17.5%. The hotel manager asks you to calculate the amount of VAT that will be shown in the VAT column of the petty cash book and the amount that will appear in the appropriate expense column.

Note that VAT amounts should always be rounded <u>down</u> to the nearest penny.

(a)	£32.90		(f)	£7.05
(b)	£25.38		(g)	£33.84
(c)	£1.88		(h)	£28.20
(d)	£4.70		(i)	94p
(e)	£ 5.64		(j)	£11.75

9 WRITING UP THE PETTY CASH BOOK

this chapter covers ...

Writing up the petty cash book involves the following:

- bringing forward the opening balance of petty cash for the beginning of the period

- ensuring each petty cash voucher has been properly authorised before entering it in the petty cash book

- entering the petty cash vouchers into the petty cash book

- entering any receipts into the petty cash book

OCR LEARNING OUTCOMES

unit 2: MAINTAINING PETTY CASH

Assessment objectives

1   **Analysed Petty Cash Books**

    (a)   Enter the opening balance

2   **Enter Petty Cash Vouchers for Payments and Receipts into Petty Cash Book**

    (a)   Enter correct date

    (b)   Enter correct folio reference

    (c)   Enter correct description

    (d)   Enter correct total amount

    (e)   Calculate VAT accurately

    (f)   Enter correct VAT amount

    (g)   Enter details into correct columns

    (h)   Enter all entries legibly

3   **Total the Petty Cash Book**

    (a)   Total all columns

    (b)   Cross-cast all analysis columns

INTRODUCTION

As mentioned in the previous chapter, the petty cashier will be responsible for entering transactions into the petty cash book. Before entering the various transactions for the period the petty cashier will need to ensure that all the petty cash vouchers and receipts for transactions carried out during the period are available. They will also need the petty cash book and the cash box.

opening balance

Whether the business uses the imprest or non-imprest system they will usually have an opening balance at the beginning of the period. The opening balance is the amount of money left over from the previous period that is carried forward to the next week or month. This is illustrated in the following Case Study.

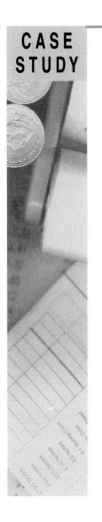

CASE STUDY

NEEDHAMS ADVERTISING AGENCY

situation
James Kerr is the petty cashier for Needhams Advertising Agency. The company operates their petty cash using the imprest system on a monthly period with a float of £100.00. At the end of May 2004 James entered the petty cash transactions and found he had spent £83.50 during May and had £16.50 left in his cash box.
As petty cashier James has been asked to carry out the following entries:

- enter the opening balance in the petty cash book at the beginning of June 2004

- enter the correct amount of cash, which has been collected from the bank to restore the imprest to £100.00.

solution
The opening balance for 1 June 2004 is £16.50, the amount of money left over from the last month. This figure needs to be brought forward to the start of the next period as follows:

Petty Cash Book (extract)

Receipts £ p	Date	Details	Voucher Number	Total £ p
16.50	1 June	Balance b/d		

James now has to enter the amount of cash collected from the bank to restore the imprest. The amount needed to restore the imprest is as follows:

	£
Amount of float	100.00
Amount spent	83.50
Cash left over	16.50

Since £83.50 of the float has been spent as shown above the amount required to restore the imprest to £100.00 will be the amount spent £83.50. This can now be entered as follows:

Petty Cash Book (extract)

Receipts £ p	Date	Details	Voucher Number	Total £ p
16.50	1 June	Balance b/d		
83.50	1 June	Cash		

Note: If a business operates a non-imprest system then only the opening balance will be entered. As discussed in the previous chapter, the petty cashier only asks the main cashier for more money as and when required. When a top-up of cash is received the amount will be entered in the petty cash book as a receipt on the actual date the money is given to the petty cashier.

entering transactions – payments

Most of the transactions recorded in the petty cash book relate to payments made by the petty cashier to members of staff to reimburse them for money spent on behalf of the business. Anyone incurring an expense on behalf of the business will have completed and signed a petty cash voucher that will also have been duly authorised by, the petty cashier, manager or perhaps the accounts line manager.

It is important that the petty cashier ensures the petty cash vouchers have been properly completed and checks the calculations before entering them into the petty cash book.

The entry of petty cash vouchers into the petty cash book is shown in the Case Study 'Evans & Co' (see below).

entering transactions – receipts

If a member of staff purchases goods, such as postage stamps, from the petty cashier and pays by cash, then a receipt is made out by the petty cashier to record the details and the amount of money received. Again, the petty cashier should check the details and calculations before entering the receipt into the petty cash book. The entry of receipts into the petty cash book is shown in the Case Study 'Evans & Co' which follows.

<table>
<tr><td>**CASE STUDY**</td><td>

EVANS AND CO

situation

You are employed as accounts assistant for Evans & Co, and one of your responsibilities is that of petty cashier.

The company uses an analytical petty cash book, ie the petty cash book has columns which analyse the types of expenses. It also operates an imprest system.

There are a number of transactions for the week commencing 1 January 2004 that require entering in the petty cash book.

The next petty cash page to use is no. 2 in the book.

All transactions, unless otherwise stated, include VAT at 17.5%.

You are required to perform the following tasks:

1   Enter the opening balance into the petty cash book.

2   Enter the correct amount of cash that has been collected from the bank to restore the imprest.

3   Enter the details of the petty cash vouchers and any receipts that are shown below.

4   Total all the analysis columns and cross-check that the total agrees with the total payments column.

</td></tr>
</table>

petty cash vouchers and receipt

2004		£ p
1 Jan	Started the week with an opening balance	20.00
1 Jan	Received cash from bank to restore imprest	80.00
2 Jan	Paid for postage stamps (no VAT) on voucher no. 21	10.00
2 Jan	Paid for taxi fare for business use, voucher no. 22 (VAT of £1.40)	9.40
3 Jan	Paid for stationery voucher no. 23 (VAT of £1.26)	8.46
3 Jan	Sold some postage stamps to a member of staff Fred Dee (receipt No 57)	3.00
4 Jan	Paid for registered package (no VAT) on voucher no. 24	12.50
5 Jan	Paid for office milk, tea and coffee (no VAT) voucher no. 25	6.24
6 Jan	Paid for postage stamps (no VAT) on voucher no. 26	10.00
6 Jan	Paid for stationery voucher no. 27 (VAT of £1.93)	13.00
7 Jan	Paid for taxi fare to station voucher no. 28 (VAT of 84p)	5.64

solution

The completed petty cash book appears as follows:

Receipts £ p	Date	Details	Voucher Number	Total £ p	VAT £ p	Postage £ p	Cleaning £ p	Travel £ p	Stationery £ p	Refresh-ments £ p
20.00	1 Jan	Balance b/d								
80.00	1 Jan	Cash								
	2 Jan	Postage stamps	21	10.00		10.00				
	2 Jan	Taxi fare	22	9.40	1.40			8.00		
	3 Jan	Stationery	23	8.46	1.26				7.20	
		Fred Dee								
3.00	3 Jan	Postage stamps	57							
	4 Jan	Registered package	24	12.50		12.50				
	5 Jan	Office milk etc	25	6.24						6.24
	6 Jan	Postage stamps	26	10.00		10.00				
	6 Jan	Stationery	27	13.00	1.93				11.07	
	7 Jan	Taxi fare	28	5.64	0.84			4.80		
				75.24	5.43	32.50		12.80	18.27	6.24

Petty Cash Book   PCB 2

notes on completion of the petty cash book

- The receipts column is the 'debit side' of the petty cash book and contains the opening balance bought down of £20.00 plus the entry to record the money received from the bank to restore the imprest, in this case £80.00.

- Each item of expenditure is then entered as follows:

  (a) Enter the date. Note that it is important to ensure that the transactions are entered in strict date order. Then enter details of the expenditure, voucher number and the total amount spent.

  The total payment column is the 'credit side' of the petty cash book.

  (b) Using the analysis columns enter the amount of VAT, if applicable, in the VAT column and the net expenditure incurred in the relevant analysis column. Using the above example, the amount paid on the taxi fare on 2 Jan was £9.40. Note that £9.40 is entered in the total payment column, £1.40 is entered in the VAT column and £8.00 entered in the travel column.

- Enter the receipt of £3.00 for the sale of postage stamps on 3 January in date order but note that this item is entered on the 'debit side' of the petty cash book under the heading 'receipts' as illustrated in the solution above

- At the end of the period each column is added up.

- It is then important to cross-check (cross cast) the additions, ie the total of all the analysis columns should equal the total payments made, this process in accounting terms is known as to cross cast. Using the above example the analysis columns are as follows:

	£
VAT	5.43
Postage	32.50
Travel	12.80
Stationery	18.27
Refreshments	6.24
Total Payments	75.24

You will note that this figure agrees with the "Total Payment Column" of £75.24.

- In the next chapter we shall see how the petty cash book is balanced and the imprest restored to the original float.

CHAPTER SUMMARY

- Entering transactions into the petty cash book starts with the opening balance. The opening balance is entered in the same way for either the imprest or the non-imprest system.

- The amount received from the bank to restore the imprest is entered next.

- It is important to ensure that the petty cash vouchers have been completed correctly, that calculations are accurate and the vouchers are properly authorised prior to entry.

- The next step is to enter the petty cash vouchers and any receipts into the petty cash book.

- Lastly, all the analysis columns in the petty cash book will be totalled and checked against the total payments column to ensure that they equal the total payments.

KEY TERMS

opening balance	the amount of cash in the petty cash tin at the start of the period
analysis column	a column into which the types of expenditure – eg stationery, postage – are entered
cross-check	adding up figures in analysis columns and ensuring that they equal the total payment column, which should be added up separately (this process is also known as to 'cross cast' in accountancy terms)

9.1*   (a)   A business operates their petty cash using the imprest system. The float for the period is £100.00 and during the period a total of £42.16 is spent. How much cash would the petty cashier need to obtain from the main cashier to restore the imprest?

(b)   Ms Ainsworth is the petty cashier in a small business. The petty cash is operated using the imprest system with a float of £250.00 for a monthly period. During May the total payments out of petty cash was £231.78. Also during the month Ms Ainsworth received the following amounts from employees who had bought some stationery and postage stamps from the business for their own use:

• Received from Alan Grimshaw £10.00 for photo-copier paper

• Received £2.30 from Betty Jones for postage stamps

Calculate the amount of cash that Ms Ainsworth will need to ask the main cashier for to restore the imprest to £250.00. Show your workings.

(c)   John is the petty cashier at a local estate agents which operates their petty cash using the imprest system. The float for a monthly period is £75.00. During December the company sends out Christmas cards and calendars to clients and by the third week of the period John realises that all the petty cash for the month has been spent and he still has several claims to pay.

Advise John what he should do in these circumstances.

(d)   A company operates their petty cash using the imprest system and at the end of the period they have £12.14 left in the cash box. The float was originally £50.00 and during the period £12.00 had been received from a member of staff who had purchased some stationery from the company.

How much cash should the petty cashier claim from the accountant to restore the imprest?

9.2* You work as an accounts clerk for a local printing company and one of your tasks is to look after the petty cash.

You are asked to write up the petty cash book, page 18, for May 2005 using the following analysis columns: VAT, postage, cleaning, travel, stationery and sundry expenses.

The cash float brought down at the beginning of the month is shown below, and the next voucher number to use is 73.

2005		£
1 May	Petty cash float brought down	100.00
3 May	Paid for postage stamps (no VAT)	18.00
7 May	Bought envelopes (including VAT of 64p)	4.30
9 May	Train fare to Manchester (no VAT)	6.50
11 May	Donation to local charity (no VAT)	25.00
18 May	Postage on parcel to customer (no VAT)	5.74
22 May	Bought stationery (including VAT of £1.37)	9.20
25 May	Window cleaning (no VAT)	8.00
30 May	Cleaning (no VAT)	10.00

A suitable blank petty cash book page is provided on the next page. You may photocopy this page for use if you wish. Alternatively you may download blank forms from the free resources section of our website: www.osbornebooks.co.uk

After entering the vouchers you are asked to total all the columns and cross-check to ensure that calculations have been carried out correctly.

State how much money is left at the end of May. What amount would the petty cashier need from the cashier to restore the imprest?

Petty Cash Book

Receipts		Date	Details	Voucher Number	Total		VAT		Postage		Cleaning		Travel		Stationery		Sundry Expenses	
£	p				£	p	£	p	£	p	£	p	£	p	£	p	£	p

9.3* Prepare a petty cash book for Wildthorn Guest House with analysis columns for VAT, postages, cleaning, travel, stationery and sundry expenses.

A suitable blank petty cash book page is provided on the opposite page. You may photocopy this page for use if you wish. Alternatively you may download blank forms from the free resources section of our website: www.osbornebooks.co.uk

Enter the following authorised transactions for the month of March 2006 on page 34 of the petty cash book.

The voucher amounts include VAT at 17.5% unless stated otherwise.

2006

1 March	Cash Balance brought down £50.00
3 March	Paid for cleaning (no VAT) £15.00, voucher no 101
7 March	Postage stamps (no VAT) £4.50, voucher no 102
11 March	Flowers for reception £6.00, including VAT of 90p, voucher no 103,
16 March	Dusters, polish for cleaning £3.75, including VAT of 56p, voucher no 104
20 March	Bus fares (no VAT) £2.50, voucher no 105
28 March	Window cleaning (no VAT) £8.00, voucher no 106
31 March	Envelopes £2.30, Note-pad & pens £3.60, including total VAT of 88p, voucher no 107
31 March	Parcel post 0.90p (no VAT), voucher no. 108

At the end of the month total all columns and cross-check against the total expenses incurred for March. Indicate to the manager of the hotel the amount of cash required to restore the imprest to £50.00.

9.4*   J. Dolan operates an analytical petty cash book using the imprest system. On 1 June 2005 there was an opening balance in the petty cash box of £26.80. As petty cashier you are asked to carry out the following tasks:

(a)   Enter the opening balance into the petty cash book on page 56.

(b)   Enter the correct amount of cash to restore the imprest to the original float of £100.00. Use cash book reference CB1.

(c)   Enter the details of the petty cash vouchers and the receipts shown on pages 200-203 into the petty cash book using the following analysis columns, VAT, postage, cleaning, sundry expenses, stationery and refreshments.

(d)   Total and cross-check the petty cash book at the end of June.

(e)   State how much money the petty cashier would have left at the end of June and how much would be required to restore the imprest.

A suitable blank petty cash book page is provided on the next page. You may photocopy this page for use if you wish. Alternatively you may download blank forms from the free resources section of our website: www.osbornebooks.co.uk

Petty Cash Book

Receipts	Date	Details	Voucher Number	Total		VAT		Postage		Cleaning		Sundry Expenses		Stationery		Refreshments	
£ p				£	p	£	p	£	p	£	p	£	p	£	p	£	p

petty cash voucher		No. 001
	date	1 June 2005

description	amount	
	£	p
Milkman (re: milk for visitors) no VAT	2	80
	2	80

signature *J. Bond*

authorised *GR*

---

petty cash voucher		No. 002
	date	4 June 2005

description	amount	
	£	p
Coffee, tea bags and biscuits (for visitors) no VAT	6	13
	6	13

signature *M. Franks*

authorised *GR*

---

petty cash voucher		No. 003
	date	9 June 2005

description	amount	
	£	p
Cleaner (no VAT)	20	–
	20	–

signature *M Bould*

authorised *GR*

petty cash voucher

No. 004

date   16 June 2005

description		amount	
		£	p
Marker pens		3	29
Envelopes		1	29
(including VAT of 68p)			
		4	58

signature   *S. Scott*

authorised   *GR*

RECEIPT

No. 36

date   23 June 2005

received from   M Parkin

the sum of   Two pounds ten pence

for   Postage stamps

cheque	—	
cash	2.10	
discount	—	
total	2.10	

signature   *G Robinson*

---

petty cash voucher

No. 005

date 24 June 2005

description		amount	
		£	p
Postage stamps		10	50
Parcel post		3	42
(no VAT)		13	92

signature   *S. Scott*

authorised   *GR*

petty cash voucher		No. 006

date 24/6/2005

description	amount	
	£	p
Donation to local junior football club (no VAT)	5	-
	5	-

signature *S. Scott*

authorised *GR*

---

petty cash voucher		No. 007

date 26/6/2005

description	amount	
	£	p
Cleaner (no VAT)	10	-
	10	-

signature *M Bould*

authorised *GR*

---

petty cash voucher		No. 008

date 27 June 2005

description	amount	
	£	p
1 pkt computer disks	3	99
Ink cartridge	11	20
(including VAT)		
	14	19

signature *S. Scott*

authorised *GR*

petty cash voucher

No. 009

date 30 June 2005

description	amount	
	£	p
Bus fares to bank (no VAT)	2	30
	2	30

signature _D. Huntley_

authorised _GR_

---

petty cash voucher

No. 010

date 30 June 2005

description	amount	
	£	p
Milk (office visitors) no VAT	2	38
	2	38

signature _Paul Brown_

authorised _GR_

---

petty cash voucher

No. 011

date 30 June 2005

description	amount	
	£	p
Postage stamps (no VAT)	4	50
	4	50

signature _S. Scott_

authorised _GR_

9.5 As accounts assistant for Blake Business Products Ltd you are required to look after the petty cash book as one of your duties. On 1 September 2005 there was £12.36 left in the petty cash box from the previous month. The cashier, Joe Morgan, gives you £62.64 to restore the imprest to £75.00.

You are to:

(a) Enter the balance brought down from the previous month £12.36 together with the amount required to restore the imprest in the petty cash book, page 24, on 1 September 2005.

(b) Your next task is to enter the petty cash vouchers and the receipts (shown on pages 206-209) for September 2005 in the petty cash book using the following analysis columns: VAT, postage, cleaning, travel, stationery and sundry expenses.

(c) At the end of September total all the columns and cross-check.

(d) State how much money the petty cashier would have left at the end of September and how much would be required to restore the imprest.

(e) You notice that over the last few months the amount of petty cash spent each month is increasing and wonder if the float should be increased to £100.00. Write a memo to the cashier requesting an increase in the float from £75.00 to £100.00

A suitable blank petty cash book page is provided on the next page. You may photocopy this page for use if you wish. Alternatively you may download blank forms from the free resources section of our website: www.osbornebooks.co.uk

Petty Cash Book

Receipts £ p	Date	Details	Voucher Number	Total £ p	VAT £ p	Postage £ p	Cleaning £ p	Travel £ p	Stationery £ p	Sundry Expenses £ p

petty cash voucher		No. 100

date **1 Sept 2005**

description			amount	
			£	p
Postage stamps (no VAT)			4	20
			4	20

signature _Simon Duffy_

authorised _JB_

---

petty cash voucher		No. 101

date **4 Sept 2005**

description			amount	
			£	p
Flowers for office reception including VAT of 56p			3	75
			3	75

signature _J. Davies_

authorised _JB_

RECEIPT No. 42

date **8 Sept 2005**

received from — M Noel

the sum of — Three pounds fifty pence

for — Stationery

cheque	———	
cash	3.50	
discount	———	
total	3.50	

signature _J Blake_

petty cash voucher   No. 102

date 8/9/2005

description		amount	
		£	p
A4 copy paper Correcting fluid (incl VAT of £1.14)		7	64
		7	64

signature _M Noel_

authorised _JB_

---

petty cash voucher   No. 103

date 9 Sept 2005

description		amount	
		£	p
Providing refreshments for meeting (incl VAT of £2.10)		14	10
		14	10

signature _S. Scott_

authorised _GR_

---

petty cash voucher   No. 104

date 10/9/05

description		amount	
		£	p
Parcel post (no VAT)		–	80
		–	80

signature _Simon Duffy_

authorised _JB_

RECEIPT		No. 43

date 11.9.2005

received from	A Bell
the sum of	One pound thirty pence
for	Postage stamps

cheque	——	
cash	1.30	
discount	——	
total	1.30	

signature *J Blake*

---

petty cash voucher No. 105

date **13 Sept 2005**

description		amount
	£	p
4 Lever arch files	10	34
4 packets dividers	4	23
(incl VAT of £2.17)		
	14	57

signature *A Bell*

authorised *JB*

---

petty cash voucher No. 106

date **15 Sept 2005**

description		amount
	£	p
Bus fare to solicitors to collect documents (no VAT)	1	20
	1	20

signature *F Oddy*

authorised *JB*

petty cash voucher		No. 107
		date 17/9/2005

description	amount	
	£	p
Cleaning materials (including VAT)	3	76
	3	76

signature _Ethel May_

authorised _JB_

petty cash voucher		No. 108
		date 29/9/2005

description	amount	
	£	p
Postage stamps (no VAT)	4	80
	4	80

signature _J. Davies_

authorised _JB_

petty cash voucher		No. 109
		date 30/9/2005

description	amount	
	£	p
Milk (for use by visitors) no VAT	3	60
	3	60

signature _A Bell_

authorised _JB_

10 BALANCING THE PETTY CASH BOOK

this chapter covers . . .

Totalling and balancing the petty cash book and restoring the imprest as follows:

- totalling the petty cash book and cross-checking the analysis columns

- balancing the petty cash book to find out how much cash remains

- completing a petty cash reimbursement request for authorisation so that the petty cash can be topped up

- preparing a cheque to reimburse the imprest so that cash can be withdrawn from the bank

OCR LEARNING OUTCOMES

unit 2: MAINTAINING PETTY CASH

Assessment objectives

3   Total the Petty Cash Book

    (a)   Total all columns

    (b)   Cross-cast all analysis columns

    (c)   Balance the petty cash book

    (d)   Enter the balance

4   Complete a Petty Cash Reimbursement request

    (a)   Identify accurate amount for reimbursement

    (b)   Complete all sections of form accurately

    (c)   Observe instructions for authorised signature(s)

5   Prepare a Cheque to Reimburse Imprest

    (a)   Enter correct date on cheque and counterfoil

    (b)   Enter correct details on cheque and counterfoil

    (c)   Enter correct amount on cheque and counterfoil

    (d)   Observe instructions for authorised signature(s)

    (e)   Present the information clearly and legibly

BALANCING THE PETTY CASH BOOK

In the previous chapter the Case Study, 'Evans & Co', showed the entry of the petty cash vouchers and receipts. In this chapter we are going to show how the petty cash book of 'Evans & Co' is totalled, balanced and the imprest restored. A petty cash reimbursement request will then be completed and finally a cheque made out. The cash will then be drawn out of the bank to restore the petty cash imprest to the original float amount.

checking the cash

At the end of a period, usually a week or month, the petty cashier completes the entries in the petty cash book, balances the account (see below) for the particular period and brings down the balance for the start of the next period. The petty cashier also needs to ensure that the 'balance' according to the petty cash book is verified by the amount of money held in the cash box. The money held in the cash box will be counted, and if no errors have been made during the period, the cash total should equal the amount of the petty cash book balance. If the money held does *not* equal the amount of the balance, then the petty cashier will need to check all the entries made into the petty cash book and recount the cash. If an error has been made it should be identified by carrying out these checks.

balancing the account

In the Case Study 'Evans & Co', in the previous chapter (see pages 192-193), the total amount spent during the first week in January was £75.24. This figure was checked when the total of all the analysis columns were added up and cross-checked as follows:

	£
VAT	5.43
Postage	32.50
Travel	12.80
Stationery	18.27
Refreshments	6.24
Total Payments	75.24

To balance the petty cash book at the end of the period it is necessary to add up the 'Receipts' column as follows:

	£
Balance b/d	20.00
Cash	80.00
Proceeds from sale of stamps	3.00
Total Receipts	103.00

Now that the totals of 'Receipts' and 'Payments' for the period are known the amount of the 'balance' can be found as follows:

	£
Total receipts	103.00
Less total payments	75.24
Balance	27.76

The 'balance' figure £27.76 is the difference between the total receipts and the total payments and should be the amount of money that the petty cashier has left in the cash box. The balance figure will now be entered in the petty cash book as shown in the illustration on the next page.

restoring the imprest

In the Case Study 'Evans & Co' the amount of the float held for the period was £100.00, therefore, the amount of money needed to restore the imprest is calculated as follows:

	£
Amount of float	100.00
Less balance of money left (see above)	27.76
Amount needed to restore the imprest	72.24

entering the balances in the petty cash book

The balance of money left at the end of the period will be entered in the petty cash book, as shown opposite.

You will notice that the balance is shown twice, once as 'Balance c/d' which stands for 'Balance carried down' and also as 'Balance b/d' for 'Balance brought down'. This is normal accounting practice and indicates that the closing balance of one period becomes the opening balance for the next period.

double entry posting of petty cash transactions

At the end of the period the totals in the analysis columns of the petty cash book are posted to the various accounts in the general ledger and the cash received to restore the imprest is posted to the cash book (see Chapter 12). However, since these entries are not part of this unit of study you need only note this procedure, details will follow in later studies.

Petty Cash Book

Receipts £ p	Date	Details	Voucher Number	Total £ p	VAT £ p	Postage £ p	Cleaning £ p	Motor Expenses £ p	Stationery £ p	Refreshments £ p
20.00	1 Jan	Balance b/d								
80.00	1 Jan	Cash								
	2 Jan	Postage stamps	21	10.00		10.00				
	2 Jan	Taxi fare	22	9.40	1.40			8.00		
	3 Jan	Stationery	23	8.46	1.26				7.20	
3.00	3 Jan	Fred Dee	57							
	3 Jan	Postage stamps	24	12.50		12.50				
	4 Jan	Registered package	25	6.24						6.24
	5 Jan	Office milk etc	26	10.00		10.00				
	6 Jan	Postage stamps								
	6 Jan	Stationery	27	13.00	1.94				11.06	
	7 Jan	Taxi fare	28	5.64	0.84			4.80		
				75.24	5.44	32.50		12.80	18.26	6.24
	7 Jan	Balance c/d		27.76						
103.00				103.00						
27.76	8 Jan	Balance b/d								

COMPLETION OF PETTY CASH REIMBURSEMENT REQUEST

When the petty cash book has been balanced off, the petty cashier will know the amount of money required to restore the imprest to the original amount. In the above case the amount required was £72.24 to restore the imprest to £100.00. In order to obtain the money the petty cashier will need to complete a Petty Cash Reimbursement Request. This is illustrated below:

PETTY CASH REIMBURSEMENT REQUEST

Please arrange for a cheque for £   72.24   to restore imprest.

Signed   *Amy Bennett*   Petty Cashier

Date   7 January 2004

Signed   *J C Evans*   Authorised Signatory

Date   7 January 2004

Note that the form is signed by the petty cashier, Amy Bennett, and will need to be authorised for payment by the main cashier or accountant before a cheque can be made out enabling the money to be withdrawn from the bank. The person authorising the form should check that the form is completed correctly and that the petty cashier is requesting the correct amount of money. This check can be carried out by verifying the balance in the petty cash book and counting the remaining cash to ensure that the two figures agree.

PREPARING A CHEQUE TO REIMBURSE IMPREST

When the Petty Cash Reimbursement Request has been completed and authorised, the petty cashier is able to obtain a cheque for the amount required. In the above Case Study a cheque for £72.24 will need to be made out as follows:

8 January 2004	**Southern Bank PLC**		date	8 January 2004		97-76-54

Mereford Branch
16 Broad Street, Mereford MR1 7TR

To

Petty Cash

Pay   Cash

Seventy two pounds 24p only   only

£ 72.24

Account payee only

Evans & Co

£ 72.24   JC Evans

123459   123459   977654   68384939

points to note when writing out a cheque

When writing out a cheque it is important that it is written out clearly and neatly. The date and details should be written on both the counterfoil and the cheque. The amount of the cheque should be written on the counterfoil and the cheque itself and the amount should also be written in words on the cheque. It is common practice to insert a line after the payee details (here 'cash') and the amount in words. This is to prevent fraud. Finally, the cheque should be signed by a person authorised to sign cheques on behalf of the business.

cashing the cheque

Once the cheque has been signed the petty cashier (or the person who does the 'banking') may take it to the bank and obtain the cash. The money is then put into the cash box that should then be kept in a secure place, ideally a fireproof safe.

entering the restored imprest

The restored imprest of £72.24 should then be entered in the petty cash book extract as shown below:

Receipts	Date	Details	Voucher Number	Total
£ p				£ p
27.76	8 Jan	Balance b/d		
72.24	8 Jan	Cash		

- When all the entries for a period have been entered into the petty cash book the petty cashier 'balances' the account.

- The petty cashier then verifies that the balance agrees with the amount of money in the cash box.

- The balance is then entered twice in the petty cash book, as 'balance c/d' and 'balance b/d'.

- A Petty Cash Reimbursement Request is completed requesting an amount of money from the cashier or accountant to enable the imprest to be restored to the original amount.

- A cheque is written out neatly and accurately enabling the money needed to restore the imprest to be withdrawn from the bank.

- The cheque is taken to the bank and the money withdrawn. The money should then be kept in a secure place.

- Finally, the cheque should be entered in the petty cash book underneath the entry of the balance brought down.

balancing the account	calculating the balance on the account by finding the difference between the total receipts and payments; the difference is the 'balance'
balance c/d	this stands for 'balance carried down' and is the balance on the account at the end of the period
balance b/d	this stands for 'balance brought down' and represents the amount or balance at the beginning on a new period

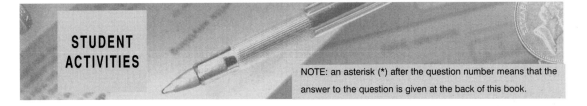

STUDENT
ACTIVITIES

NOTE: an asterisk (*) after the question number means that the answer to the question is given at the back of this book.

10.1* You are employed as Accounts Assistant for Hulme Bros. Ltd. The company operates their petty cash using the imprest system on a weekly basis with a float of £50.00. On 1 March 2004 there was £4.36 left in the petty cash box from the previous week. David Dyson, the accountant, hands you £45.64 in cash to restore the imprest to its original float of £50.00.

The following are details of the petty cash vouchers and receipts which have been authorised for payment by Mr Dyson for the week commencing 1 March 2004.

A suitable blank petty cash book page is provided on the next page. You may photocopy this page for use if you wish. Alternatively you may download blank forms from the free resources section of our website: www.osbornebooks.co.uk

		£
1 March	Cleaning windows in office (no VAT)	8.50
3 March	Postage stamps (no VAT)	4.50
4 March	Petrol (including VAT of £2.50)	16.80
5 March	Coffee, tea and biscuits for visitors (no VAT)	5.70
5 March	Parcel post (no VAT)	3.60
6 March	Sold stamps to Ben Read for £3.00 (Receipt no. 7)	
6 March	Stationery (including VAT)	6.40
7 March	Cleaning material (including VAT of 36p)	2.38

Tasks:

(a) Enter the balance brought down and the cash received to restore the imprest in the petty cash book page no.12. Date the entries 1 March 2004.

(b) Enter the above transactions into the petty cash book using the following analysis columns, VAT, postage, cleaning, motor expenses, stationery and refreshments. The next voucher number to use is 42. You may have to calculate some of the VAT.

(c) Total and cross-check the petty cash book.

(d) Balance the petty cash book as at 7 March 2004 and bring down the balance for next week commencing 8 March 2004.

(e) State how much cash is required to restore the imprest to £50.00

Petty Cash Book

Receipts		Date	Details	Voucher Number	Total		VAT		Postage		Cleaning		Motor Expenses		Stationery		Refresh-ments	
£	p				£	p	£	p	£	p	£	p	£	p	£	p	£	p

10.2* As junior assistant in the offices of Chell Construction Co one of your duties is to look after the petty cash. The company uses an analytical petty cash book with columns for VAT, postage, cleaning, motor expenses, stationery and sundry expenses.

A suitable blank petty cash book page is provided on the next page. You may photocopy this page for use if you wish. Alternatively you may download blank forms from the free resources section of our website: www.osbornebooks.co.uk

The petty cash is operated using the imprest system with a float of £100.00 per month. All claims must be authorised for payment by the accountant, John Dean.

On 1 January 2004 the balance of cash in hand brought down from December 2003 is £16.22 and on the same day John Dean gives you cash of £83.78 to restore the imprest to £100.00.

As petty cashier carry out the following tasks:

(a)   Enter the opening balance in the petty cash book on page 43.

(b)   Enter the amount of cash received from the accountant to restore the imprest.

(c)   Enter the details of the petty cash vouchers and receipts (see below). You may have to calculate some of the VAT.

(d)   Total and cross-cast the petty cash book.

(e)   Balance the petty cash book at 31 January 2004 and bring down the balance for the next month starting 1 February 2004.

(f)   State how much cash is needed at the end of January to restore the imprest.

Details of transactions for January 2004:		£
1 January	Construction trade magazine for reception (no VAT)	3.30
3 January	Postage stamps (no VAT)	8.00
7 January	Petrol (including VAT of £4.26)	28.60
10 January	Parcel to London (no VAT)	4.20
13 January	Sold stamps to Clive Taylor £1.35 (Receipt No. 8)	
17 January	Cleaner (no VAT)	22.00
22 January	Stationery (including VAT)	5.05
25 January	Postage stamps (no VAT)	4.00
27 January	Petrol (including VAT of £2.24)	15.00

The next petty cash voucher number to use is 27.

Petty Cash Book

Receipts	Date	Details	Voucher Number	Total		VAT		Postage		Cleaning		Motor Expenses		Stationery		Sundry expenses	
£ p				£	p	£	p	£	p	£	p	£	p	£	p	£	p

10.3* D Ashcroft Ltd operates an analytical petty cash book using the imprest system.

On 1 July 2005 there was an opening balance of £56.40. As petty cashier you are required to carry out the following tasks:

(a)   Enter the opening balance into the petty cash book on page 11.

(b)   Enter the correct amount of cash which has been collected from the bank to restore the imprest to £150.00.

(c)   Enter the details of the petty cash vouchers and the receipts in the petty cash book on page 11 using the following analysis columns VAT, postage, cleaning, motor expenses, stationery and refreshments. The manager, Clare Riley, has authorised all the vouchers for payment.

(d)   Total and cross-cast the petty cash book.

(e)   Balance the petty cash book on 31 July 2005 and bring down the balance ready for 1 August 2005.

(f)   Prepare the petty cash reimbursement request form ready for authorisation by the manager, Clare Riley.

(g)   Prepare the cheque for petty cash reimbursement for signing by the owner, Don Ashcroft. Date the cheque 31 July 2005.

A suitable blank petty cash book page is provided on page 227. A blank reimbursement form and cheque are provided on page 226. You may photocopy these pages for use   if you wish. Alternatively you may download blank forms from the free resources section of our website: www.osbornebooks.co.uk

The petty cash vouchers and receipts are shown on the pages that follow:

petty cash voucher		No. 50
	date	1 July 2005

description		amount
	£	p
Envelopes	1	30
4 Files	12	00
VAT	2	33
	15	63

signature   *J Scott*

authorised   *C Riley*

petty cash voucher

No. 51

date   3 July 2005

description		amount	
		£	p
Petrol		20	30
(including VAT of £3.02)			
		20	30

signature   *Antony Morris*

authorised   *C Riley*

---

petty cash voucher

No. 52

date   4 July 2005

description		amount	
		£	p
Postage - special delivery (no VAT)		4	00
		4	00

signature   *J Scott*

authorised   *C Riley*

---

petty cash voucher

No. 53

date   5 July 2005

description		amount	
		£	p
Cleaner (no VAT)		15	-
		15	-

signature   *Ada Wynn*

authorised   *C Riley*

petty cash voucher   No. 54

date   6 July 2005

description			amount	
			£	p
Tea, coffee and biscuits (no VAT)			5	32
			5	32

signature   *J Scott*

authorised   *C Riley*

RECEIPT   No. 5

date   6 July 2005

received from   Kim Stead

the sum of   One pound twenty pence

for   Postage stamps

cheque	——
cash	1.20
discount	——
total	1.20

signature   *C Riley*

---

petty cash voucher   No. 55

date   10 July 2005

description			amount	
			£	p
Postage stamps (no VAT)			6	00
			6	00

signature   *Bob Greaves*

authorised   *C Riley*

petty cash voucher   No. 56

date   15 July 2005

description		amount
	£	p
Petrol (including VAT of £2.68)	18	00
	18	00

signature   *Anthony Morris*

authorised   *C Riley*

---

petty cash voucher   No. 57

date   17 July 2005

description		amount
	£	p
Refreshments for meeting (including VAT of £2.26)	15	20
	15	20

signature   *J Scott*

authorised   *C Riley*

---

petty cash voucher   No. 58

date   23 July 2005

description		amount
	£	p
Photocopy paper (including VAT - amount not on receipt)	9	40
	9	40

signature   *J Scott*

authorised   *C Riley*

petty cash voucher

No. 59

date 25 July 2005

description	amount	
	£	p
Cleaner (no VAT)	20	–
	20	–

signature _Ada Wynn_

authorised _C Riley_

RECEIPT

No. 6

date 30 July 2005

received from Anthony Morris

the sum of Two pounds fifteen pence

for Postage stamps

cheque	——	
cash	2.15	
discount	——	
total	2.15	

signature _C Riley_

PETTY CASH REIMBURSEMENT REQUEST

Please arrange for a cheque for £ _____ to restore imprest.

Signed _____ Petty Cashier

Date _____

Signed _____ Authorised Signatory

Date _____

Date	**Southern Bank PLC**	date	97-76-54

Date _____

To _____

_____

_____

£ _____

734017

Southern Bank PLC
Mereford Branch
16 Broad Street, Mereford MR1 7TR

date _____ 97-76-54

Pay _____ only

Account payee only

£

_____

_____

D ASHCROFT LIMITED

734017   977654   68384939

Petty Cash Book

Receipts £ p	Date	Details	Voucher Number	Total £ p	VAT £ p	Postage £ p	Cleaning £ p	Motor Expenses £ p	Stationery £ p	Refresh-ments £ p

10.4 Fairacres Garden Centre operates an analytical petty cash book using the imprest system. The layout is on the previous page. The garden centre manager Philip Mellor authorises all petty cash vouchers on behalf of the owner Jane Belfield. On 1 June 2004 there was an opening balance in the petty cash box of £18.48. As petty cashier you are required to carry out the following tasks:

(a)   Enter the opening balance into the petty cash book on page 20.

(b)   Enter the correct amount of cash which has been collected from the bank to restore the imprest to £200.00.

(c)   Enter the details of the petty cash vouchers and the receipts in the petty cash book, using the following analysis columns (see page 232 for a photocopiable petty cash book page):

VAT, postage, cleaning, motor expenses, stationery and refreshments

(d)   Total and cross-check the petty cash book.

(e)   Balance the petty cash book on 30 June 2004 and bring down the balance ready for 1 July 2004.

(f)   Prepare the petty cash reimbursement request form ready for authorisation by the manager, Philip Mellor (please see page 233 for a photocopiable form).

(g)   Prepare the cheque for petty cash reimbursement for signing by the owner, Jane Belfield. Date the cheque 30 June 2004 (please see page 233 for a photocopiable cheque).

Petty cash vouchers and receipts are shown below:

petty cash voucher		No. 1
	date	2 June 2004

description	amount	
	£	p
String and labels (inc VAT of 63p)	4	20
	4	20

signature   Barbara Blinston

authorised   P Mellor

petty cash voucher		No. 2
	date	3 June 2004

description	amount	
	£	p
Cleaner (no VAT)	20	-
	20	-

signature   Mary Lawson

authorised   P Mellor

RECEIPT   No. 61

                                    date   5 June 2004

received from   Robert Jones

the sum of   Two pounds

for   Postage stamps

cheque	———
cash	2.00
discount	———
total	2.00

signature   *P Cashier*

---

petty cash voucher   No. 3

                                    date   8 June 2004

description		amount
	£	p
Petrol (incl VAT of £3.72)	25	00
	25	00

signature   *F Dawes*

authorised *P Mellor*

---

petty cash voucher   No. 4

                                    date   12 June 2004

description		amount
	£	p
Postage stamps (no VAT)	10	00
	10	00

signature   *Jane Simpson*

authorised *P Mellor*

petty cash voucher			No. 5
		date	16 June 2004

description	amount	
	£	p
Coffee, tea, sugar for staff (provided by Garden Centre) no VAT	6	30
	6	30

signature _Jane Simpson_

authorised _P Mellor_

---

petty cash voucher			No. 6
		date	23 June 2004

description	amount	
	£	p
Envelopes	2	20
White card size A3	6	40
(inc VAT)		
	8	60

signature _Barbara Blinston_

authorised _P Mellor_

RECEIPT   No. 62

date   24 June 2004

received from	Jane Simpson
the sum of	Eighty pence
for	Postage stamps

cheque	——
cash	0.80
discount	——
total	0.80

signature   _P Cashier_

petty cash voucher No. 7

date 25 June 2004

description		amount	
		£	p
Cleaner (no VAT)		20	00
		20	00

signature *Mary Lawson*

authorised *P Mellor*

---

petty cash voucher No. 8

date 26 June 2004

description		amount	
		£	p
Petrol (incl VAT of £3.40)		22	80
		22	80

signature *J Belfield*

authorised *P Mellor*

---

petty cash voucher No. 9

date 30 June 2004

description		amount	
		£	p
Cleaner (no VAT)		20	–
		20	–

signature *Mary Lawson*

authorised *P Mellor*

Petty Cash Book

Receipts £ p	Date	Details	Voucher Number	Total £ p	VAT £ p	Postage £ p	Cleaning £ p	Motor Expenses £ p	Stationery £ p	Refresh-ments £ p

PETTY CASH REIMBURSEMENT REQUEST

Please arrange for a cheque for £ _____ to restore imprest.

Signed _____ Petty Cashier

Date _____

Signed _____ Authorised Signatory

Date _____

Date	Southern Bank PLC	date	97-76-54
_____	Mereford Branch		
To	16 Broad Street, Mereford MR1 7TR		

Pay _____ only

Account payee only

£

FAIRACRES GARDEN CENTRE

£

652414   652414   977654   68384939

11 SOURCE DOCUMENTS FOR THE CASH BOOK

this chapter covers . . .

The cash book is the main bookkeeping record of receipts and payments made in cash and through the bank account.

In order to make entries in the cash book the person writing the entries obtains data from a number of different financial documents, and sometimes makes calculations based on the figures from those documents.

The object of this chapter is to familiarise you with these financial documents and the data they provide. The documents include:

- receipts received and issued
- cheques received and issued – including cheque counterfoils

The next chapter explains how the information from the documents is entered into the cash book.

OCR LEARNING OUTCOMES

Knowledge and Understanding – Unit 3 Maintaining the Cash Book

This chapter does not cover any of the specific Assessment Objectives of Unit 3 of the Level 1 Bookkeeping course, but instead concentrates on the underlying Knowledge and Understanding involved when writing up the cash book:

- use and purpose of a three-column Cash Book
- discount, cash and bank columns

The process of writing up the cash book will be explained in full in the next chapter.

THE CASH BOOK

an introduction

The layout, operation and balancing of the cash book will be covered in full in the next chapter. But in order that you can appreciate what it looks like and where the entries generated by the documents go, it is illustrated below, together with a few sample entries.

Study the layout and read the notes that follow.

cash book: receipts side (debits)   **cash book: payments side (credits)**

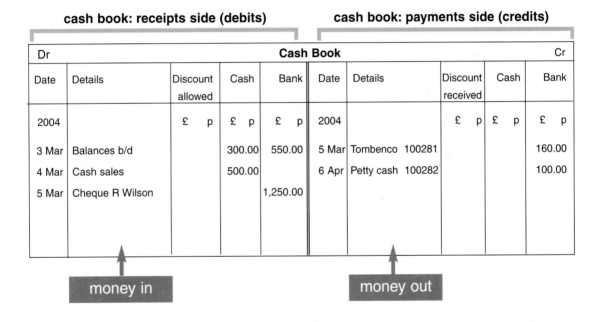

Dr										Cr
					Cash Book					
Date	Details	Discount allowed	Cash	Bank	Date	Details	Discount received	Cash	Bank
2004		£ p	£ p	£ p	2004		£ p	£ p	£ p
3 Mar	Balances b/d		300.00	550.00	5 Mar	Tombenco 100281			160.00
4 Mar	Cash sales		500.00		6 Apr	Petty cash 100282			100.00
5 Mar	Cheque R Wilson			1,250.00					

money in   money out

Notes

- the cash book is set up on the same principles as any double-entry account, with balances brought down
- payments received are recorded on the left, and payments made are recorded on the right
- examples of payments received are cash sales (cash kept in the business), and a cheque received from a customer (debtor)
- examples of payments made are a cheque paid to a supplier (creditor) and cash taken out of the bank to top up into the petty cash float (see the previous chapter)

At this stage you do not need to study the cash book any further. We will now look in detail at the documents which provide the information for the entries.

CASH TRANSACTIONS: RECEIPTS

a note on 'cash' and 'credit'

Business terminology uses the word 'cash' in two ways:

- 'cash' can mean notes and coins – this is what most people understand by the word 'cash'
- a 'cash' transaction can also mean a transaction for 'immediate payment' – as opposed to a 'credit' transaction which means payment can be made at a later date

In this chapter the term 'cash' is mostly used in the first sense – ie using notes and coins.

receipts for cash sales

When a business sells goods or services for cash it may issue a receipt to the buyer, or possibly an invoice marked 'cash sale'. A copy of the document will be kept by the business and used as a source document by the person writing up the receipts (left-hand) side of the cash book.

A cash sales receipt, with sample details, is shown below. Study the receipt and the explanations, and read the notes that follow.

the business issuing the receipt	**RECEIPT** **Osborne Fashion Limited** Unit 16 Millyard Estate Fencote Road, Worcester WR2 6HY
receipt number	No. 3
receipt date	date 12 May 2004
the person paying by cash	received with thanks from A Partridge (cash sales)
cash amount in words	the sum of Twenty pounds and fifty pence
	for Goods sold
cash amount in figures	cheque —— cash £20.50 discount —— total £20.50
signature of the seller	signature A Guest

cash receipt – details needed for the cash book

The details required for the cash book are very simple:

- the date of the receipt – this is the date of the cash sale, ie the date the cash is received by the business
- the amount of cash received

The description of the transaction in the cash book is simply 'Cash Sales', as the name of the customer is not needed.

It is possible that if there are a number of cash sales during the day, the amounts will be added up and only the total entered in the cash book (and also on the bank paying-in slip). You are not likely, however, to see this in your assignments.

receipts for cash payments

When a business buys goods or services for cash it may receive a receipt (or possibly an invoice) from the supplier. A copy of the document will be kept by the business and used as a source document by the person writing up the cash book.

A sample 'cash purchases' receipt is shown below.

The details entered in the cash book are similar to the details taken from a cash sales receipt – date, description 'cash purchases' and amount – but they are entered on the payments side of the cash book. Study the example and explanations shown below.

the seller issuing the receipt	**RECEIPT** → **Hughes Hire Services**
	17 Westway
	Bournemouth BH1 5RT
receipt number	→ No. 56
receipt date	→ date 24 May 2004
the buyer paying by cash	received with thanks from Brian Potter (cash purchases)
cash amount in words	the sum of → Eighty five pounds only
	for Plant hire
cash amount in figures	cheque ——
	cash £85.00
	discount ——
	total £85.00
signature of the supplier	signature T Hughes

CREDIT TRANSACTIONS: CHEQUES RECEIVED

The receipts on the last two pages have been for **cash** sales and purchases – cash (notes and coins) has been used, and payment is immediate.

As we have already seen, many business transactions are on **credit** – the sale or purchase takes place, an invoice is issued, and payment is made later. Payment may be made through the bank BACS computer system, but a common and traditional method of payment is to use a **cheque**.

A business may deal with cheques in a number of situations:

- a business receives cheques from customers in settlement of accounts
- a business writes cheques when paying suppliers
- a business writes cheques when paying expenses such as wages and electricity bills
- a business writes a cheque when drawing (taking) cash out of the bank

This chapter focuses on dealing with cheques received from customers settling accounts and cheques issued to pay suppliers.

First, however, we look at the definition and format of a cheque.

A cheque is a written instruction to the bank signed by its customer (known as the 'drawer' or 'issuer') to pay a stated amount to a named person (known as the 'payee').

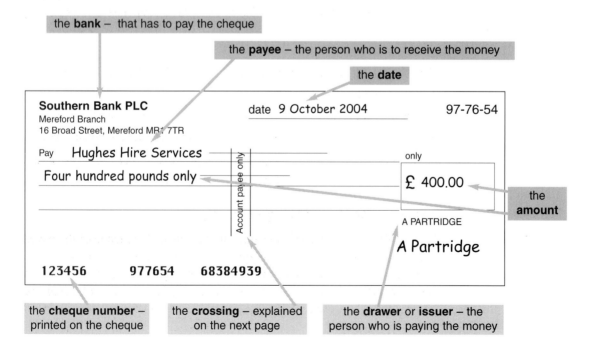

important details on the cheque

The bank customer, known as the **drawer** or issuer, writes out a cheque requiring the **bank** to pay the money to the **payee**. The payee is the person who is due to get the money (eg a supplier being paid by a business).

The two parallel lines on the cheque, the **crossing**, mean that the cheque has to be paid into a bank account, which, of course, it will be. The lines are likely to have words printed between them, eg 'account payee only', which state that the cheque has to paid into the account of the payee (the person who is to receive the money). The main purpose of the crossing and the words in the crossing is a security measure to prevent fraud.

The cheque is paid into the bank by the payee on a paying-in slip and in due course the money will be added to the payee's account. This process can be summarised as follows:

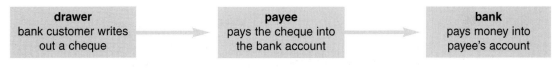

The **amount** is written in words and figures. Note also the lines drawn after the name of the payee and the amount. These are intended to prevent fraud, eg some unscrupulous person changing the amount, or the payee's name!

The **cheque number** is printed on the cheque by the bank and will be entered in the cash book by the business when issuing cheques. It will also appear on the bank statement and enable the business to reconcile ('tie up') entries in the cash book with entries on the bank statement (see Chapter 14).

checking the cheque

When receiving a cheque from a customer, you should always check that:

• it is signed

• the amount in words and the amount in figures are the same

• it is in date – cheques go out of date six months after the cheque date

Similarly, when writing out a cheque you should check all the details carefully before signing it, or passing it on for signature.

the counterfoil (cheque stub)

The details on the cheque – the amount, the date and the name of the payee – should also be noted on the cheque stub or counterfoil, as once the cheque is issued it will be the main record of the cheque payment. It is possible that the counterfoil details will be used by the business to record details of payments made in the cash book. A cheque and its counterfoil are illustrated on the next page.

cheque torn off here

| Date 31/10/04 | **Albion Bank PLC** | Date | 31 October 2004 | 90-47-17 |

7 The Avenue
Broadfield BR1 2AJ

Pay
Cool Socks
Limited

Pay Cool Socks Limited

(CREDITOR)

Two hundred and forty nine pounds 57p   £ 249.57

A/c payee only

TRENDS

£ 249.57

V Williams

238628

238628   90 47 17   11719512

counterfoil   **cheque**

The counterfoil can also be used to note details of any cash discount received from suppliers (see page 242). First, however, we will deal with the practical issues of receiving cheques from customers.

DEALING WITH CHEQUES FROM CUSTOMERS

When you are writing up the cash book, you will need to record the receipt of cheques from customers. In addition to the name of the customer and the amount received you will need to record:

- the date it is going to be banked
- details of any cash discount that has been allowed to the customer

These details are normally given to you in your assignments as a note written against each cheque, as in the examples shown on the next page.

example 1

On this example, cash discount has not been taken. The amount of the cheque is the full amount owing, ie £400.

example 2

On this example, cash discount of 2.5% has been allowed by the seller, and deducted by the customer.

Read the notes on the next page to see what entries need to be made in the cash book for these two examples.

example 1 – no cash discount taken

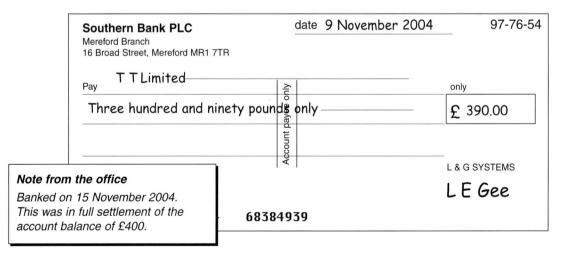

The details that go into the cash book (left-hand 'receipts' side) are:

- the date the cheque is banked – 15 October 2004
- name of the customer – L & G Systems
- the amount of £400 goes in the bank column – no cash discount has been taken because the cheque amount is the same as the account balance

example 2 – cash discount of 2.5% taken

The date and customer name are the same, but the amounts that go into the cash book (left-hand 'receipts' side) are different:

- the amount of the cheque, ie £390, goes in the bank column
- the discount amount, ie the account balance of £400 minus £390 = £10, goes in the discount allowed column

DEALING WITH CHEQUES ISSUED TO SUPPLIERS

When you write up the cash book, you need to record details of cheques issued to suppliers and for other expenses. The details you need to know are:

- the date the cheque has been written out
- the name of the customer
- cheque number
- details of any cash discount that has been received
- the amount of the cheque, ie the amount paid to the supplier

These details are normally written on the cheque counterfoils, as in the examples shown below.

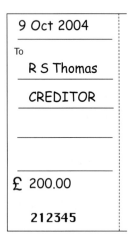

example 1 – no cash discount received

The details that go into the cash book (right-hand 'payments' side) are:

- the date the cheque is issued – 9 October 2004
- name of the supplier (creditor) – R S Thomas
- cheque number – 212345

The amount entered in the bank column of the cash book is £200 – the counterfoil does not mention any cash discount and so you can assume that none has been taken.

example 2 – cash discount of 5% received

The details that go into the cash book (right-hand 'payments' side) are:

- the date the cheque is issued – 9 October 2004
- name of the supplier (creditor) – G M Hopkins
- cheque number – 212346

The amounts here show that cash discount of 5% has been taken, (£200 x 5% = £10). The cash book procedure is very simple and no calculation is required. The money amount details that go into the cash book from the counterfoil are:

- amount paid £190 (into the bank column)
- discount received £10 (into the discount received column)

- The cash book is the bookkeeping record which shows cash received and paid out by a business and transactions through the bank account.

- The cash book is written up from financial documents processed by the business.

- Financial documents for money received include:
  - receipts for cash sales made to customers
  - cheques received from customers for credit sales

- Financial documents for money paid out include:
  - receipts for cash purchases made from suppliers
  - cheques (or cheque counterfoils) for payments made to suppliers

- Details to be entered in the cash book include:
  - date of the transaction
  - details of the transaction
  - amount of the cheque/receipt
  - any cash discount allowed or received

- Discount allowed on payments received from customers
  = full amount owing from customer *minus* amount received

- Discount received on amounts paid to suppliers
  = full amount owing to supplier *minus* amount actually paid

cash payment	can mean both notes and coins and immediate payment
credit payment	payment made at a later date than the sale or purchase
discount allowed	cash discount allowed by a seller of goods or services in return for early payment
discount received	cash discount received by a buyer of goods or services in return for early payment
cheque	a written instruction to the bank from its customer to pay a stated amount to a named person
drawer	the person paying the money who signs the cheque
payee	the person who is to receive payment of a cheque
counterfoil	cheque 'stub' which records the details of the cheque, ie date, amount, payee and any cash discount received

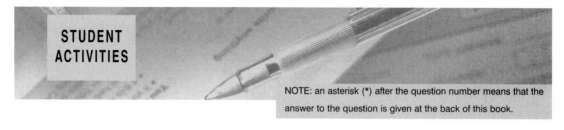

STUDENT ACTIVITIES

NOTE: an asterisk (*) after the question number means that the answer to the question is given at the back of this book.

11.1* List the details (including the date) that will be recorded in the cash book (receipts side) from the documents on the next three pages. The three money columns are:

– discount allowed

– cash

– bank

You can use (or photocopy) the following table for your answer:

Cash Book (receipts side)

Date	Customer name	Discount allowed £ p	Cash £ p	Bank £ p

(a)

RECEIPT

Osborne Fashion Limited

Unit 16 Millyard Estate
Fencote Road, Worcester WR2 6HY

No. 3

date   12 May 2004

received with thanks from   A Partridge (cash sales)

the sum of   Twenty pounds

and fifty pence

for   Goods sold

cheque	———
cash	£20.50
discount	———
total	£20.50

signature   A Guest

(b)

RECEIPT

Osborne Fashion Limited

Unit 16 Millyard Estate
Fencote Road, Worcester WR2 6HY

No. 4

date   13 May 2004

received with thanks from   J Singh (cash sales)

the sum of   Thirty pounds

and seventy pence

for   Goods sold

cheque	———
cash	£30.70
discount	———
total	£30.70

signature   A Guest

(c)

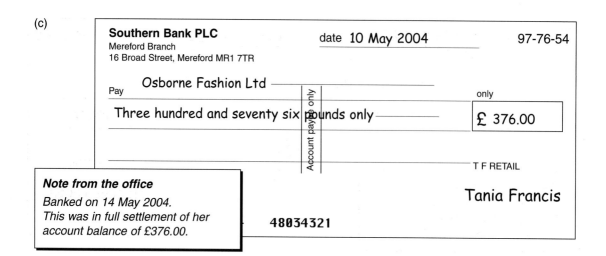

Southern Bank PLC
Mereford Branch
16 Broad Street, Mereford MR1 7TR

date 10 May 2004   97-76-54

Pay   Osborne Fashion Ltd ————————————————

Three hundred and seventy six pounds only ————

Account payee only

only

£ 376.00

T F RETAIL

Tania Francis

48034321

Note from the office
Banked on 14 May 2004.
This was in full settlement of her
account balance of £376.00.

(d)

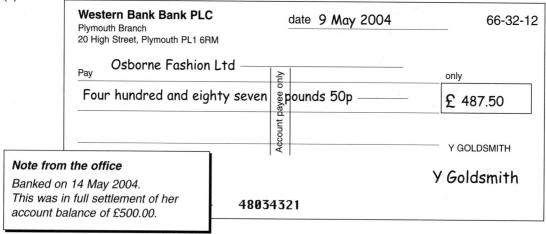

Western Bank Bank PLC
Plymouth Branch
20 High Street, Plymouth PL1 6RM

date 9 May 2004   66-32-12

Pay   Osborne Fashion Ltd ————————————

Four hundred and eighty seven pounds 50p ———

Account payee only

only

£ 487.50

Y GOLDSMITH

Y Goldsmith

48034321

Note from the office
Banked on 14 May 2004.
This was in full settlement of her
account balance of £500.00.

(e)

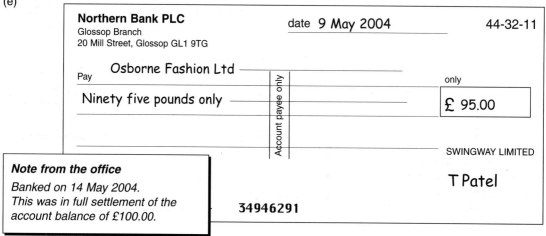

Northern Bank PLC
Glossop Branch
20 Mill Street, Glossop GL1 9TG

date 9 May 2004   44-32-11

Pay   Osborne Fashion Ltd ————————————

Ninety five pounds only ————

Account payee only

only

£ 95.00

SWINGWAY LIMITED

T Patel

34946291

Note from the office
Banked on 14 May 2004.
This was in full settlement of the
account balance of £100.00.

(f)

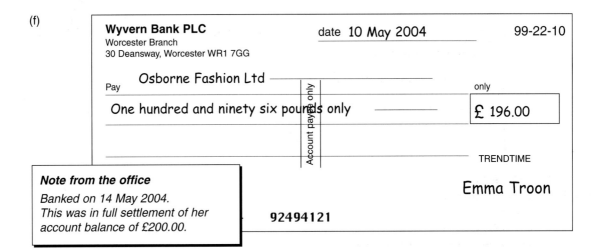

Wyvern Bank PLC
Worcester Branch
30 Deansway, Worcester WR1 7GG

date 10 May 2004

99-22-10

Pay   Osborne Fashion Ltd

only

One hundred and ninety six pounds only

£ 196.00

Account payee only

TRENDTIME

Emma Troon

92494121

Note from the office
Banked on 14 May 2004.
This was in full settlement of her
account balance of £200.00.

(g)

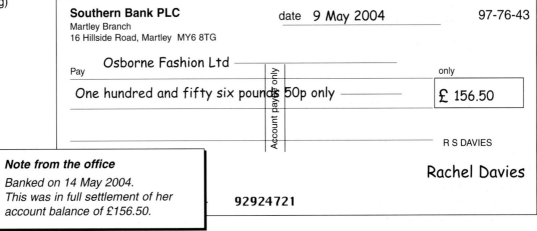

Southern Bank PLC
Martley Branch
16 Hillside Road, Martley MY6 8TG

date 9 May 2004

97-76-43

Pay   Osborne Fashion Ltd

only

One hundred and fifty six pounds 50p only

£ 156.50

Account payee only

R S DAVIES

Rachel Davies

92924721

Note from the office
Banked on 14 May 2004.
This was in full settlement of her
account balance of £156.50.

(h)

Wyvern Bank PLC
Worcester Branch
30 Deansway, Worcester WR1 7GG

date 10 May 2004

99-22-10

Pay   Osborne Fashion Ltd

only

Ninety seven pounds 50p only

£ 97.50

Account payee only

PATRICIA SMITH

P Smith

92494121

Note from the office
Banked on 14 May 2004.
This was in full settlement of her
account balance of £100.00.

11.2   List the details (including the date) that will be recorded in the cash book (payments side) from the documents on the next three pages. The three money columns are:

– discount received

– cash

– bank

Remember to record the cheque numbers next to the supplier names.

You can use (or photocopy) the following table for your answer:

Cash Book (payments side)

Date	Supplier name	Discount received £ p	Cash £ p	Bank £ p

(a)

RECEIPT	Hermes Car Hire
	17 Chepstow Way
	Bromswich B17 8GH

No. 103

date 24 May 2004

received with thanks from Osborne Fashion (cash purchases)

the sum of Seventy five pounds only

for Peugeot 307 hire

cheque	—
cash	£75.00
discount	—
total	£75.00

signature K Singh

(b)

RECEIPT	Ludlow Leather
	17 Tenbury Way
	Ludlow SY6 8VF

No. 76

date 25 May 2004

received with thanks from Osborne Fashion (cash purchases)

the sum of Twenty pounds only

for 4 x leather belts @ £5

cheque	—
cash	£20.00
discount	—
total	£20.00

signature R Marchant

(c)

RECEIPT	ACJ Fashions
	3 Nansen Road
	Stockport ST1 5FG

No. 121

date   25 May 2004

received with thanks from   Osborne Fashion (cash purchases)

the sum of   Ten pounds only

for   4 x pairs black tights @ £2.50

cheque	——
cash	£10.00
discount	——
total	£10.00

signature   A C Jones

(d)
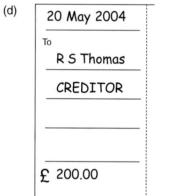

20 May 2004

To
R S Thomas

CREDITOR

£ 200.00

212345

(e)

20 May 2004

To
G M Hopkins

CREDITOR

Discount £10

£ 190.00

212346

(f)

20 May 2004

To
J Keats Ltd

CREDITOR

Discount £8.75

£ 341.25

212347

(g)

21 May 2004
To
R Graves & Co
CREDITOR
Discount £20
£380.00
212348

(h)

21 May 2004
To
W Owen
CREDITOR
£ 245.95
212349

(i)

21 May 2004
To
W Blake Ltd
CREDITOR
Discount £3.75
£71.25
212350

(j)

23 May 2004
To
T Hughes
CREDITOR
Discount £4
£ 76.00
212351

(k)

23 May 2004
To
T Hardy
Insurance
CREDITOR
Discount £3.60
£140.40
212352

(l)

23 May 2004
To
S Plath &
Associates
CREDITOR
£ 195.00
212353

12 WRITING UP AND BALANCING THE CASH BOOK

this chapter covers . . .

This chapter will explain the layout of the cash book and entries made in its columns:

* details of cash and cheques received and paid in

* details of cash discount allowed

* payments made by cash, cheque, and other forms of bank payment

* details of cash discount received from suppliers

The chapter will also explain how the columns of the cash book are balanced and describe the significance of the balances. It will also explain the role and duties of the cashier.

A fully-worked Case Study will show how a variety of transactions is entered by the cashier in the cash book.

OCR LEARNING OUTCOMES

unit 3: MAINTAINING THE CASH BOOK

Assessment objectives

1 **Entering Opening Balances in the Cash Book**

   (a) Enter opening balance

2 **Enter Transactions in the Cash Book**

   (a) Enter details of transactions on the correct side

   (b) Enter correct dates of transactions

   (c) Enter the correct folio reference

   (d) Calculate and enter cash discounts

   (e) Enter accurate amounts in the correct column(s)

3 **Balancing the Cash Book**

   (a) Calculate accurate balances

   (b) Enter accurate Cash Book totals

   (c) Enter balances

   (d) Total discount columns

INTRODUCTION TO THE CASH BOOK

One of the most important books of account kept by firms is the **cash book**. The cash book contains records of money received and payments made out of the business, including both cash and bank (cheque, bank giro credit, and other bank transfers) transactions. It is important to keep the cash book up to date since it enables the owner(s) of the business to know how much money the business has in cash and at the bank at any moment of time.

The cash book has two functions in the accounting procedure:

- firstly, all cash and bank transactions are recorded in the cash book and it therefore acts as a book of prime entry (in other words, it is where transactions are entered first)

- secondly, it combines the double-entry accounts for the cash and bank accounts

In addition to the cash book many firms also keep a petty cash book to record small items of expenditure such as the purchase of postage stamps and incidental expenses. The petty cash book is dealt with in Unit 2 Maintaining Petty Cash (see Chapters 9 – 10).

USES AND PURPOSE OF THE CASH BOOK

a cash and bank book

The cash book is used to record both the cash and bank transactions in one book. Some students may find the name "cash book" confusing in that it contains both cash and bank transactions so why not call it the cash/bank book? However, in accounting terms it has always been known as the cash book.

The cash book is used to record the money aspect of bookkeeping transactions such as:

- **cash transactions**

   - all receipts in cash

   - most payments for cash, except for small value expense payments (which as mentioned above are paid through the petty cash book)

- **bank transactions**

   - all receipts through the bank (including payment of cash into the bank)

   - all payments through the bank (including the withdrawal of cash from the bank)

purposes of the cash book

The activities of businesses involve cash or bank transactions at some point. The entry of these transactions into the cash book is carried out by the cashier, who is responsible for maintaining and controlling the cash book.

One of the main purposes of the cash book is to maintain a record of the amount of money held in cash and the bank balance at any point in time. The cash book acts as a ledger account for the cash and bank balances.

Another purpose of maintaining a cash book is to keep a permanent record of money received and payments made into and out of a business. As mentioned earlier, a cash book is a book of prime entry (where a transaction is entered first). It is important to note that any transaction entered into the cash book must be supported by documentary evidence such as an invoice, statement or receipt.

THE ROLE OF THE CASHIER

The cashier has the important role of maintaining and controlling the money coming into and going out of a business and providing up-to-date information on the organisation's cash position at any time. The cashier's duties and responsibilities include the following:

- issuing receipts for cash (and sometimes cheques) received
- recording receipts for cash and bank transactions (cheques and bank giro credits)
- making authorised payments in cash and by cheque against documents received (such as invoices and statements) showing amounts due
- recording payments by cash, cheque or bank transfers
- checking expense claims from employees and ensuring they have been properly authorised before making payment
- entering expense claims into the cash book
- paying cash and cheques received into the bank
- issuing cash to the petty cashier who operates the firm's petty cash book (see Chapters 8 – 10)
- controlling the firm's cash, using a secure cash till or cash box
- checking the accuracy of the cash and bank balances at regular intervals

the importance of accuracy and security

With so many transactions being entered into the cash book, the cashier must ensure that the accounting procedures are followed at all times. These involve:

- **Accuracy** – making sure each transaction is entered correctly in the cash book. The entry should be in strict date order using the correct date, description and amount. Any payment made must be supported by the correct documentation and be properly authorised.

  At intervals, usually one month, the cash book is checked against the bank statement and a bank reconciliation statement prepared (this is dealt with in Chapter 14). It is therefore important to ensure that all entries made in the cash book are accurate and all additions correct to enable the reconciliation to be made quickly and efficiently.

- **Security** – the cash box and the cheque books must be kept in a safe and secure place. It is also important to ensure all payments have been correctly authorised before payment is made.

- **Confidentiality** – it is important that all information contained in the cash book is kept confidential and not revealed to unauthorised people or organisations. This includes details of individual entries and the cash and bank balances of the organisation.

LAYOUT OF THE CASH BOOK

There are a number of cash book layouts that may be used by a business, but the most common format is the use of three money columns on each side of the cash book, as illustrated below. Note that the cash book is divided into two sides. The left-hand side is the **Receipts** side in which all receipts are entered, and the right-hand side is the **Payments** side where all the payments are recorded.

cash book: receipts side (debits)   **cash book: payments side (credits)**

| Dr | | | | | | | | | Cash Book | | | | | Cr |
Date	Details	Discount allowed	Cash	Bank	Date	Details	Discount received	Cash	Bank
2004		£ p	£ p	£ p	2004		£ p	£ p	£ p
3 Mar	Balances b/d		300.00	550.00	5 Mar	Tombenco 100281			160.00
4 Mar	Cash sales		500.00		6 Apr	Petty cash 100282			100.00
5 Mar	Cheque R Wilson			1,250.00					

money in   money out

the receipts side of the cash book

The left-hand side of the cash book is the debit side in which all the receipts are entered. You may like to refer to the debit side as the "in" side where all the monies received "into" the business will be entered. As can be seen from the illustration of the cash book on the previous page, there are three money columns on the debit (left-hand) side:

- discount allowed
- cash
- bank

In the column headed "cash" all cash receipts into the business (but not into the bank) are entered and in the "bank" column all the money paid into the bank (eg cheques, cash, bank giro credits, standing orders, direct debits received) are entered. A third money column is used to record cash "discount allowed" to customers (see below).

the payments side of the cash book

The right-hand side of the cash book is the credit side where all the payments are entered. Again, you may find it useful to refer to the credit side as the "out" side where all the payments "out of" the business are recorded. Again, there are three money columns on this side of the cash book for discount received, cash and bank.

In the column headed "cash" all cash payments "out of" the business are entered and in the "bank" column all bank payments (eg cheques, cash withdrawals, standing orders, direct debits paid) are entered. The "discount received" column relates to cash discounts that have been received by the business in respect of prompt payments made to its suppliers.

CASH DISCOUNT

definition of cash discount

Cash discount is an amount offered by the seller of goods and/or services to the buyer to encourage the buyer to pay their account promptly. For example, on the bottom of an invoice the terms may state "Cash discount of 2.5% for settlement within 7 days". This means that the seller will allow 2.5% off the net price (ie the price before VAT is added on) if the account is paid within seven days of the invoice date.

This type of discount should not be confused with "trade discount" given to regular customers. Trade discount is not dependent on early payment.

cash discount allowed and received

There are two ways of looking at cash discount, depending on whether you are the supplier or the buyer:

- **Discount allowed** is when the supplier allows the buyer to deduct cash discount when the account is settled – the supplier "allows" the discount

- **Discount received** is where the buyer deducts the cash discount from the amount outstanding before making payment – the buyer "receives" the discount

Now read through and study the two Case Studies that follow. One deals with the receipts side of the cash book, the other with the payments side.

CASE STUDY

ACE ADVERTISING AGENCY: WRITING UP THE CASH BOOK – RECEIPTS SIDE

situation

Kulvinder is assistant cashier at Ace Advertising Agency. One of Kulvinder's tasks is to bank any cheques received and enter them in the cash book. The advertising agency offers cash discount to their clients to encourage them to pay their accounts quickly.

The list below shows the clients who have paid their outstanding accounts by cheque, less cash discount of 2.5% for prompt payment, during June 2004.

Kulvinder is asked to enter the receipts in the cash book. This is shown on the next page.

List of cheques received during June 2004

Name of client	Amount Due	Cheque amount	Discount allowed
	£	£	£
Bennetts Ltd	425.58	414.94	10.64
J Chadwick Ltd	138.00	134.55	3.45
Green's Solicitors	564.67	550.56	14.11
Marsh Motors	220.50	214.99	5.51
Owen & Owen Ltd	330.00	321.75	8.25
Taylors Ltd	95.90	93.50	2.40

Dr					Ace Advertising Agency: Cash Book					Cr
Date	Details	Discount allowed	Cash	Bank	Date	Details	Discount received	Cash	Bank
2004		£ p	£ p	£ p	2004		£ p	£ p	£ p
1 Jun	Balances b/d		200.00	750.00					
4 Jun	Bennetts Ltd	10.64		414.94					
11 Jun	J Chadwick Ltd	3.45		134.55					
16 Jun	Greens Solicitors	14.11		550.56					
23 Jun	Marsh Motors	5.51		214.99					
28 Jun	Owen & Owen	8.25		321.75					
29 Jun	Taylors Ltd	2.40		93.50					

Notes to the above

- The first entry in the cash book is 'Balances b/d'. This is the amount of cash held by the business and the balance of the bank account at the beginning of June. We will deal with balancing these accounts later in the chapter.

- The amounts then entered in the cash book are the cash discount and the amount of the cheque.

  For example, the total amount due by Bennetts Ltd is £425.58, the net amount received from them is £414.94, therefore, the cash discount is the difference between £425.58 and £414.94 = £10.64. The £10.64 is entered in the Discount Allowed column and the net (cheque) amount £414.94 is entered in the Bank column.

CASE STUDY

ACE ADVERTISING AGENCY: WRITING UP THE CASH BOOK – PAYMENTS SIDE

situation

One of Kulvinder's tasks as accounts assistant is to prepare a schedule of suppliers that require payment at the month end. The schedule will list the name of the supplier, the total amount due, the cash discount that may be deducted and the net amount to be paid.

A list of the suppliers and the amounts outstanding on their accounts at the end of April is shown below. You are to assume that all accounts are paid by the due date and the next cheque number is 404520.

Kulvinder's tasks are to prepare the cheques for payment and the appropriate counterfoils, and then to enter the payments into the right-hand side of the cash book.

Name of supplier	Amount Due	Usual payment terms
Halls Ltd	£152.00	Cash discount received for settlement within 7 days
Business Supplies Co.	£325.70	Net monthly
Frank Osborne Ltd	£87.60	Cash discount received for settlement within 15 days
Paper & Printing Supplies	£400.00	Cash discount received for settlement within 7 days
White Office Supplies	£116.80	Cash discount received for settlement within 7 days
Shaftesbury Partners	£ 85.00	Net monthly

Kulvinder first calculates the amounts of cash discount that will be available:

Name of supplier	Amount Due £	Cash Discount £	Net Amount Due £
Halls Ltd	152.00	3.80	148.20
Business Supplies	325.70	-	325.70
Frank Osborne Ltd	87.60	2.19	85.41
Paper & Printing	400.00	10.00	390.00
White Office Supplies	116.80	3.50	113.30
Shaftesbury Partners	85.00	-	85.00

Kulvinder then writes out the six cheques on the due date of 30 June.

The cheque book counterfoils (cheque stubs) that she has made out are shown on the next page.

Note that all the suppliers are marked 'CREDITOR' (someone to whom you owe money) and that the cash discount has been deducted wherever it is available.

30 June 2004
To
Halls Limited
CREDITOR
Discount
£3.80
£148.20
404520

30 June 2004
To
Business
Supplies Co.
CREDITOR
£325.70
404521

30 June 2004
To
Frank
Osborne Ltd
CREDITOR
Discount £2.19
£ 85.41
404522

30 June 2004
To
Paper & Printing
CREDITOR
Discount
£10.00
£390.00
404523

30 June 2004
To
White Office
Supplies
CREDITOR
Discount £3.50
£113.30
404524

30 June 2004
To
Shaftesbury
Partners
CREDITOR
£ 85.00
404525

Kulvinder then writes the cheque details in the cash book on the 'payments' side (right-hand side), as shown below.

Dr						Ace Advertising Agency: Cash Book				Cr
Date	Details	Discount allowed	Cash	Bank	Date	Details	Discount received	Cash	Bank
2004		£ p	£ p	£ p	2004		£ p	£ p	£ p
1 Jun	Balances b/d		200.00	750.00	30 Jun	Halls Ltd 404520	3.80		148.20
4 Jun	Bennetts Ltd	10.64		414.94	30 Jun	Business Supplies			
11 Jun	J Chadwick Ltd	3.45		134.55		404521			325.70
16 Jun	Greens Solicitors	14.11		550.56	30 Jun	Frank Osborne Ltd			
23 Jun	Marsh Motors	5.51		214.99		404522	2.19		85.41
28 Jun	Owen & Owen	8.25		321.75	30 Jun	Paper & Printing			
29 Jun	Taylors Ltd	2.40		93.50		404523	10.00		390.00
					30 Jun	White Office			
						Supplies 404524	3.50		113.30
					30 Jun	Shaftesbury Ptnrs			
						404525			85.00

- In the above illustration the cash discount is entered in the Discount Received column and the net amount entered in the Bank column, because the payment is being made by cheque. If a payment is made in cash to the business, then the amount would be entered in the Cash column.

- The cash discount on the payments side is 'Discount received' because the discount is 'received' by Ace Advertising Agency as a reduction in the amount owed.

- When entering the cheques in the cash book it is important to include the cheque number, this makes the payment easier to identify when checking the cash book against the bank statement.

BALANCING THE CASH BOOK

The cash book contains the accounts for cash and bank transactions and, like other accounts, needs to be balanced at regular intervals.

The debit (receipts) and credit (payments) sides of the cash book include columns for bank and cash transactions, and, as we have seen in this chapter, other columns – such as discount allowed and discount received – may also be incorporated.

Illustrated below is the cash book of Attwood Limited showing the transactions for the first week in April. As you will see there are entries in all the money columns, and at the end of the week they have all been totalled. In addition the cash and bank columns have been *balanced*.

Study the format below and then read the explanation on the next page. Note that the grey arrows and boxes below have been added to help with the explanation. They do not appear in the actual cash book.

cash book: receipts side (debits)   **cash book: payments side (credits)**

Dr					Attwood Limited: Cash Book					Cr
Date	Details	Discount allowed	Cash	Bank	Date	Details	Discount received	Cash	Bank
2004		£	£	£	2004		£	£	£
5 Apr	Balances b/d		300	1,550	5 Apr	E Lee & Co 616001			160
5 Apr	Cash sales		235		6 Apr	Hayes Ltd 616002			200
6 Apr	Mango Designs	2		98	6 Apr	S Crane 616003	5		145
6 Apr	John Mason &				7 Apr	Cash purchases		94	
	Associates			205	8 Apr	R Jameson 616004			282
7 Apr	J Jones	4		76	9 Apr	S Maverick 616005	5		70
7 Apr	R Singh			94		the balancing figure, ie the difference between the debit and credit total is entered on the side of the lower total – this is the 'balance'			
9 Apr	D Whiteman Ltd	3		45					
9 Apr	Natasha Barclay								
	and Co			110					
					11 Apr	Balances c/d		441	1,321
		9	535	2,178			10	535	2,178
12 Apr	Balances b/d		441	1,321		totals box			

balance brought down for the following week = balance carried down from this week

balancing the cash and bank columns

The cash and bank columns are balanced as follows:

step 1	Add up the figures in all the cash and bank columns and make a note of the totals.
step 2	Compare the totals of the cash columns – they are £535 and £94.
step 3	Take away the lower figure from the higher to give the *balance* of the cash remaining (£535 – £94 = £441).
step 4	Write down the *higher* of the two totals at the bottom of *both* cash columns in a totals 'box' (£535).
step 5	The balance of cash remaining (£441) is entered as a balancing item *above* the totals box on the side which gave the lower total, ie the credit (right-hand) side. This £441 is written down again (brought down) below the cash total on the *other* side, the debit (left-hand) side as the opening balance for next week (£441).
step 6	The two bank columns are dealt with in the same way: £2,178 is the higher of the two column totals and is entered in the totals box on both sides, the balance is the difference between the subtotals, ie
	£2,178 – £857 = £1,321 (the balance of money in the bank)
	This is entered above the totals box in the bank column which had the lower initial total, in this case the credit side.

Note that in the cash book shown on the previous page the cash and bank balances have been brought down on the debit (left-hand) side, which indicates a positive bank balance. It is very important to appreciate that the bank columns of the cash book represent the firm's own records of bank transactions and the balance at the bank, but the bank statement may well show different figures. Chapter 14 explains how to reconcile the two figures.

dealing with the discount columns

Each discount column is totalled separately on a regular basis, as in the cash book on page 262. Note that *no attempt should be made to balance them*. At this point, amounts recorded in the columns and the totals are *not* part of the double-entry system. The two totals are transferred to the double-entry system as follows:

- the total on the debit side (£9 in the example opposite) is debited to discount allowed account in the nominal ledger

- the total on the credit side (£10 in the example) is credited to discount received account, also in the nominal ledger

GEE TRADING COMPANY CASH BOOK: A WORKED EXAMPLE

situation

Anton is employed by The Gee Trading Company as a cashier.

Set out below are the receipts and payments that require entering in the firm's cash book for the week commencing 3 May 2004.

2004

1 May	Balances at start of week: cash £150.00, bank £1,200.00.
3 May	Received a cheque from J Kirk, a debtor, for £136.50 (no cash discount).
3 May	Received a cheque from Peak Products Ltd £421.00 (no cash discount).
3 May	Paid C. Wager Ltd, a creditor, £80.00 by cheque no. 201334 (no cash discount).
4 May	Paid for purchases in cash £42.00.
4 May	Received £64.00 cash into the business from cash sales.
5 May	Paid Lee & Sons, a creditor, £133.60 by cheque no. 201335, having deducted cash discount of £3.40.
5 May	Received £54.00 cash into the business from cash sales.
5 May	Cashed cheque for £81.70 (no. 201336) at bank to reimburse petty cashier to top up petty cash imprest.
6 May	Received cheque from Albert Brown Ltd for £298.35 (cash discount allowed £7.65).
6 May	Paid £125.00 to Ace Insurance, cheque no. 201337.
6 May	Paid cash £20.00 donation to local charity.
7 May	Received cheque from D Patel for £210.60, Mr Patel having deducted £5.40 cash discount.
7 May	Paid cheque to D Hunt Ltd £72.00, cheque no. 201338.

On 7 May Anton has to balance off the cash book and bring down the balances.

solution

Anton writes up and balances the cash book :

Dr										Cr
					Gee Trading Company:Cash Book					
Date	Details	Discount Allowed £ p	Cash £ p	Bank £ p	Date	Details		Discount Received £ p	Cash £ p	Bank £ p
2004					2004					
1 May	Balances b/d		150.00	1,200.00	3 May	C Wager Limited	201334			80.00
3 May	J Kirk			136.50	4 May	Cash purchases			42.00	
3 May	Peak Products Limited			421.00	5 May	Lee & Sons	201335	3.40		133.60
4 May	Cash sales		64.00		5 May	Petty cash	201336			81.70
5 May	Cash sales		54.00		6 May	Ace Insurance	201337			125.00
6 May	Albert Brown Limited	7.65		298.35	6 May	Donation			20.00	
7 May	D Patel	5.40		210.60	7 May	D Hunt Limited	201338			72.00
					7 May	Balance c/d			206.00	1,774.15
		13.05	268.00	2,266.45				3.40	268.00	2,266.45
8 May	Balance b/d		206.00	1,774.15						

The balancing is carried out as follows:

totalling the discount columns

The discount columns act as a list or 'memorandum' column and as such each column only needs totalling. Thus on the receipts (left-hand) side of the cash book the column headed Discount Allowed has been added up giving a total of £13.05, which has been entered as the total.

On the payments (right-hand) side of the cash book the Discount Received column has been added to give a total of £3.40, this too has been entered as the total.

These totals are later transferred into the double-entry system through the General Ledger.

balancing the cash columns

The cash columns are balanced as follows:

- Add up all the cash receipts in the cash column on the receipts ("in") side:
  £150.00 + £64.00 + £54.00 = £268.00

- Add up all the cash payments in the cash column on the payments ("out") side:
  £42.00 + £20.00 = £62.00

- From the total cash receipts (the higher figure) deduct the total cash payments (the lower figure):   £268.00 – £62.00 = £206.00

- The difference of £206.00 represents the cash left over at the end of the period, and is the 'balance' of cash account.

- This balance of £206.00 is entered on the credit (payments) side of the cash book as 'Balance c/d' which stands for 'balance carried down'. The cash columns are then totalled off at the end of the period, producing a total on both sides of £268.00. The balance of £206.00 is then entered again on the debit (receipts) side of the cash book as 'Balance b/d' which stands for 'balance brought down'.

- This means that the opening balance on 8 May 2004 is £206.00, the amount of cash which the firm is holding at the beginning of the next period.

balancing the bank columns

The bank columns are balanced off in exactly the same way:

- Add up all the bank receipts in the bank column on the receipts ('in') side:

  £1,200.00 + £136.50 + £421.00 + £298.35 + £210.60 = £2,266.45

- Add up all the bank payments in the bank column on the payments ('out') side:

  £80.00 + £133.60 + £81.70 + £125.00 + £72.00 = £492.30

- Deduct the lower figure from the higher figure:

  £2,266.45 – £492.30 = £1,774.15

- The difference of £1,774.15 represents the amount of money in the firm's bank account at the end of the period according to our records, this is known as the 'balance'.

- The balance of £1,774.15 is entered at the bottom of the bank column which had the lower total, as 'Balance c/d' . In this case the bank column is on the credit (right-hand) side of the cash book.

- The bank columns are then added up, and should produce the same total of £2,266.45.

- The bank balance 'Balance c/d' (£1,774.15) is then entered again on the debit (receipts) side of the cash book as 'Balance b/d' which stands for 'balance brought down'.

- This means that the opening bank balance on 8 May 2004 is £1,774.15, the amount of money in the bank account, according to the firm's records, which it has available for the beginning of the next period.

note

It is possible that when you balance the bank columns the bank 'balance b/d' is on the opposite 'payments' side of the cash book. This means that the business has a bank overdraft. This is explained in the next Case Study.

CASE STUDY

GEE TRADING COMPANY GOES OVERDRAWN

situation

If a business spends more than it receives through the bank account, the result is a bank overdraft. In other words, the business will be borrowing from the bank.

If in the Case Study on the previous pages, Gee Trading Company issued a cheque to C. Wager Ltd for £2,080.00 instead of £80.00, the effect would be to increase the total of the bank payments by £2,000. The effect on the cash book would be:

- Total receipts would still be £ 2,266.45, but . . .

- Total payments are now £2,080.00 + £133.60 + £81.70 + £125.00 + £72.00 = £2,492.30.

- Total payments of £2,492.30 less total receipts £2,266.45 = £225.85 (ie the business has paid out more than it has received)

- The balancing figure of £225.85 is entered above the total box on the debit (left-hand) side as 'balance c/d' and then on the credit (right-hand) side as 'balance b/d'. This represents a bank overdraft of £225.85.

The amended cash book is shown below.

Dr					Gee Trading Company:Cash Book				Cr
Date	Details	Discount Allowed £ p	Cash £ p	Bank £ p	Date	Details	Discount Received £ p	Cash £ p	Bank £ p
2004					2004				
1 May	Balances b/d		150.00	1,200.00	3 May	C Wager Limited 201334			2,080.00
3 May	J Kirk			136.50	4 May	Cash purchases		42.00	
3 May	Peak Products Limited			421.00	5 May	Lee & Sons 201335	3.40		133.60
4 May	Cash sales		64.00		5 May	Petty cash 201336			81.70
5 May	Cash sales		54.00		6 May	Ace Insurance 201337			125.00
6 May	Albert Brown Limited	7.65		298.35	6 May	Donation		20.00	
7 May	D Patel	5.40		210.60	7 May	D Hunt Limited 201338			72.00
7 May	Balance c/d			225.85	7 May	Balance c/d		206.00	
		13.05	268.00	2,492.30			3.40	268.00	2,492.30
8 May	Balance b/d		206.00		8 May	Balance b/d			225.85

The rule is therefore:

- bank balance on the debit (left-hand) side = money in the bank

- bank balance on the credit (right-hand) side = bank overdraft (money owed)

CHAPTER SUMMARY

- A cash book is maintained to record both cash and bank transactions on a regular basis, for example, once a month, so that the business can assess its financial position.

- The role of the cashier is vital in assessing the financial position since his/her duties include recording the money coming into the business and the money going out. After entering the various receipts and payments he/she will calculate the amount of cash held by the business and the bank balance.

- When entering transactions in the cash book it is important to ensure that items are entered accurately and confidentiality is maintained at all times. The cash and the cheque books should be kept in a secure place.

- The cash book layout used in this chapter follows that used by many businesses. The layout incorporates both receipts and the payments.

- Cash discounts are both allowed and received by businesses. They are entered in memorandum columns in the cash book.

- The cash book is balanced on a regular basis. The cash account will always show a positive (debit) balance, but the bank account balance may be either debit (money in the bank) or credit (a bank overdraft).

KEY TERMS

cash book	a record of cash and bank transactions, combining the roles of primary accounting record and double-entry bookkeeping
cashier	the person in a business responsible for maintaining and controlling the money that flows into and out of a business; their role is one of importance since they provide up-to-date information about the business cash position at any point
cash discount	an amount (often a percentage reduction) offered by the seller of goods and/or services to the buyer to encourage the buyer to pay their account promptly
discount allowed	is where the supplier allows the buyer to deduct cash discount on settlement of their account
discount received	is where the buyer deducts the cash discount from the outstanding account before making payment
overdraft	borrowing from the bank on the bank account, (shown in the cash book as a credit balance, brought down on the right-hand side)

STUDENT
ACTIVITIES

NOTE: an asterisk (*) after the question number means that the
answer to the question is given at the back of this book.

12.1* Jenkins Products Limited uses a three column cash book to maintain its cash and bank transactions.

The following transactions took place during January 2004.

1 Jan	Opening Balances of £78.50 in the cash account and £567.20 (Dr) in the bank account.
2 Jan	Received cheque from P. Simms Ltd, a debtor, £390.00, cash discount allowed £10.00.
2 Jan	Paid expenses to the Company Secretary £27.00 by cash.
5 Jan	Paid Ace Advertising Agency £378.00 by cheque no. 100559, having deducted £9.50 cash discount.
7 Jan	Received £120.00 cash into the business from cash sales.
8 Jan	Received cheque from Smart Trading for £625.00 (no cash discount).
12 Jan	Paid £89.00 to Star Insurance by cheque 100560.
15 Jan	Sold goods to A Lucas and received a cheque for £144.30, cash discount allowed £3.70.
19 Jan	Received cheque from J. Jackson, a debtor, £220.00 (no cash discount).
23 Jan	Paid M Evans, a creditor, £635.00 by cheque no. 100561 (no cash discount).
27 Jan	Received cheque from W Little Ltd, £438.75, cash discount of £11.25 having been taken.
30 Jan	Paid travelling expenses in cash £22.78.
31 Jan	Paid Logan Products, a creditor, by cheque no. 100562, £185.25, having deducted £4.75 cash discount.

You are required to

(a)   Enter the opening balances in the cash book (see next page for a cash book format).

(b)   Enter the details of receipts and payments including the cash discounts.

(c)   Total and balance the cash book and bring down the balance.

(d)   Total the discount columns.

Note

A blank cash book page is reproduced on the next page. You may photocopy this page.
Blank forms are also available for download from the resources sections of www.osbornebooks.co.uk

Cash Book

Date	Details	Discount Allowed £ p	Cash £ p	Bank £ p

Date	Details	Discount Received £ p	Cash £ p	Bank £ p

12.2* You are employed as cashier by Flynn Motor Parts Company. The company maintains a three column cash book.

You have been asked to write up the cash book for April 2004 from the following details.

| 1 Apr | Balances brought down: | Cash Account | £105.00 Dr |
| | | Bank Account | £900.00 Dr |

2 Apr   Received cheque from Hartwell Motors, a debtor, £399.75, having allowed £10.25 cash discount.

2 Apr   Received £98 cash into the business from cash sales.

5 Apr   Paid Cohen Ltd, a creditor, £380.00 by cheque no. 004243 (no cash discount).

6 Apr   Received cheque from Weir & Co £760.50 (having allowed £19.50 cash discount).

9 Apr   Paid travelling expenses to Company Secretary £45.00 in cash.

9 Apr   Paid for fixtures £400.00, cheque no. 004244.

13 Apr   Received cheque from Bates Engineering for £117.00, having allowed £3.00 cash discount.

16 Apr   Received cheque £95.00 from Garners Ltd, a creditor.

21 Apr   Paid premium by cheque 004245 to Oak Insurance Co £105.00.

23 Apr   Received cheque from W Curtis for £45.00 in full settlement of the account of £48.00.

26 Apr   Paid Car Breakdown Service £75.00 by cheque 004246.

30 Apr   Paid cheque no 004247 to Brook Motors £234.00 (cash discount of £6.00 deducted).

30 Apr   Paid for sundry purchases £69.50 in cash.

You are required to

(a)   Enter the opening balances in the cash book.

(b)   Enter the details of receipts and payments including the cash discounts.

(c)   Total and balance the cash book and bring down the balance.

(d)   Total the discount columns.

12.3   As cashier for Spencer's Office Supplies your task is to maintain the firm's three column cash book. Below are the details of the receipts and payments of cash and bank for the month of March 2004. The firm offers cash discounts to encourage their clients to pay their accounts promptly.

1 Mar   Opening balances of cash in hand £235.00 and balance at bank £2,345.00 (Dr).

3 Mar   Paid cleaner in cash £40.00.

4 Mar   Received cheques from:

Peak Dental Practice £44.85 – cash discount allowed £1.15

Rippon (Estate Agents) £79.00 – no cash discount

9 Mar   Received cheque from Premier Garage £144.25. cash discount of £3.75 having been deducted.

12 Mar   Paid motor expenses in cash £17.89, to Bill Healey the Office Manager.

12 Mar   Cash sales – £92.34 received into the business.

15 Mar   Paid Office Supplies Ltd, a creditor, £750.75 cheque no. 925001, cash discount of £19.24 having been deducted.

16 Mar   Paid a creditor, Cox & Co, by cheque no. 925002, £550.00 (no cash discount).

18 Mar   Received cheque from Halls Ltd, a debtor, £106.00 (no cash discount).

25 Mar   Cash sales – £67.00 received into the business.

26 Mar   Paid wages £1,010 by cheque no. 925003.

30 Mar   Received cash sales £123.00 into the business.

30 Mar   Paid business rates by cheque 925004 for £400.00 to SMDC.

31 Mar   Bought fixtures for office use paying by cheque no. 925005, £330.00.

You are required to

(a)   Enter the opening balances.

(b)   Enter the details of receipts and payments including the cash discounts.

(c)   Total and balance the cash book and bring down the balance.

(d)   Total the discount columns.

12.4 Firbank & Worrall run a haulage company in Cheshire. Their cashier, Roger, is responsible for the company's three column cash book. Roger is asked to write up the cash book for June 2004 from the following details:

1 Jun   Balances brought down: Cash Account   £205.00 (Dr)

                                                  Bank overdraft   £733.20 (Cr)

2 Jun   Received cheque from Mr Wilshaw, a creditor, £129.00 (no cash discount).

3 Jun   Paid for sundry purchases by cash £132.00.

4 Jun   Received cheque from Browns Products £2,340.00 in full settlement of their account for £2,400.00.

8 Jun   Paid cheque to Ace Insurance £300.00, cheque no. 511615.

9 Jun   Cheque 511616 for £85.00 cashed at bank, for petty cash imprest top up.

10 Jun   Received cheque from Akhash Foods £419.25, cash discount of £10.75 allowed.

12 Jun   Paid the following by cheque:

Bowman Products   £300.00   Cheque no. 511617, cash discount £8.00

Goddard's Machines   £ 75.00   Cheque no. 511618, cash discount £2.00

Pete's Garage   £ 526.00 Cheque no. 511619, cash discount £12.50

17 Jun   Paid rates £250.00 by cheque 511620.

23 Jun   Received cheque from K Green, a creditor, £600.00 cash discount of £16.00 allowed.

24 Jun   Cash sales £80.00 received into the business.

26 Jun   Paid wages £1,254.00 by cheque no. 511621.

27 Jun   Received cheque £421.00 from Polar Foods Ltd in full settlement of their account for £430.00.

You are required to

(a)   Enter the opening balances.

(b)   Enter the details of receipts and payments including the cash discounts.

(c)   Total and balance the cash book and bring down the balance.

(d)   Total the discount columns.

12.5 Julie Capper has recently opened a new business called 'Capper's Crafts' It sells craft and art materials to schools and retail shops.

Julie has appointed Jo to help her with the book-keeping side of the business. One of Jo's tasks is to enter the daily transactions into the business's three column cash book.

Julie offers cash discount for prompt payment and she also receives cash discount provided she pays within the payment terms.

At the beginning of March 2004 the following balances were brought down:

      Cash in hand   £252.00

      Balance of money in the bank   £1,300.00

Documentation relating to all the transactions involving the receipt and payment of money during March 2004 are shown on the next seven pages:

You are required to carry out the following tasks

(a)   Enter the opening balances.

(b)   Enter details of receipts and calculate the cash discounts using the documents shown on pages 275 to 278.

(c)   Enter details of payments and cash discounts using the documents shown on pages 279 to 281.

(d)   Total and balance the cash book and bring down the balance.

(e)   Total the discount columns.

Important note: ensure that you enter all the transactions in strict date order.

cheques received by Cappers Crafts

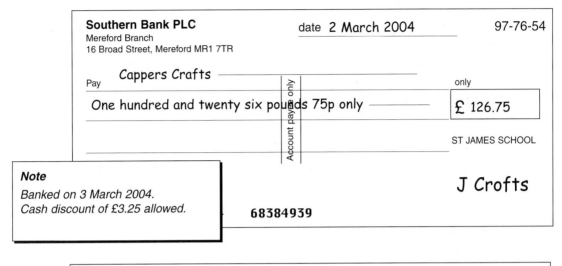

Southern Bank PLC
Mereford Branch
16 Broad Street, Mereford MR1 7TR

date 2 March 2004

97-76-54

Pay   Cappers Crafts ——————————————————— only

One hundred and twenty six pounds 75p only ————

£ 126.75

Account payee only

ST JAMES SCHOOL

J Crofts

68384939

Note
Banked on 3 March 2004.
Cash discount of £3.25 allowed.

TUDOR BANK PLC
Market Place
Crewe CW1 2TG

date 4 March 2004

72-31-03

Pay   Cappers Crafts ——————————————— only

Fifty seven pounds 20p only ———

£ 57.20

Account payee only

ARTS & CRAFTS

Ann Ball

32511891

Note
Banked on 5 March 2004.
No cash discount.

Regency Bank PLC
Bridge Street
Nantwich CW3 4RF

date 15 March 2004

42-21-03

Pay   Cappers Crafts ——————————————— only

Three hundred and thirty three pounds 45p only ———

£ 333.45

Account payee only

GODDARDS LIMITED

G Goddard

02368093

Note
Banked on 16 March 2004.
This was in full settlement of their
account balance of £342.00.

cheques received by Cappers Crafts

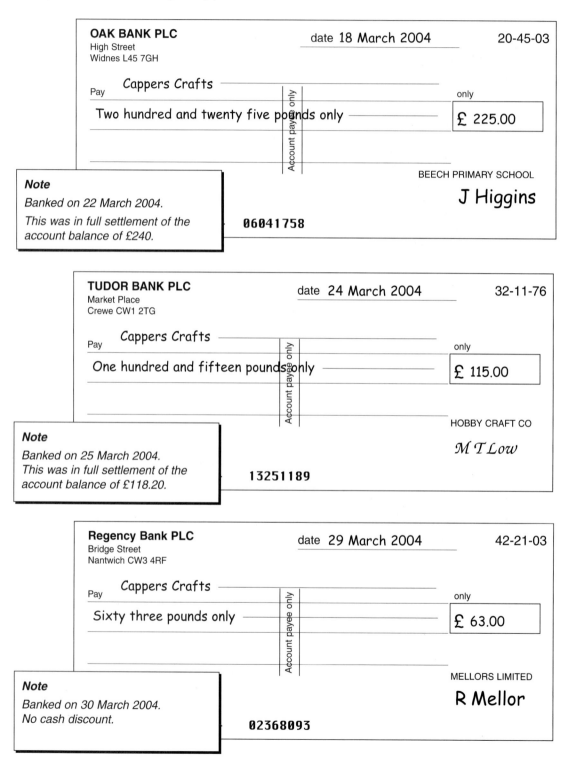

OAK BANK PLC
High Street
Widnes L45 7GH

date 18 March 2004   20-45-03

Pay   Cappers Crafts   only

Two hundred and twenty five pounds only ————   £ 225.00

Account payee only

BEECH PRIMARY SCHOOL

J Higgins

06041758

Note
Banked on 22 March 2004.
This was in full settlement of the
account balance of £240.

TUDOR BANK PLC
Market Place
Crewe CW1 2TG

date 24 March 2004   32-11-76

Pay   Cappers Crafts   only

One hundred and fifteen pounds only ————   £ 115.00

Account payee only

HOBBY CRAFT CO

M T Low

13251189

Note
Banked on 25 March 2004.
This was in full settlement of the
account balance of £118.20.

Regency Bank PLC
Bridge Street
Nantwich CW3 4RF

date 29 March 2004   42-21-03

Pay   Cappers Crafts   only

Sixty three pounds only ————   £ 63.00

Account payee only

MELLORS LIMITED

R Mellor

02368093

Note
Banked on 30 March 2004.
No cash discount.

receipts issued by Cappers Crafts for cash sales

CAPPERS CRAFTS
RECEIPT

No. 101

date 6 March 2004

received from T Ahmed

the sum of Forty two pounds fifty pence

for Goods supplied

cheque	——
cash	£42.50
discount	-
total	£42.50

signature Jo Dunn

CAPPERS CRAFTS
RECEIPT

No. 102

date 10 March 2004

received from Banks Lane School

the sum of Fifty one pounds only

for Goods supplied

cheque	——
cash	£51.00
discount	-
total	£51.00

signature Jo Dunn

receipts issued by Cappers Crafts for cash sales

CAPPERS CRAFTS	No. 103
RECEIPT	date 12 March 2004

received from Judith's Art Materials

the sum of Seventy six pounds only

for Goods supplied

cheque	———
cash	£76.00
discount	-
total	£76.00

signature Julie Capper

CAPPERS CRAFTS	No. 104
RECEIPT	date 24 March 2004

received from Worrall's Workshop

the sum of Twenty three pounds only

for Goods supplied

cheque	———
cash	£23.00
discount	-
total	£23.00

signature Jo Dunn

cash receipts issued by Cappers Crafts' suppliers

DOBBY ARTS & CRAFTS   No. 27

RECEIPT   date   4 March 2004

received from   Cappers Crafts

the sum of   Two hundred and forty three pounds 75p

for   Goods supplied

cheque	——
cash	£243.75
discount	£6.25
total	£250.00

signature   E Firth

BURGESS SUPPLIES   No. 201

RECEIPT   date 15 March 2004

received from   Cappers Crafts

the sum of   Forty two pounds only

for   Goods supplied

cheque	——
cash	£42.00
discount	£2.00
total	£44.00

signature   Mary Grainger

PATEL WHOLESALE   No. 89

RECEIPT   date 31 March 2004

received from   Cappers Crafts

the sum of   Twenty seven pounds fifty pence

for   Goods supplied

cheque	——
cash	£27.50
discount	-
total	£27.50

signature   D P A Patel

cheque counterfoils written out by Cappers Crafts

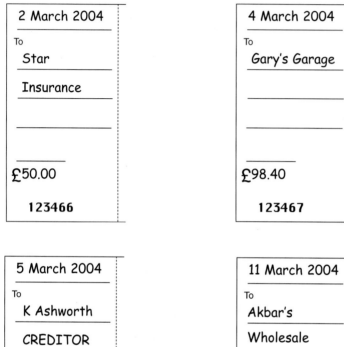

| 2 March 2004 |
| To |
| Star |
| Insurance |
| |
| |
| £50.00 |
| **123466** |

| 4 March 2004 |
| To |
| Gary's Garage |
| |
| |
| £98.40 |
| **123467** |

| 5 March 2004 |
| To |
| K Ashworth |
| CREDITOR |
| Discount £5.95 |
| £ 232.05 |
| **123468** |

| 11 March 2004 |
| To |
| Akbar's |
| Wholesale |
| CREDITOR |
| Discount £10.50 |
| £ 409.50 |
| **123469** |

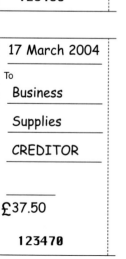

| 17 March 2004 |
| To |
| Business |
| Supplies |
| CREDITOR |
| |
| £37.50 |
| **123470** |

| 22 March 2004 |
| To |
| Southern |
| Electric |
| |
| |
| £ 108.20 |
| **123471** |

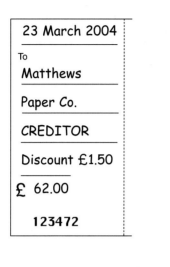

23 March 2004

To

Matthews

Paper Co.

CREDITOR

Discount £1.50

£ 62.00

123472

26 March 2004

To

Blakes

Advertising

CREDITOR

Discount £3.00

£ 117.00

123473

29 March 2004

To

Rates

£ 122.00

123474

31 March 2004

To

Gee

Wholesale

CREDITOR

Discount £12.30

£ 570.00

123475

13 BANK TRANSACTIONS

this chapter covers . . .

A business records its banking transactions in the bank columns of its cash book. The bank also records the account transactions of the business on its computers, and regularly produces a bank statement showing those transactions.

This chapter explains the various receipts and payments items recorded on the bank statement, some of which may not yet be recorded in the cash book of the business.

Receipt items in addition to cash and cheques include:

- BACS (computer processed) payments received
- bank giro credit transfers
- interest received from the bank

Payment items in addition to cash and cheques include:

- BACS (computer processed) payments made – standing orders and direct debits
- bank transaction charges
- interest charged by the bank
- unpaid ('bounced') cheques

The next chapter explains how the business reconciles ('ties up') the transactions on the bank statement with the transactions recorded in the bank columns of its cash book.

OCR LEARNING OUTCOMES

unit 3: MAINTAINING THE CASH BOOK

Assessment objectives

4   Prepare a bank reconciliation statement

    (a)   Compare transactions that appear on both cash book and bank statement

    (b)   Update cash book from details of transactions appearing on bank statement

THE BANK STATEMENT

The bank statement is printed by the bank and sent to the bank customer on a regular basis – daily, weekly, monthly – depending on the number of transactions passing through the account. Banks are increasingly offering an online banking service which enables customers to view bank transactions on screen, but the traditional paper-based statement is still required by these customers.

bank statement format

The format of a bank statement varies from bank to bank, but the example shown and explained below is fairly typical of the monthly statement which is likely to appear in your assignments. Study the format and read the explanatory notes. Details of the receipts and payments are explained in the pages that follow.

STATEMENT

the bank issuing the statement

National Bank PLC
5-6 Christmas Square
Mereford
MR1 7GH

Account	Teme Computers
Account Number	12037661
Sheet	17
Date	31 October 2004

the account name and account number of the customer and the date and sheet number of the statement

Date	Details	Debit	Credit	Balance
2004				
01 Oct	Balance			405.93 CR
01 Oct	Cheques		590.53	996.46 CR
07 Oct	619651	298.64		697.82 CR

the date of the transaction

the details of the transaction, eg cheques, bank charges

debit = money paid out of the bank account

credit = money paid into the bank account

the running balance of the bank account

CR = credit (money in the bank)

DR = debit (an overdraft)

the opening balance of the bank account at the beginning of the period covered by the statement

a note on debit and credit balances

You will see from the illustration of the bank statement that it works in a similar way to a double-entry account, recording for each transaction

- the date
- details
- money amount – payments out as a debit, receipts in as a credit

It also calculates a balance after each transaction, money in the bank being a credit (shown as CR) and an overdraft (borrowing) as a debit (shown as DR). Like any double-entry account it always shows an opening balance on the first line.

You will notice that the debits and credits appear to be the wrong way round. In fact the bank sees the customer as a creditor, so if there is money in the bank, it owes the money to the customer and the balance will be a credit balance. Similarly if the customer is borrowing and the account is overdrawn, the balance will show as a debit balance because the customer is effectively a debtor. This takes a bit of getting used to, but it is logical.

We will now look at receipts and payments in turn.

RECEIPTS TO THE BANK ACCOUNT

As we have just seen, receipts to the bank account are recorded as credits in a credit column on the bank statement (highlighted in the example on the opposite page).

cheques and cash

We have already seen in the last chapter that cheques from debtors and cash from sales are commonly paid into the bank account. The description in the details column of the bank statement may vary from bank to bank. The description on the statement illustrated on the opposite page is self-explanatory as 'Cheques' and 'Cash'. You may also find the description 'Credit' and also possibly the reference number of the paying-in slip used.

It is common to pay in a batch of cheques using a single paying-in slip. It is the total of the cheques on the paying-in slip which shows on the bank statement.

a preprinted paying-in slip

STATEMENT

National Bank PLC

5-6 Christmas Square
Mereford
MR1 7GH

Account	Teme Computers
Account Number	12037661
Sheet	17
Date	31 October 2004

Date	Details	Debit	Credit	Balance	
2004			**RECEIPTS**		
01 Oct	Balance			405.93	CR
01 Oct	Cheques		590.53	996.46	CR
07 Oct	619651	298.64		697.82	CR
07 Oct	619652	100.00		597.82	CR
13 Oct	RT Telecom (DD)	154.00		443.82	CR
15 Oct	619653	58.90		384.92	CR
17 Oct	Mereford City Council (SO)	240.00		144.92	CR
20 Oct	GH Trading (BGC)		230.00	374.92	CR
20 Oct	Cheque		127.80	502.72	CR
23 Oct	Cash		450.00	952.72	CR
24 Oct	Tombenco (BACS)		120.50	1073.22	CR
27 Oct	Unpaid cheque	127.80		945.42	CR
31 Oct	619654	45.75		899.67	CR
31 Oct	Bank charges	24.30		875.37	CR

bank giro credit (BGC)

A bank giro credit is a slip of paper which is processed through the bank clearing system and is originated by the person making the payment. It is commonly attached as a tear-off slip on credit card and electricity or water bills (see the next page).

If you want to pay the bill you can make out a cheque for the payment amount, complete the bank giro credit and pay it through your bank. The giro credit is then processed through the banking system and is credited to the bank account of the organisation receiving the money.

Pre-printed bank giro credits are also used by trade customers settling accounts. In the example above, a bank giro credit (BGC) for £230 has been received from GH Trading.

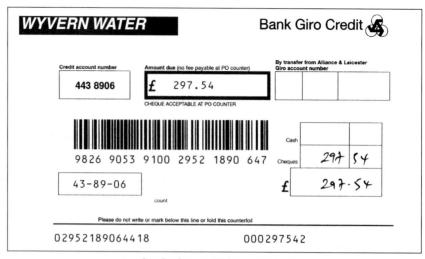

a bank giro credit for a water bill

The important point about bank giro credits is that they may not initially be recorded in the cash book of the organisation receiving the money, as the payment may have bypassed the organisation and gone straight to the bank. The cash book will have to be updated and the entry made after the bank statement has been received (see next chapter).

BACS receipts

Bankers Automated Clearing Services (BACS) is a computer transfer payment system owned by the banks. It is widely used for regular payments such as insurance premiums, settlement of trade debts, wages and salaries. BACS is a cheap and efficient means of payment because, instead of a payslip having to be prepared and processed, the transfer is set up on a computer file and transferred between the banks' computers – the payment goes direct from account to account.

BACS payments are made in a number of situations:

- by customers who buy from a business regularly settling invoices for variable amounts – all the customer has to do is to set up the payment system with their bank and then instruct the bank in writing (or online) each month the amount to be paid and the date of payment – the bank does the rest

- by customers paying **standing orders** (regular payments for the same amount) – the BACS payment is set up with the bank by the person sending the money, for example by a tenant renting office space from a business and paying a regular amount each month

```
BACS REMITTANCE ADVICE                      FROM: Tombenco
                                            4 Fleet Street
                                            Broadfield BR1 3RF

TO
Teme Computers
Unit 3 Elgar Estate, Mereford, MR7 4ER      20 10 04


Your ref          Our ref                               Amount

787923            47609      BACS TRANSFER               120.50


                                            TOTAL     120.50


THIS HAS BEEN PAID BY BACS CREDIT TRANSFER DIRECTLY INTO YOUR BANK ACCOUNT AT
NATIONAL BANK NO 12037661 SORT CODE 89 47 17
```

remittance advice sent to advise of a BACS payment

- by bank customers paying **direct debits** – a regular payment of possibly variable amounts from bank account to bank account where the payment is set up by the business receiving the money, for example an insurance company 'collecting' an insurance premium

In the case of the statement on the next page, a BACS payment of £120.50 has been received from Tombenco. The business will have received from Tombenco a BACS remittance advice setting out the details of the payment. This is illustrated above. As with bank giro credits, BACS payments received may initially bypass the cash book of the business receiving payment and appear first on the bank statement. The organisation receiving payment must check the BACS remittance advice carefully against the bank statement when it arrives to ensure that the correct amount has been received by the bank. An entry can then be made in the cash book.

interest and refunds

Payments into a bank account may also be made by the bank itself, and like a number of other receipts explained earlier in this chapter, will need to be entered in the cash book after the receipt of the bank statement by the business.

Interest may be paid on the account for credit balances held. The amount will appear in the credit column of the bank statement, and the business will record the amount on the receipts side of the cash book accordingly.

Refunds may also be paid by the bank to the business, if, for example, the business has complained about bank charges or if an amount has been deducted from the bank account in error – it does happen!

BANK PAYMENTS

The bank statement below highlights the payments made out of the bank account. Study the bank statement and then read the explanations which follow.

STATEMENT   **National Bank PLC**
                                                  5-6 Christmas Square
                                                  Mereford
                                                  MR1 7GH

Account   Teme Computers
Account Number   12037661
Sheet   17
Date   31 October 2004

Date	Details	Debit	Credit	Balance	
2004		PAYMENTS			
01 Oct	Balance			405.93	CR
01 Oct	Cheques		590.53	996.46	CR
07 Oct	619651	298.64		697.82	CR
07 Oct	619652	100.00		597.82	CR
13 Oct	RT Telecom (DD)	154.00		443.82	CR
15 Oct	619653	58.90		384.92	CR
17 Oct	Mereford City Council (SO)	240.00		144.92	CR
20 Oct	GH Trading (BGC)		230.00	374.92	CR
20 Oct	Cheque		127.80	502.72	CR
23 Oct	Cash		450.00	952.72	CR
24 Oct	Tombenco (BACS)		120.50	1073.22	CR
27 Oct	Unpaid cheque	127.80		945.42	CR
31 Oct	619654	45.75		899.67	CR
31 Oct	Bank charges	24.30		875.37	CR

cheques

Cheques issued by the business and paid in by the payees of the cheques pass through the bank cheque clearing system and are deducted from the bank account. They appear on the bank statement in the debit column and are referenced by the cheque number (which will also be recorded in the bank column of the business cash book). Here cheques numbered 619651, 619652, 619653 and 619654 have been deducted.

If a business wishes to take cash out of the bank – for example to pay wages or top up the petty cash – it will write out a cheque, take it to the bank and collect the cash. The cheque number appears on the bank statement in the normal way.

It should also be noted that businesses are increasingly using the BACS automated payments system to pay suppliers (see page 286), in which case the bank statement would show a reference to 'BACS' or the name of the individual bank's own payment system – eg 'Autopay'.

standing orders and direct debits

As noted earlier (page 286), a **standing order (SO)** is a regular automatic payment which is set up by the bank customer and processed through the banks' BACS system. For example, if a business pays the same amount each month for office rent, instead of writing out a cheque each time, it can set up a standing order and payment can be made automatically.

The one bookkeeping problem with this system is that the payments need to be recorded in the cash book. Common practice is for the bookkeeper to keep a list of standing order payments and then make the entries from the list on, say, a monthly basis. An alternative, of course, is to wait for the bank statement to arrive and then make the entries from the bank statement.

The standing order (SO) payment on the statement on the opposite page is £240 to Mereford City Council, in this case a payment of business rates made on the 17th of each month.

Direct debit (DD) payments are also processed automatically through the BACS system, but may be for variable amounts, eg telephone bills. In the statement on the previous page a payment for £154.00 has been made to RT Telecom. Direct debits are different from standing orders in that it is the business receiving the money which sets up the payment. Direct debits can be more unpredictable, although the business has certain safeguards when a direct debit is set up. The text below is taken from a typical direct debit agreement for payments to be made to an insurance company.

> - I instruct you to pay direct debits from my account at the request of Tradesure Insurance Company.
> - The amounts are variable and may be debited on various dates.
> - I understand that Tradesure Insurance Company may change the amounts and dates after giving me prior notice.
> - I will inform the bank/building society if I wish to cancel this instruction.
> - I understand that if any direct debit is paid which breaks the terms of this instruction, the bank/building society will make a refund.

It is common practice to enter direct debits into the cash book after the bank statement has been received.

bank charges and interest

Other payment items which appear on the bank statement and will have to be entered in the cash book are **bank charges** and **interest** deducted by the bank.

Bank charges are the fees paid to the bank for operating the account.They may be based on the number of items paid in and out of the bank account, or they may be based on the amounts involved, or a combination of the two.

Interest is the cost to the customer of borrowing from the bank, normally on overdraft – in other words when the bank account goes overdrawn (shown as a debit balance ['DR'] on the bank statement). Interest is usually worked out on a percentage rate, and is calculated on the amount borrowed.

When the bank statement is received, as mentioned above, bank charges and interest will have to be entered in the cash book. The bank statement on page 288 shows bank charges of £24.30. There is no interest payable because the account has remained in credit all month (shown by the 'CR' in the right-hand column) and there has been no borrowing on overdraft.

unpaid cheques

Sometimes a business pays in a cheque received from one of its customers, and that cheque 'bounces'. In other words the customer's bank for one of a number of reasons decides that it will not pay the cheque, which will then become an 'unpaid cheque'. The practical consequences of this is that the cheque is then deducted from the business bank account and sent back to the business which paid it in. It will show on the bank statement in the debit column with the description 'unpaid cheque', as shown below.

Date	Details	Debit	Credit	Balance
20 Oct	Cheque (paid in)		127.80	502.72 Cr
23 Oct	Cash		450.00	952.72 Cr
24 Oct	Tombenco (BACS)		120.50	1073.22 Cr
27 Oct	Unpaid cheque	127.80		945.42 Cr

The reason for the bank returning the cheque can vary. It may be 'stopped' by the customer, there may be something technically wrong with it (it may not have been signed), or the person issuing the cheque may not have the money in the bank account. In this case the cheque will be returned 'refer to drawer' and this normally means the issuer is in financial difficulties; this is bad news for the business which should have received the money.

An unpaid cheque, like any payment out, has to be entered in the bank column of the cash book (credit side) when it is received back.

CHAPTER

SUMMARY

- Banks issue statements of account to their customers on a regular basis.

- A bank statement works in a similar way to a double-entry account, recording the date, details and amount of each transaction.

- A bank statement also shows the running balance of the account. Money in the account is a credit balance (abbreviated to 'CR') and borrowing on the account is a debit balance (abbreviated to 'DR').

- Payments on a bank statement appear in the debit column (payments made) and receipts in the credit column (payments received).

- Receipts on the bank statement include cash and cheques paid in, bank giro credits, BACS payments from customers and interest received.

- Payments on the bank statement include cheques issued, BACS payments (paying suppliers, standing orders, direct debits), unpaid cheques, bank charges and interest paid on borrowing.

- Some transactions which appear on the bank statement will already have been entered in the cash book of the business – and some will not. The updating of the cash book to allow for these items is covered in full in the next chapter.

KEY

TERMS

bank giro credit	a paper slip pre-printed with the bank details of a business, used for paying money due to the business through a different bank or bank branch
BACS	**B**ankers **A**utomated **C**learing **S**ervices is a computer payment system operated by the banks, used for payroll, regular supplier payments, standing orders and direct debits
standing order	a series of regular payments set up by the bank customer, using the BACS system
direct debit	a series of BACS payments (which can be variable) set up by the business receiving the money and authorised by the person making the payments
interest	money paid into the bank account in respect of a bank deposit held, or deducted from the bank account as the cost of borrowing from the bank
unpaid cheque	a cheque which is paid into a bank account, but is returned unpaid by the bank; it is then deducted from the account of the business or person that paid it in

STUDENT
ACTIVITIES

NOTE: an asterisk (*) after the question number means that the
answer to the question is given at the back of this book.

13.1* (a)   In which column of a bank statement are payments out of a bank account recorded?

(b)   In which column of a bank statement are receipts into a bank account recorded?

13.2* (a)   The first entry on a bank statement reads:

'01 Sept   Balance   £450.95 DR'

What does this mean?

(b)   The first entry on a bank statement reads:

'01 Nov   Balance   £1,096.70 CR'

What does this mean?

13.3* (a)   Give an example of an item appearing on a bank statement which should already have been recorded in the cash book of a business.

(b)   Give an example of an item appearing on a bank statement which is unlikely to have already been recorded in the cash book of a business.

13.4* Give two examples of payments out of a bank account which make use of the BACS payment system. Write a short explanation of the way in which each of the two payments works.

13.5* What is the purpose of a BACS remittance advice?

13.6* Explain why you might see the description 'Interest' on a bank statement in either the debit or the credit column.

13.7 You work in the Accounts Department of Teme Computers and are looking after Abdul, a keen new trainee.

You have just received the November statement for the business (shown on the next page).

 Abdul asks you a number of questions.

What would your replies be?

In each case give a clear explanation of the entries that Abdul is enquiring about.

(a)   What does the first entry 'Balance' mean?

(b)   Cheques paid in on 5 November are recorded in the bank statement credit column. This looks wrong because in Teme Computers' cash book, payments received are recorded in the debit column. What is going on here?

(c)   What does the entry 'unpaid cheque' on 10 November mean?

(d)   On 10 November and 11 November the balance of the account is showing as 'DR'. What does this mean?

(e)   What is the 'BGC' received from F Singh on 13 November?

(f)   What is the 'SO' paid to Mereford City Council on 17 November?

(g)   What is the 'BACS' payment received from Wilson & Co on 24 November?

(h)   What is the 'DD' paid to Hellfire Insurance on 27 November?

(i)   Why should Teme Computers have interest and bank charges deducted on 28 November?

STATEMENT	**National Bank PLC**
	5-6 Christmas Square
	Mereford
	MR1 7GH

Account	Teme Computers
Account Number	12037661
Sheet	18
Date	30 November 2004

Date	Details	Debit	Credit	Balance	
2004					
03 Nov	Balance			875.37	CR
05 Nov	Cheques		1230.60	2105.97	CR
07 Nov	619655	130.89		1975.08	CR
07 Nov	619656	1500.00		475.08	CR
10 Nov	Unpaid cheque	750.00		274.92	DR
11 Nov	619657	120.00		394.92	DR
12 Nov	Cheques		890.70	495.78	CR
13 Nov	F Singh (BGC)		450.00	945.78	CR
17 Nov	Mereford City Council (SO)	240.00		705.78	CR
24 Nov	Wilson & Co (BACS)		118.75	824.54	CR
27 Nov	Hellfire insurance (DD)	134.76		689.77	CR
28 Nov	Interest	4.53		685.24	CR
28 Nov	Bank charges	19.78		665.46	CR

14 BANK RECONCILIATION STATEMENTS

this chapter covers ...

In the last chapter we balanced the cash book of a business to find out the balance of the bank account.

In this chapter we look at the way in which a business deals with any differences between the balance of the bank account in the cash book and the closing balance of the bank account shown by the bank statement for the same period.

These differences are explained by a document known as a bank reconciliation statement: which lists

- items which are in the cash book but not on the bank statement
- items which are on the bank statement but not in the cash book

This process is an important one: it enables the business to update its cash book and also helps to prove the accuracy of the bookkeeping of the business and the bank.

OCR LEARNING OUTCOMES

unit 3: MAINTAINING THE CASH BOOK

Assessment objectives

4   Prepare a Bank Reconciliation Statement

(a) Compare transactions that appear on both Cash Book and Bank Statement

(b) Update Cash Book from details of transactions appearing on Bank Statement

(c) Balance the bank columns of the Cash Book to calculate the revised balance

5   Complete a Bank Reconciliation Statement

(a) Enter correct date of the statement

(b) Enter the balance at bank as per the Cash Book

(c) Enter details of unpresented cheques

(d) Enter sub-total on reconciliation statement

(e) Enter details of bank lodgements

(f) Calculate balance as per Bank Statement

THE NEED FOR AN ACCURATE CASH BOOK

Most organisations keep a record of their cash and bank transactions in a cash book (see Chapter 12). The cash book contains a record of both the cash account and the bank account and shows the balance in each account at the end of a period. Once the cash book has been balanced off it is usual to check the details with the records of the firm's bank transactions as recorded by the bank.

To enable this check to be made the cashier will need to ensure that the cash book is completely up-to-date and a recent bank statement has been obtained from the bank.

Often, when a comparison is made between the bank balance as shown in the firm's cash book with that shown on the bank statement, the two balances will be different. It is for this reason that a **bank reconciliation statement** is prepared to **reconcile** ('tally up') the two balances. The reconciliation may identify errors that may have been made in either the firm's cash book or in the bank's records. Any corrections can then be made.

An example of a bank reconciliation statement is shown below. As you can see, it is a very simple calculation. The process of drawing up a bank reconciliation statement will be explained in full on pages 297-299.

CECILIA WHOLESALE LIMITED
Bank Reconciliation Statement as at 31 October 2004

	£	£
Balance at bank as per Cash Book		525
Add: unpresented cheques		
Taverner Trading Company	60	
Puccini Partnership	100	
B Britten Ltd	80	
		240
		765
Less: outstanding lodgements	220	
	300	
		520
Balance at bank as per bank statement		545

THE BANK STATEMENT

A bank statement is a copy of a bank account as shown by the bank records. Bank statements are sent out to customers on a regular basis, for example every month. This enables the customer to check their funds in the bank (or borrowing on overdraft) regularly and to update their own records of transactions that have occurred. It could be, for example, that the bank has not previously notified them of a certain deduction from the account, for example bank charges.

An example of a bank statement is shown below: If you are not familiar with the details of payments – eg SO (standing order), DD (direct debit), BGC (bank giro credit), BACS (Bankers Automated Clearing Services) – you should read the last chapter which introduces these terms.

STATEMENT				**National Bank PLC**	
				5-6 Christmas Square	
				Mereford	
				MR1 7GH	
Account	Teme Computers				
Account Number	12037661				
Sheet	17				
Date	31 October 2004				

Date	Details	Debit	Credit	Balance	
2004					
01 Oct	Balance			405.93	CR
01 Oct	Cheques		590.53	996.46	CR
07 Oct	619651	298.64		697.82	CR
07 Oct	619652	100.00		597.82	CR
13 Oct	RT Telecom (DD)	154.00		443.82	CR
15 Oct	619653	58.90		384.92	CR
17 Oct	Mereford City Council (SO)	240.00		144.92	CR
20 Oct	GH Trading (BGC)		230.00	374.92	CR
20 Oct	Cheque		127.80	502.72	CR
23 Oct	Cash		450.00	952.72	CR
24 Oct	Tombenco (BACS)		120.50	1073.22	CR
27 Oct	Unpaid cheque	127.80		945.42	CR
31 Oct	619654	45.75		899.67	CR
31 Oct	Bank charges	24.30		875.37	CR

WHY DO YOU NEED A BANK RECONCILIATION STATEMENT?

reconciliation

'Reconciliation' between the cash book and the bank statement final balance simply means **an explanation of the differences**. This explanation takes the form of a written calculation (see page 295 for an example). The process can be seen as follows:

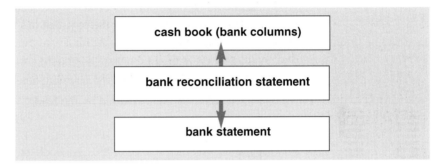

Differences between the cash book and the bank statement can arise from:

*   **timing** of the recording of the transactions
*   **errors** made by the business, or by the bank

We will explain each of these in turn.

timing differences – items recorded in the cash book

When a business compares the balance according to its cash book with the balance as shown by the bank statement there is often a difference. This difference can be caused by the **timing** of payments. For example:

*   A cashier may send cheques out to suppliers, some of whom may pay in the cheque at the bank immediately while others may keep the cheque for several days before paying it in. When this happens the cashier will have recorded all the payments in the cash book. However, the bank records will only show the cheques that have actually been paid in by the suppliers and deducted from the business bank account.

    These cheques are known as **unpresented cheques**.

*   With another type of timing difference – known as **outstanding lodgements** – the firm's cashier records a receipt in the cash book as he or she prepares the bank paying-in slip. However, the receipt may not be recorded by the bank on the bank statement for a day or so, particularly if it is paid in late in the day (when the bank will put it into the next day's work), or if it is paid in at a bank branch other than the one at which the account is maintained.

timing differences – items not recorded in the cash book

payments in

Another timing difference may also occur when the bank has received a direct payment from a customer of the business. In this instance the bank will have recorded the receipt in the business's account at the bank but the business will be unaware of the payment and will not, therefore, have recorded the receipt in the cash book. This type of payment includes:

–   standing order and BACS (Bankers' Automated Clearing Services), ie incoming payments received on the account, eg payments from debtors (customers) when the payment has not been advised to the business

–   bank giro credit amounts received by the bank, eg payments from debtors (customers) when the payment has not been advised

–   interest and refunds credited by the bank

payments out

Another reason why the balance of the cash book and the balance of the bank statement may not agree is because the bank may have deducted items from the customer's account, but the customer may not be aware of the deduction until the bank statement arrives. Examples of these deductions include:

–   standing order and direct debit payments which the customer did not know about

–   bank charges for running the account

–   interest charged for overdrawn balances

–   unpaid cheques deducted by the bank – ie stopped and 'bounced' cheques (see page 290)

differences caused by errors

Sometimes the difference between the two balances may be accounted for by an error on the part of the bank or an error in the cash book of the business. It is for this reason that a bank reconciliation is carried out frequently so that errors may be identified and rectified as soon as possible.

It is good business practice to prepare a bank reconciliation statement each time a bank statement is received. The reconciliation statement should be prepared as quickly as possible so that any queries – either with the bank statement or in the firm's cash book – can be resolved. Many firms will specify to their accounting staff the timescales for preparing bank reconciliation statements. For example, if the bank statement is received weekly, then the reconciliation statement should be prepared within five working days.

PREPARING THE BANK RECONCILIATION STATEMENT

When a bank statement has been received, reconciliation of the two balances is carried out in the following way:

step 1   The cashier will tick off the items that appear in both the cash book and the bank statement.

step 2   The unticked items on the bank statement are entered into the bank columns of the cash book to bring it up to date.

step 3   The bank columns of the cash book are now balanced to find the revised figure.

step 4   The remaining unticked items from the cash book will be the timing differences.

step 5   The timing differences are used to prepare the bank reconciliation statement (see below).

We will explain how this procedure is carried out in the Case Study which follows on the next page. First, however, we will revise what we have covered in this chapter so far by looking at a specimen bank reconciliation statement. Study the format shown below and the explanatory notes. Relate them to the text on the previous two pages.

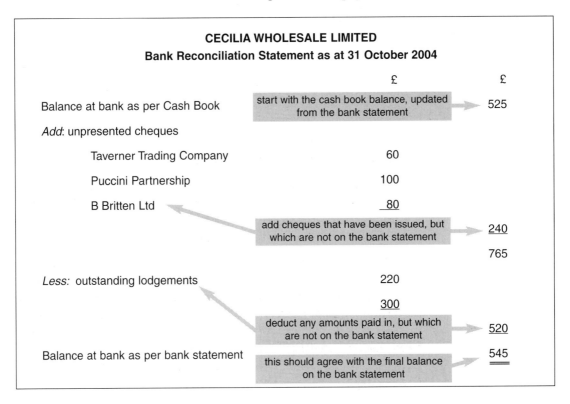

CECILIA WHOLESALE LIMITED
Bank Reconciliation Statement as at 31 October 2004

	£	£
Balance at bank as per Cash Book	*start with the cash book balance, updated from the bank statement*	525
Add: unpresented cheques		
Taverner Trading Company	60	
Puccini Partnership	100	
B Britten Ltd	80	
	add cheques that have been issued, but which are not on the bank statement	240
		765
Less: outstanding lodgements	220	
	300	
	deduct any amounts paid in, but which are not on the bank statement	520
Balance at bank as per bank statement	*this should agree with the final balance on the bank statement*	545

CASE STUDY

HURST & CO: BANK RECONCILIATION STATEMENT

situation

Carol works as a cashier for Hurst & Co., Solicitors. Her responsibilities include entering and maintaining the firm's cash book and preparing a bank reconciliation statement at the end of the month.

The firm's cash book for July 2004 which Carol has just finished entering and balancing for the month end is shown below (Note: for the sake of clarity the cash and discount columns have been omitted.) A copy of the firm's bank statement from the Star Bank Limited dated 31 July 2004 has just been received and is also illustrated. The numerical difference between the two is:

Bank statement £903.00 *minus* cash book £641.70 = £261.30

This is the difference which Carol will have to 'reconcile'.

Carol now follows the five steps outlined on the previous page.

Step 1 – tick off the items in both cash book and bank statement

Carol ticks off the items that appear in both the cash book and the bank statement.

Hurst & Co – Cash Book

	RECEIPTS				PAYMENTS		
Date	Details	Bank		Date	Details		Bank
2004		£		2004			£
1 July	Balance b/d	756.20 ✓		2 July	T Able	004450	50.00 ✓
3 July	Kershaw Ltd	220.00 ✓		2 July	Broad & Co	004451	130.00
15 July	Morris & Son	330.00 ✓		2 July	Gee & Co	004452	10.00 ✓
31 July	Pott Bros	63.00		8 July	Minter Ltd	004453	27.50
				14 July	Liverport City Council (DD)		89.00 ✓
				14 July	F D Jewell	004454	49.00 ✓
				15 July	Kirk Ltd	004455	250.00 ✓
				26 July	Bond Insurance (SO)		122.00 ✓
				31 July	Balance c/d		641.70
		1,369.20					1,369.20
31 July	Balance b/d	641.70					

STATEMENT

Star Bank PLC
23 Market Street
Liverport
LP1 6TG

Account	Hurst & Co
Account Number	79014456
Sheet	17
Date	31 July 2004

Date	Details	Debit	Credit	Balance	
2004					
01 July	Balance			756.20	Cr ✓
04 July	Cheques		220.00 ✓	976.20	Cr
09 July	004450	50.00 ✓		926.20	Cr
14 July	004452	10.00 ✓		916.20	Cr
16 July	Liverport City Council (DD)	89.00 ✓		827.20	Cr
19 July	Cheques		330.00 ✓	1,157.20	Cr
24 July	004455	250.00 ✓		907.20	Cr
26 July	Bond Insurance (SO)	122.00 ✓		785.20	Cr
30 July	004454	49.00 ✓		736.20	Cr
31 July	Bank charges	12.95		723.25	Cr
31 July	Ricardo Limited (BGC)		179.75	903.00	Cr

step 2 – update the cash book from the bank statement
The unticked items on the bank statement indicate items that have gone through the bank account but have not yet been entered in Hurst & Co's cash book. These are:

Receipt	31 July	BGC credit, Ricardo Limited	£179.75
Payment	31 July	Bank Charges	£12.95

Carol will now need to enter these items in the cash book to bring it up to date (see next page). The new entries are shown in darker type, the previous entries are in lighter type.

step 3 – balance the cash book bank columns to produce an updated balance
Carol now balances the bank columns of the cash book off again, as shown on the next page.

Hurst & Co – Cash Book (extract)

	RECEIPTS				PAYMENTS	
Date 2004	Details	Bank £	Date 2004	Details		Bank £
			31 July	Balance c/d		641.70
		1,369.20				1,369.20
31 July	Balance b/d	641.70	31 July	Bank Charges		12.95
31 July	Ricardo Limited (BGC)	179.75	31 July	Balance c/d		808.50
		821.45				821.45
1 Aug	Balance b/d	808.50				

The balance of the bank column now stands at £808.50. This still differs from the bank statement balance of £903.00.

The numerical difference between the two is:

Bank statement £903.00 *minus* cash book £808.50 = £94.50

This remaining difference is dealt with in the bank reconciliation statement.

step 4 – identify the remaining unticked items from the cash book
There are some items that remain unticked in the cash book. These are:

Receipt	31 July	Potts Bros	£63.00
Payments	2 July	Broad & Co (cheque no. 004451)	£130.00
	8 July	Minter Ltd (cheque no. 004453)	£ 27.50

These items should appear on next month's bank statement and are timing differences. These are the items which will be required in the preparation of the bank reconciliation statement, which is Carol's next step.

step 5 – preparation of the bank reconciliation statement
The completed statement is shown on the next page. The stages followed in its completion are as follows:

1   **enter the cash book balance**
     The balance figure to use, as 'per the cash book', is the revised cash book balance after entering the items that appeared on the bank statement which had not previously been entered, ie £808.50

2   add unpresented cheques

The unpresented cheques are the cheques that Hurst & Co has issued, but which have not yet been deducted from the firm's bank account, probably because they have not yet been paid in by the suppliers. They are:

Broad & Co (cheque no. 004451)	£130.00
Minter Ltd (cheque no. 004453)	£ 27.50
Total	£157.50

The unpresented cheques totalling £157.50 are added to the cash book balance in the bank reconciliation statement, bringing the revised cash book balance to £966.00. They are added back to the cash book balance so that both the cash book and the bank account contain the same items.

3   deduct outstanding bank lodgement

A 'bank lodgement' represents money, ie cheques and or cash, that has been received by a business, entered into the cash book and paid into the bank. In this case, however, the deposit has been made too late to appear on the firm's bank statement, and so forms part of the difference, as an 'outstanding' lodgement.

Here the bank lodgement of £63.00 is deducted in the bank reconciliation statement from the sub-total of £966.00, ie £966.00 − £63.00 = £903.00.

4   completing the reconciliation

Now that all the outstanding items have been added or deducted, the recalculated balance on the bank reconciliation statement should be the same as the final bank statement balance. A comparison of the two show that they are both £903.00. Carol has successfully completed the reconciliation.

HURST & CO
Bank Reconciliation Statement as at 31 July 2004

	£	£
Balance at bank as per Cash Book		808.50
Add: unpresented cheques		
Broad & Co	130.00	
Minter Ltd	27.50	
		157.50
		966.00
Less: outstanding lodgement		63.00
Balance at bank as per bank statement		903.00

DEALING WITH OVERDRAFTS

positive bank balances

In the Case Study and examples so far in this chapter we have dealt with bank reconciliation statements where the bank balance has been positive – ie there has been money in the bank account. We have also dealt with cash books which have shown that there there is money in the bank.

A positive bank balance has been indicated by:

- in the **cash book** – a debit (left-hand) brought down balance
- a **bank statement** where the balance is followed by 'CR' – which to the bank and the customer means that there is money in the account (remember that the 'credit' column on the bank statement is used for payments into the account)

negative bank balances

Businesses sometimes have overdrafts at the bank. Overdrafts are where the bank account becomes negative and the business in effect borrows from the bank. This is shown:

- in the **cash book** as a credit (right-hand) brought down balance
- on the **bank statement** where the balance is followed by 'DR' (or sometimes by 'OD') – which to the bank and the customer means that there is an overdraft

reconciliation statements and overdrafts

If you want to show an overdraft on a bank reconciliation statement, you should treat it as a negative figure by placing it in brackets. As far as the calculation is concerned, it is simply a matter of using the minus key on the calculator. If in the Case Study earlier in this chapter, Hurst & Co had started the month with an overdraft of £808.50 (a credit balance in the cash book), you would key the following into the calculator (the black boxes represent the calculator keys):

–	£808.50
+	£157.50
–	£63
=	*produces a total of (£714.00)*

Now look at how the bank reconciliation statement is set out on the next page, using brackets for negative figures (ie overdrafts).

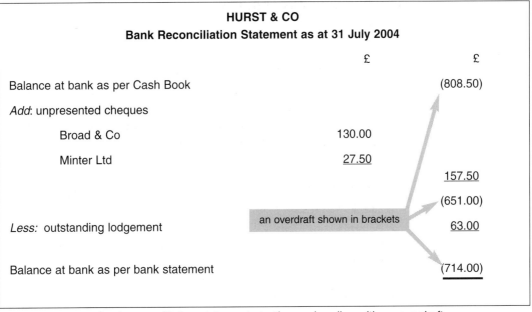

HURST & CO
Bank Reconciliation Statement as at 31 July 2004

	£	£
Balance at bank as per Cash Book		(808.50)
Add: unpresented cheques		
Broad & Co	130.00	
Minter Ltd	27.50	
		157.50
		(651.00)
Less: outstanding lodgement		63.00
Balance at bank as per bank statement		(714.00)

an overdraft shown in brackets

a bank reconciliation statement starting and ending with an overdraft

CHAPTER SUMMARY

- The balance of the bank account in the cash book of a business is regularly compared with the balance on the bank statement to ensure that the accounting records of both the business and the bank contain the same transactions and that no errors have occurred.

- There are inevitably differences between the cash book balance and the bank statement balance. These are caused either by errors in the cash book or bank statement, or by timing differences between the two documents.

- Timing differences may arise from items recorded in the bank statement and not in the cash book, bank charges and bank giro credits, for example. Normally the cash book is updated when these items are identified on the bank statement.

- Other timing differences might arise from items recorded in the cash book and not on the bank statement, unpresented cheques and outstanding lodgements, for example.

- These items are recorded in a bank reconciliation statement which is a calculation explaining how the unpresented cheques and outstanding lodgements are causing the difference between the cash book and the bank statement balances.

- The formula of the bank reconciliation statement commonly starts with the cash book:

	balance as per cash book
plus	unpresented cheques
less	outstanding lodgements
equals	balance as per bank statement

- The bank reconciliation statement can also be used when the bank balance is an overdraft. In this case, the overdrawn balance is shown as a negative figure, enclosed in brackets.

bank reconciliation statement	a statement prepared to link the bank balance shown in the cash book with the balance shown on the bank statement
timing differences	discrepancies between the bank statement and the cash book that will be corrected over time, such as unpresented cheques and outstanding lodgements
outstanding lodgements	amounts that have been paid into the bank, but not yet recorded on the bank statement
unpresented cheques	cheques that have been issued but have not yet been paid in and deducted from the account of the business

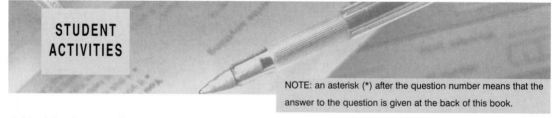

**STUDENT
ACTIVITIES**

NOTE: an asterisk (*) after the question number means that the answer to the question is given at the back of this book.

A blank bank reconciliation statement is reproduced on the next page and the format for setting out the cash book is shown below. You may photocopy and adapt these formats.

Blank forms are also available for download from the resources sections of <u>www.osbornebooks.co.uk</u>

CASH BOOK					
RECEIPTS			PAYMENTS		
Date	Details	Bank	Date	Details	Bank
2004		£	2004		£

name of
business...

Bank Reconciliation Statement as at ....

	£	£

Balance at bank as per Cash Book

Add: unpresented cheque(s)

Less: outstanding lodgement(s) not yet entered on bank statement

Balance at bank as per bank statement

Note
Negative bank balances (ie overdrafts) should be shown in brackets.

14.1* You are a trainee accountant for Fern Limited, a small printing company. One of your tasks is to enter transactions in the company's cash book, check the entries on receipt of the bank statement, update the cash book and make any amendments as necessary. You are then asked to prepare a bank reconciliation statement at the end of the month.

The company's cash book (showing the bank money columns only) and the bank statement are shown below.

You are to:

- Reconcile the cash book with the bank statement.

- Make the entries necessary to update the cash book.

- Balance the bank columns of the cash book and calculate the revised bank balance.

- Draw up or obtain a photocopy of a blank bank reconciliation statement.

- Start with the balance as per the cash book, list any unpresented cheques and sub-total on the reconciliation statement.

- Enter details of bank lodgements.

- Calculate the balance as per the bank statement and check your total against the bank statement for accuracy.

Fern Ltd – Cash Book

CASH BOOK

	RECEIPTS				PAYMENTS		
Date	Details	Bank		Date	Details		Bank
2004		£		2004			£
1 Aug	Balance b/d	1,946		2 Aug	DD Bell Insurance		75
1 Aug	I Watts & Co	249		2 Aug	Harvey & Co	200100	206
5 Aug	B Rogers (BACS)	188		4 Aug	Durose Ltd	200101	315
8 Aug	E Shaw	150		7 Aug	Motts Garage	200102	211
10 Aug	J Moore Ltd	440		9 Aug	SO Rock Finance		120
18 Aug	Simms Ltd	65		13 Aug	Hill Bros	200103	22
27 Aug	Martin Black	520		20 Aug	Ashleys Ltd	200104	137
30 Aug	Davies Partners	82		27 Aug	DD Rates		270
				31 Aug	Balance c/d		2,284
		3,640					3,640
31 Aug	Balance b/d	2,284					

ALBION BANK				**STATEMENT**	
12 Market Street, Bury BU1 2GH					
Account Fern Limited			**Account no.** 78300582		
Date 31 August 2004			**Statement No.** 16		

Date 2004	Details	Debit	Credit	Balance	
1 Aug	Balance			1,946	CR
2 Aug	Cheques		249	2,195	CR
4 Aug	Bell Insurance (DD)	75		2,120	CR
4 Aug	200101	315		1,805	CR
5 Aug	B Rogers (BACS)		188	1,993	CR
8 Aug	Cheques		150	2,143	CR
9 Aug	200102	211		1,932	CR
12 Aug	Cheques		440	2,372	CR
12 Aug	Rock Finance (SO)	120		2,252	CR
20 Aug	Cheques		65	2,317	CR
27 Aug	DD Rates	270		2,047	CR
30 Aug	Torr Bros (BGC)		92	2,139	CR
31 Aug	Bank Charges	55		2,084	CR
31 Aug	City Finance (SO)	1,000		1,084	CR

14.2* You are employed by Brooklyn Ltd as their cashier. Your main responsibility is to maintain the company's cash book and prepare a bank reconciliation statement at the end of each month.

The cash book (showing the bank money columns only) is set out below together with a copy of the bank statement for February 2004.

You are to:

- Reconcile the cash book with the bank statement.

- Make the entries necessary to update the cash book.

- Balance the bank columns of the cash book and calculate the revised bank balance.

- Draw up or obtain a photocopy of a blank bank reconciliation statement.

- Start with the balance as per the cash book, list any unpresented cheques and sub-total on the reconciliation statement.

- Enter details of bank lodgements.

- Calculate the balance as per the bank statement and check your total against the bank statement for accuracy.

Brooklyn Ltd – Cash Book

CASH BOOK

	RECEIPTS				PAYMENTS		
Date	Details	Bank		Date	Details		Bank
2004				2004			
1 Feb	Balance b/d	1,425		1 Feb	Barton Bros	400460	98
1 Feb	Worrall & Co	157		1 Feb	SO Road Car Co		50
4 Feb	Brindle's (BGC)	243		3 Feb	R Jackson Ltd	400461	540
8 Feb	Robinson Ltd	91		9 Feb	Spencer Partners	400462	42
13 Feb	Moore & Cox (BGC)	75		9 Feb	Avery Computers	400463	490
20 Feb	Riley & Co	420		10 Feb	DD Ajax Insurance		300
28 Feb	Howard Ltd	94		16 Feb	Shanklin Garage	400464	110
				23 Feb	Petty Cash	400465	50
				27 Feb	White & Co	400466	120
				28 Feb	Balance c/d		705
		2,505					2,505
28 Feb	Balance b/d	705					

REGENCY BANK			STATEMENT		
10 The Parade, Cheltenham G12 6YG					
Account Brooklyn Limited			**Account no.** 29842943		
Date 28 February 2004			**Statement No.** 35		

Date 2004	Details	Debit	Credit	Balance	
1 Feb	Balance			1,425	CR
2 Feb	Cheques		157	1,582	CR
2 Feb	Road Car Co (SO)	50		1,532	CR
4 Feb	400460	98		1,434	CR
6 Feb	Brindle's (BGC)		243	1,677	CR
10 Feb	Cheques		91	1,768	CR
12 Feb	Ajax Insurance (DD)	300		1,468	CR
14 Feb	Moore & Cox (BGC)		75	1,543	CR
14 Feb	400463	490		1,053	CR
23 Feb	Cheques		420	1,473	CR
26 Feb	Rates (DD)	103		1,370	CR
26 Feb	400465	50		1,320	CR
27 Feb	D Stead (BACS)		220	1,540	CR
28 Feb	Bank Charges	38		1,502	CR

14.3* As accounts assistant for O'Connor Limited your main task is to enter transactions into the company's cash book, check the entries against the bank statement and prepare a monthly bank reconciliation statement.

The cash book (showing the bank money columns only) and bank statement for October 2004 are set out below.

You are to:

- Reconcile the cash book with the bank statement.

- Make the entries necessary to update the cash book.

- Balance the bank columns of the cash book and calculate the revised bank balance.

- Draw up or obtain a photocopy of a blank bank reconciliation statement.

- Start with the balance as per the cash book, list any unpresented cheques and sub-total on the reconciliation statement.

- Enter details of bank lodgements.

- Calculate the balance as per the bank statement and check your total against the bank statement for accuracy.

<table>
<tr><td colspan="7" align="center">**O'Connor Limited – Cash Book**</td></tr>
<tr><td colspan="7" align="center">**CASH BOOK**</td></tr>
<tr><td colspan="3" align="center">RECEIPTS</td><td colspan="4" align="center">PAYMENTS</td></tr>
<tr><td>Date</td><td>Details</td><td>Bank</td><td>Date</td><td colspan="2">Details</td><td>Bank</td></tr>
<tr><td>2004</td><td></td><td></td><td>2004</td><td colspan="2"></td><td></td></tr>
<tr><td>1 Oct</td><td>Balance b/d</td><td>2,521</td><td>1 Oct</td><td>Sharp & Co Rent (SO)</td><td></td><td>400</td></tr>
<tr><td>4 Oct</td><td>Allen Ltd (BACS)</td><td>620</td><td>4 Oct</td><td>G Orwell</td><td>210526</td><td>367</td></tr>
<tr><td>8 Oct</td><td>Mason & Moore</td><td>27</td><td>5 Oct</td><td>Heath & Co</td><td>210527</td><td>1,108</td></tr>
<tr><td>11 Oct</td><td>Howard Limited</td><td>48</td><td>8 Oct</td><td>Ellis & Son</td><td>210528</td><td>320</td></tr>
<tr><td>11 Oct</td><td>Barrett & Bryson</td><td>106</td><td>13 Oct</td><td>Kerr's Garage</td><td>210529</td><td>32</td></tr>
<tr><td>12 Oct</td><td>D Patel (BGC)</td><td>301</td><td>14 Oct</td><td>J Choudrey</td><td>210530</td><td>28</td></tr>
<tr><td>20 Oct</td><td>Cohen & Co</td><td>58</td><td>22 Oct</td><td>Astley Insurance (DD)</td><td></td><td>139</td></tr>
<tr><td>25 Oct</td><td>J McGilvery</td><td>209</td><td>25 Oct</td><td>Text Computers</td><td>210531</td><td>1,800</td></tr>
<tr><td>31 Oct</td><td>Balance c/d</td><td>604</td><td>30 Oct</td><td>Rates (DD)</td><td></td><td>300</td></tr>
<tr><td></td><td></td><td>4,494</td><td></td><td colspan="2"></td><td>4,494</td></tr>
<tr><td></td><td></td><td></td><td>1 Nov</td><td>Balance b/d</td><td></td><td>604</td></tr>
</table>

OAK BANK			STATEMENT		
99 Bank Chambers, Nottingham NG1 7FG					
Account O'Connor Limited			**Account no.** 06618432		
Date 31 October 2004			**Statement No.** 45		

Date 2004	Details	Debit	Credit	Balance	
1Oct	Balance			2,521	CR
1 Oct	Sharp & Co (SO)	400		2,121	CR
4 Oct	Allen Ltd (BACS)		620	2,741	CR
7 Oct	210526	367		2,374	CR
11 Oct	Cheques		154	2,528	CR
13 Oct	D Patel (BGC)		301	2,829	CR
15 Oct	Cheques		27	2,856	CR
18 Oct	210528	320		2,536	CR
18 Oct	210527	1,108		1,428	CR
22 Oct	Astley Insurance (DD)	139		1,289	CR
27 Oct	210531	1,800		511	DR
28 Oct	Bayley's (BACS)		114	397	DR
29 Oct	Rates (SO)	300		697	DR
29 Oct	Bank Interest	53		750	DR
29 Oct	Bank Charges	45		795	DR

14.4 You are the cashier of Chowda Trading Limited and have written up the firm's cash book (bank money columns only) for the month of September 2004. You have also received the bank statement for the same period.

You are to:

- Reconcile the cash book with the bank statement.

- Make the entries necessary to update the cash book.

- Balance the bank columns of the cash book and calculate the revised bank balance.

- Draw up or obtain a photocopy of a blank bank reconciliation statement.

- Start with the balance as per the cash book, list any unpresented cheques and sub-total on the reconciliation statement.

- Enter details of bank lodgements.

- Calculate the balance as per the bank statement and check your total against the bank statement for accuracy.

Chowda Trading Limited – Cash Book

CASH BOOK

	RECEIPTS				PAYMENTS	
Date	Details	Bank	Date	Details		Bank
2004				2004		
1 Sept	Rogers & Co	2,710	1 Sept	Balance b/d		4,223
6 Sept	Chapman Ltd	252	3 Sept	Park Lane Garage	043173	236
8 Sept	F Sanderson (BACS)	121	3 Sept	Wages	043174	1,723
10 Sept	Booth (BACS)	379	7 Sept	Otis Electronics	043175	110
16 Sept	Rushton Associates	1,200	12 Sept	Fraser & Co	043176	46
20 Sept	I Campbell	28	17 Sept	United Insurance (DD)		175
27 Sept	W Blake (BGC)	1,320	23 Sept	Beet & Malkin	043177	1,052
28 Sept	Chapman Ltd	540	24 Sept	Rates (SO)		220
28 Sept	Balance c/d	1,235				
		7,785				7,785
			1 Oct	Balance b/d		1,235

	STAR BANK		STATEMENT	
	16, South Parade, Offerton OF1 8BN			
	Account Chowda Trading Limited		**Account no.** 77650017	
	Date 30 September 2004		**Statement No.** 16	

Date 2004	Details	Debit	Credit	Balance	
1 Sept	Balance			4,223	DR
6 Sept	043174	1,723		5,946	DR
6 Sept	043173	236		6,182	DR
7 Sept	Cheque		2,710	3,472	DR
7 Sept	Cheque		252	3,220	DR
9 Sept	Sanderson (BACS)		121	3,099	DR
13 Sept	Booth (BACS)		379	2,720	DR
14 Sept	Bank Charges	20		2,740	DR
14 Sept	Bank Interest	92		2,832	DR
17 Sept	Cheque		1,200	1,632	DR
17 Sept	United Insurance (DD)	175		1,807	DR
17 Sept	0043176	46		1,853	DR
23 Sept	Cheque		28	1,825	DR
28 Sept	W Blake (BGC)		1,320	505	DR
28 Sept	Rates (SO)	220		725	DR
28 Sept	Hunt & Associates (BACS)		26	699	DR

answers to selected student activities

The answers provided here are to the questions which have asterisks.

The answers to the remaining questions are included in the Level 1 Bookkeeping Tutor Pack, available direct from Osborne Books (Telephone 01905 748071).

CHAPTER 1 – BUSINESS AND BOOKKEEPING

1.1   (a) & (b) See text page 3

1.2   (a) See text page 4   (b) See text page 5

1.3   See text page 7

1.4   A cash fund kept on the business premises to pay for small expense items.

1.5   Capital, liabilities, assets, expenses, cash sales, credit sales, cash purchases, credit purchases, payments received, payments made.

1.6   (a)   the owner will want to know how profitable the business is

    (b)   the bank will want to know if any borrowing is likely to be repaid

    (c)   the Inland Revenue will want to know what tax the business will have to pay

    (d)   the VAT authorities will want to know how much VAT the business will be due to pay

CHAPTER 2 – DOCUMENTS FOR SALES AND PURCHASES

2.1   (a)   Buying now and being allowed to pay later by a specified date.

    (b)   Invoice

    (c)   Credit note

2.2   (a)   Osborne Fashion Limited

    (b)   £63.45

    (c)   Within 30 days from 24 October 2004.

    (d)   10 large T shirts and 2 blue sweatshirts.

    (e)   Trade discount of 10% has been given.

    (f)   £54.00

    (g)   £9.45. VAT is a Government tax charged by businesses on the sale of goods and services.

2.3   (a)   To reduce the amount owing on an invoice if there is a problem with the goods or services supplied.

    (b)   Osborne Fashion Limited is crediting Gullwing Limited.

    (c)   The sweatshirts that were supplied were incorrect.

    (d)   £63.45 (invoice amount) – £15.86 (credit note amount) = £47.59

    (e)   Statement

2.4   (a)   Date of cheque, amount, name of the person/business receiving the money.

    (b)   These are the details of the transaction needed by the business when it comes to write up its accounts.

    (c)   A person or business to whom money is owed.

    (d)   Remittance advice.

CHAPTER 3: ACCOUNTS AND LEDGERS FOR CREDIT SALES AND RETURNS

Tutorial note: answers may be set out in two-column format

3.1

NOMINAL LEDGER

Dr		Sales Account		Cr
2004		£	2004	£
			2 Feb Severn Supplies	221.30
			3 Feb Malvern Stores	173.35
			6 Feb A Cox Ltd	85.47
			12 Feb Roper & Sons	196.33
			16 Feb A Cox Ltd	274.83
			20 Feb Malvern Stores	362.13
			24 Feb Severn Supplies	46.20
			27 Feb A Cox Ltd	169.30

Dr		Value Added Tax Account		Cr
2004		£	2004	£
			2 Feb Severn Supplies	38.72
			3 Feb Malvern Stores	30.33
			6 Feb A Cox Ltd	14.95
			12 Feb Roper & Sons	34.35
			16 Feb A Cox Ltd	48.09
			20 Feb Malvern Stores	63.37
			24 Feb Severn Supplies	8.08
			27 Feb A Cox Ltd	29.62

SALES LEDGER

Dr		Severn Supplies		Cr
2004		£	2004	£
2 Feb	Sales	260.02		
24 Feb	Sales	54.28		

Dr		Malvern Stores		Cr
2004		£	2004	£
3 Feb	Sales	203.68		
20 Feb	Sales	425.50		

Dr		A Cox Limited			Cr
2004			£	2004	£
6 Feb	Sales		100.42		
16 Feb	Sales		322.92		
27 Feb	Sales		198.92		

Dr		Roper & Sons			Cr
2004			£	2004	£
12 Feb	Sales		230.68		

3.2

NOMINAL LEDGER

Dr		Sales Returns Account		Cr
2004		£	2004	£
3 Mar	A Cox Ltd	47.25		
11 Mar	Roper & Sons	55.31		
16 Mar	A Cox Ltd	102.33		

Dr		Value Added Tax Account			Cr
2004		£	2004		£
3 Mar	A Cox Ltd	8.26	1 Mar	Balance b/d	267.51
11 Mar	Roper & Sons	9.67			
16 Mar	A Cox Ltd	17.90			

SALES LEDGER

Dr		A Cox Limited				Cr
2004		£	2004			£
1 Mar	Balance b/d	622.26	3 Mar	Sales returns		55.51
			16 Mar	Sales returns		120.23

Dr		Roper & Sons				Cr
2004		£	2004			£
1 Mar	Balance b/d	230.68	11 Mar	Sales returns		64.98

CHAPTER 4: PAYMENTS FROM DEBTORS

Tutorial note: answers may be set out in two-column format

4.1

NOMINAL LEDGER

Dr				**Bank Account**			Cr
2004			£	2004			£
1 Mar	Balance b/d		1,022.48				
18 Mar	Roper & Sons		165.70				
24 Mar	A Cox Ltd		300.00				
25 Mar	Severn Supplies		314.30				

SALES LEDGER

Dr				**Severn Supplies**			Cr
2004			£	2004			£
1 Mar	Balance b/d		314.30	25 Mar	Bank		314.30

Dr				**A Cox Limited**			Cr
2004			£	2004			£
1 Mar	Balance b/d		622.26	3 Mar	Sales returns		55.51
				16 Mar	Sales returns		120.23
				24 Mar	Bank		300.00

Dr				**Roper & Sons**			Cr
2004			£	2004			£
1 Mar	Balance b/d		230.68	11 Mar	Sales returns		64.98
				18 Mar	Bank		165.70

CHAPTER 5: ACCOUNTS AND LEDGERS FOR CREDIT PURCHASES AND RETURNS

Tutorial note: answers may be set out in two-column format

5.1

NOMINAL LEDGER

Dr				**Purchases Account**			Cr
2004			£	2004			£
3 Feb	Perran & Sons		305.47				
5 Feb	Durning Supplies		247.80				
7 Feb	Zelah Trading Co		110.54				
10 Feb	Bissoe Ltd		278.11				
14 Feb	Zelah Trading Co		358.15				
18 Feb	Durning Supplies		122.19				
23 Feb	Perran & Sons		162.48				
26 Feb	Zelah Trading Co		87.40				

Dr		Value Added Tax Account			Cr
2004			£	2004	£
3 Feb	Perran & Sons		53.45		
5 Feb	Durning Supplies		43.36		
7 Feb	Zelah Trading Co		19.34		
10 Feb	Bissoe Ltd		48.66		
14 Feb	Zelah Trading Co		62.67		
18 Feb	Durning Supplies		21.38		
23 Feb	Perran & Sons		28.43		
26 Feb	Zelah Trading Co		15.29		

PURCHASES LEDGER

Dr		Perran & Sons			Cr
2004		£	2004		£
			3 Feb	Purchases	358.92
			23 Feb	Purchases	190.91

Dr		Durning Supplies			Cr
2004		£	2004		£
			5 Feb	Purchases	291.16
			18 Feb	Purchases	143.57

Dr		Zelah Trading Company			Cr
2004		£	2004		£
			7 Feb	Purchases	129.88
			14 Feb	Purchases	420.82
			26 Feb	Purchases	102.69

Dr		Bissoe Limited			Cr
2004		£	2004		£
			10 Feb	Purchases	326.77

5.2

NOMINAL LEDGER

Dr		Purchases Returns Account			Cr
2004		£	2004		£
			5 Mar	Durning Supplies	25.46
			10 Mar	Zelah Trading Co	53.80
			14 Mar	Durning Supplies	15.62

Dr	Value Added Tax Account				Cr
2004		£	2004		£
1 Mar	Balance b/d	292.58	5 Mar	Durning Supplies	4.45
			10 Mar	Zelah Trading Co	9.41
			14 Mar	Durning Supplies	2.73

PURCHASES LEDGER

Dr	Durning Supplies				Cr
2004		£	2004		£
5 Mar	Purchases returns	29.91	1 Mar	Balance b/d	434.73
14 Mar	Purchases returns	18.35			

Dr	Zelah Trading Company				Cr
2004		£	2004		£
10 Mar	Purchases returns	63.21	1 Mar	Balance b/d	653.39

CHAPTER 6: PAYMENTS FOR PURCHASES AND EXPENSES

Tutorial note: answers may be set out in two-column format

6.1

NOMINAL LEDGER

Dr	Bank Account				Cr
2004		£	2004		£
1 Mar	Balance b/d	2,386.45	5 Mar	Perran & Sons	549.83
			12 Mar	Zelah Trading Co	300.00
			18 Mar	Durning Supplies	386.47
			18 Mar	Bissoe Ltd	326.77

PURCHASES LEDGER

Dr	Perran & Sons				Cr
2004		£	2004		£
5 Mar	Bank	549.83	1 Mar	Balance b/d	549.83

Dr	Durning Supplies				Cr
2004		£	2004		£
5 Mar	Purchases returns	29.91	1 Mar	Balance b/d	434.73
14 Mar	Purchases returns	18.35			
18 Mar	Bank	386.47			

Dr	Zelah Trading Company			Cr
2004		£	2004	£
10 Mar Purchases returns		63.21	1 Mar Balance b/d	653.39
12 Mar Bank		300.00		

Dr	Bissoe Limited			Cr
2004		£	2004	£
18 Mar Bank		326.77	1 Mar Balance b/d	326.77

6.4   **PURCHASES LEDGER**

Dr	Stardust & Company			Cr
2004		£	2004	£
5 Aug Bank		654.91	1 Aug Balance b/d	1,328.43

Dr	Nova Limited			Cr
2004		£	2004	£
15 Aug Bank		610.58	1 Aug Balance b/d	851.24

NOMINAL LEDGER

Dr	General Expenses Account			Cr
2004		£	2004	£
1 Aug Balance b/d		638.49		
16 Aug Bank		96.40		

Dr	Furniture and Fittings Account			Cr
2004		£	2004	£
1 Aug Balance b/d		3,295.00		
12 Aug Bank		210.30		
20 Aug Bank		86.00		

Dr	Value Added Tax Account			Cr
2004		£	2004	£
9 Aug Bank		564.97	1 Aug Balance b/d	564.97
12 Aug Furniture and fittings		36.80		
16 Aug General expenses		16.87		
20 Aug Furniture and fittings		15.05		

Dr		**Bank Account**		Cr
2004		£	2004		£
1 Aug	Balance b/d	3,628.98	5 Aug	Stardust & Co	654.91
			9 Aug	HM Customs & Excise	564.97
			12 Aug	Furniture and fittings	247.10
			15 Aug	Nova Ltd	610.58
			16 Aug	General expenses	113.27
			20 Aug	Furniture and fittings	101.05

CHAPTER 7: BALANCING ACCOUNTS

'T' account format

7.1

Dr		**Sales Account**			Cr
2005		£	2005		£
30 Apr	Balance c/d	4,633.60	1 Apr	Balance b/d	2,468.30
			5 Apr	Perran Stores	532.18
			11 Apr	L Johnson	386.97
			20 Apr	Doyle & Co	1,246.15
		4,633.60			4,633.60
			1 May	Balance b/d	4,633.60

Dr		**Purchases Account**			Cr
2005		£	2005		£
1 Apr	Balance b/d	1,524.92	30 Apr	Balance c/d	2,591.92
7 Apr	Shah & Co	345.99			
18 Apr	P Devoran	211.63			
27 Apr	Bissoe Ltd	509.38			
		2,591.92			2,591.92
1 May	Balance b/d	2,591.92			

Dr		**Perran Stores**			Cr
2005		£	2005		£
1 Apr	Balance b/d	826.91	12 Apr	Sales returns	86.24
5 Apr	Sales	532.18	20 Apr	Bank	826.91
			30 Apr	Balance c/d	445.94
		1,359.09			1,359.09
1 May	Balance b/d	445.94			

Dr			Shah & Co			Cr
2005		£	2005			£
14 Apr	Purchases returns	96.45	1 Apr	Balance b/d		826.15
28 Apr	Bank	1,075.69	7 Apr	Purchases		345.99
		1,172.14				1,172.14

two-column account format

	Sales		**Account**			
Date	**Details**	**£**	**p**	**£**	**p**	
2005						
1 Apr	Balance b/d			2,468	30	
5 Apr	Perran Stores			532	18	
11 Apr	L Johnson			386	97	
20 Apr	Doyle & Co			1,246	15	
				4,633	60	
1 May	Balance b/d			4,633	60	

	Purchases		**Account**			
Date	**Details**	**£**	**p**	**£**	**p**	
2005						
1 Apr	Balance b/d	1,524	92			
7 Apr	Shah & Co	345	99			
18 Apr	P Devoran	211	63			
27 Apr	Bissoe Ltd	509	38			
		2,591	92			
1 May	Balance b/d	2,591	92			

Perran Stores		**Account**				
Date	**Details**	**£**	**p**	**£**	**p**	
2005						
1 Apr	Balance b/d	826	91			
5 Apr	Sales	532	18			
12 Apr	Sales returns			86	24	
20 Apr	Bank			826	91	
		1,359	09	913	15	
1 May	Balance b/d	445	94			

Shah & Co		**Account**				
Date	**Details**	**£**	**p**	**£**	**p**	
2005						
1 Apr	Balance b/d			826	15	
7 Apr	Purchases			345	99	
14 Apr	Purchases returns	96	45			
28 Apr	Bank	1,075	69			
		1,172	14	1,172	14	

CHAPTER 8: PRINCIPLES OF PETTY CASH

8.1

(a)	Photocopier paper	pay from petty cash
(b)	Office cleaner	item over the £25 limit, accountant to pay by cheque
(c)	Postage	pay from petty cash
(d)	Secretary's train ticket	personal expense – cannot be paid out of petty cash
(e)	Tea, sugar and milk	pay from petty cash as these items are for visitors use
(f)	Coffee for staff	coffee for staff use – cannot be paid out of petty cash
(g)	Postage	pay from petty cash
(h)	Card, fabric, staples	item over the £25 limit, accountant to pay by cheque
(i)	Job advert in local press	pay from petty cash
(j)	Flowers for reception area	pay from petty cash

8.2   Morgan's Garages Ltd

Petty Cash Procedures – Brief Notes for Louise

- At the start of the new period make sure your petty cash balance equals the amount of cash in the petty cash box – do check by counting the cash in the petty cash box.

- Keep the petty cash box locked and keep the key in a safe place. Remember to put the petty cash box in the safe when not in use and especially each night on leaving the office.

- When making payments:

  1   Make sure that the person making the claim has completed the petty cash voucher correctly and if possible supplied a receipt. Check all calculations.

  2   The voucher must be signed by the person making the claim and to whom the money will be paid.

  3   Check that the voucher has been authorised for payment by John Morgan.

- Enter the voucher details in the petty cash book. Remember to enter the VAT in the VAT column (if appropriate) and the expense under the relevant column.

- File the petty cash vouchers in number order.

- At the end of the month you will need to add up the amount of money spent during the month and claim this amount back from the accountant. See example below:

	£	
Our float for the month is	200.00	
Assume we spend	160.00	during the month
Amount left over	40.00	

If you add up the money left in the petty cash box it should equal £40.00.

You will then have to ask the accountant for £160.00 cash to make the float back up to £200.00 for the next month. Hopefully I should be back at work at the end of the month and will complete the balancing off procedures.

Best of Luck,

James

8.3

petty cash voucher   No. 22

date   today

description	amount	
	£	p
Postage on special delivery parcel (no VAT)	18	30
Documentation will be a receipt from the Post Office for £18.30		
	18	30

signature   *Louise Carter*

authorised   *A Student*

---

petty cash voucher   No. 23

date   today

description	amount	
	£	p
2 packets of computer disks @ £4.70 each includes total VAT of £1.40	9	40
Documentation will be a till receipt from stationery shop for £9.40		
	9	40

signature   *Martin Gould*

authorised   *A Student*

---

petty cash voucher   No. 24

date   today

description	amount	
	£	p
Train fare to London to attend Health and Safety conference (no VAT)	35	00
Documentation will be a receipt from the train company for £35.00 or the train ticket.		
	35	00

signature   *C Edge*

authorised   *Bob Allen*

8.5   Bode Manufacturers Ltd

	Total	VAT	Expense
	£	£	£
(a)	21.30	3.17	18.13
(b)	2.35	35p	2.00
(c)	8.40	1.25	7.15
(d)	1.41	21p	1.20
(e)	15.60	2.32	13.28
(f)	3.30	49p	2.81
(g)	90p	13p	77p
(h)	7.75	1.15	6.60
(i)	10.10	1.50	8.60
(j)	14.10	2.10	12.00

CHAPTER 9: WRITING UP THE PETTY CASH BOOK

			£
9.1	(a)	Petty cash float	100.00
		Less: Amount spent during the period	42.16
		Cash in hand	57.84
		Amount required to restore the imprest	42.16
	(b)	Petty cash float	250.00
		Less: Amount spent during May	231.78
			18.22
		Add: Amounts received during May	
		Alan Grimshaw	10.00
		Betty Jones	2.30
			30.52
		Amount required to restore the imprest	
		Petty cash float	250.00
		Less: Cash in hand (*see above*)	30.52
		Amount required	219.48

(c) Since the petty cash float of £75.00 is not enough for the expenses John has to pay during December, more money will be needed. John will have to put in a request to the main cashier for the float to be increased from £75.00 to the amount required to cover the expenses for December. After these have been paid the float can return to the original amount or if John thinks the existing float is too small it may be necessary to increase the float permanently.

			£	£
(d)	Petty cash float			50.00
		Amount left over for month	12.14	
		Amounts received during month	12.00	24.14
		Amount required to restore the imprest		25.86

9.2 Printing Company

Petty Cash Book

PCB 18

Receipts £ p	Date	Details	Voucher Number	Total £ p	VAT £ p	Postage £ p	Cleaning £ p	Travel £ p	Stationery £ p	Sundry expenses £ p
100.00	2005 1 May	Balance b/d								
	3 May	Postage	73	18.00		18.00				
	7 May	Stationery	74	4.30	0.64				3.66	
	9 May	Train fare	75	6.50				6.50		
	11 May	Donation	76	25.00						25.00
	18 May	Postage	77	5.74		5.74				
	22 May	Stationery	78	9.20	1.37				7.83	
	25 May	Window cleaning	79	8.00			8.00			
	30 May	Cleaning	80	10.00			10.00			
				86.74	2.01	23.74	18.00	6.50	11.49	25.00
100.00										

Amount of cash left at the end of May is (£100.00 − £86.74) = £13.26

Amount required to restore the imprest is (£100.00 − £13.26) = £86.74

9.3 Wildthorn Guest House

Petty Cash Book

PCB 34

Receipts £ p	Date	Details	Voucher Number	Total £ p	VAT £ p	Postage £ p	Cleaning £ p	Travel £ p	Stationery £ p	Sundry expenses £ p
50.00	2006 1 March	Balance b/d								
	3 March	Cleaning	101	15.00			15.00			
	7 March	Postage	102	4.50		4.50				
	11 March	Flowers	103	6.00	0.90					5.10
	16 March	Cleaning materials	104	3.75	0.56		3.19			
	20 March	Bus fares	105	2.50				2.50		
	28 March	Window cleaning	106	8.00			8.00			
	31 March	Stationery	107	5.90	0.88				5.02	
	31 March	Postage	108	0.90		0.90				
				46.55	2.34	5.40	26.19	2.50	5.02	5.10
50.00										

Amount of cash required to restore the imprest = £46.55

9.4   J Dolan

Petty Cash Book

PCB 56

Receipts £ p	Date	Details	Voucher Number	Total £ p	VAT £ p	Postage £ p	Cleaning £ p	Sundry expenses £ p	Stationery £ p	Refreshments £ p
	2005									
26.80	1 June	Balance b/d	CB1							
73.20	1 June	Cash								
	1 June	Milk	001	2.80						2.80
	4 June	Coffee, tea etc	002	6.13						6.13
	9 June	Cleaner	003	20.00			20.00			
	16 June	Marker pens etc	004	4.58	0.68				3.90	
2.10	23 June	M Parkin								
		Postage stamps	36							
	24 June	Postage	005	13.92		13.92				
	24 June	Donation	006	5.00				5.00		
	26 June	Cleaner	007	10.00			10.00			
	27 June	Stationery	008	14.19	2.11				12.08	
	30 June	Bus fare	009	2.30				2.30		
	30 June	Milk	010	2.38						2.38
	30 June	Postage	011	4.50		4.50				
				85.80	2.79	18.42	30.00	7.30	15.98	11.31
102.10										

Amount of cash left at 30 June is £102.10 – £85.80 = £16.30
Amount required to restore the imprest is £100.00 – £16.30 = £83.70

CHAPTER 10: BALANCING THE PETTY CASH BOOK

Petty Cash Book   10.1   Hulme Bros Ltd   PCB 12

Receipts £ p	Date	Details	Voucher Number	Total £ p	VAT £ p	Postage £ p	Cleaning £ p	Motor expenses £ p	Stationery £ p	Refreshments £ p
		2004								
4.36	1 March	Balance b/d								
45.64	1 March	Cash	CB12							
	1 March	Window cleaner	42	8.50			8.50			
	3 March	Postage	43	4.50		4.50				
	4 March	Petrol	44	16.80	2.50			14.30		
	5 March	Coffee, tea etc	45	5.70						5.70
	5 March	Parcel post	46	3.60		3.60				
3.00	6 March	Ben Read	7							
		Postage stamps								
	6 March	Stationery	47	6.40	0.95				5.45	
	7 March	Cleaning materials	48	2.38	0.36		2.02			
				47.88	3.81	8.10	10.52	14.30	5.45	5.70
	7 March	Balance c/d		5.12						
53.00				53.00						
5.12	8 March	Balance b/d								

(e) Amount required to restore the imprest is £50.00 – £5.12 = £44.88

10.2 Chell Construction Co

Petty Cash Book PCB 43

Receipts £ p	Date	Details	Voucher Number	Total £ p	VAT £ p	Postage £ p	Cleaning £ p	Motor expenses £ p	Stationery £ p	Sundry expenses £ p
	2004									
16.22	1 Jan	Balance b/d								
83.78	1 Jan	Cash								
	1 Jan	Trade magazine	27	3.30						3.30
	3 Jan	Postage	28	8.00		8.00				
	7 Jan	Petrol	29	28.60	4.26			24.34		
	10 Jan	Parcel post	30	4.20		4.20				
1.35	13 Jan	Clive Taylor								
		Postage stamps	8							
	17 Jan	Cleaner	31	22.00			22.00			
	22 Jan	Stationery	32	5.05	0.75				4.30	
	25 Jan	Postage	33	4.00		4.00				
	27 Jan	Petrol	34	15.00	2.24			12.76		
				90.15	7.25	16.20	22.00	37.10	4.30	3.30
	31 Jan	Balance c/d		11.20						
101.35				101.35						
11.20	1 Feb	Balance b/d								

Amount required to restore the imprest is £100.00 − £11.20 = £88.80

10.3 D Ashcroft Ltd

Petty Cash Book

PCB 11

Receipts £ p	Date	Details	Voucher Number	Total £ p	VAT £ p	Postage £ p	Cleaning £ p	Motor expenses £ p	Stationery £ p	Refresh-ments £ p
56.40	2005 1 July	Balance b/d								
93.60	1 July	Cash								
	1 July	Stationery	50	15.63	2.33				13.30	
	3 July	Petrol	51	20.30	3.02			17.28		
	4 July	Postage	52	4.00		4.00				
	5 July	Cleaner	53	15.00			15.00			
	6 July	Tea, coffee etc	54	5.32						5.32
1.20	6 July	Kim Stead	5							
		Postage stamps								
	10 July	Postage stamps	55	6.00		6.00				
	15 July	Petrol	56	18.00	2.68			15.32		
	17 July	Refreshments	57	15.20	2.26					12.94
	23 July	Photocopy paper	58	9.40	1.40				8.00	
	25 July	Cleaner	59	20.00			20.00			
2.15	30 July	Anthony Morris	6							
		Postage stamps								
				128.85	11.69	10.00	35.00	32.60	21.30	18.26
153.35	31 July	Balance c/d		24.50						
				153.35						
24.50	1 Aug	Balance b/d								

(f)

PETTY CASH REIMBURSEMENT REQUEST

Please arrange for a cheque for £ _____125.50_____ to restore imprest.

Signed _____A Student_____   Petty Cashier

Date _____31 July 2005_____

Signed _____   Authorised Signatory

Date _____

(g)

| 31.7.05 | Southern Bank PLC | date | 31 July 2005 | 97-76-54 |

31.7.05
To
Cash
restore
imprest –
petty cash
£ 125.50
734017

Southern Bank PLC
Mereford Branch
16 Broad Street, Mereford MR1 7TR

date   31 July 2005   97-76-54

Pay   Cash _____   only

One hundred and twenty five pounds and fifty pence ——   £ 125.50

Account payee only

D ASHCROFT LIMITED

734017   977654   24941017

CHAPTER 11 – SOURCE DOCUMENTS FOR THE CASH BOOK

11.1

Cash Book (receipts side)

	Date	Customer name	Discount allowed £ p	Cash £ p	Bank £ p
	2004				
(a)	12 May	A Partridge		20.50	
(b)	13 May	J Singh		30.70	
(c)	14 May	T F Retail			376.00
(d)	14 May	Y Goldsmith	12.50		487.50
(e)	14 May	Swingway Limited	5.00		95.00
(f)	14 May	Trendtime	4.00		196.00
(g)	14 May	R S Davies			156.50
(h)	14 May	Patricia Smith	2.50		97.50

CHAPTER 12 – WRITING UP AND BALANCING THE CASH BOOK

12.1

Dr   Jenkins Products Ltd: Cash Book   **Cr**

Date	Details	Discount Allowed £ p	Cash £ p	Bank £ p	Date	Details		Discount Received £ p	Cash £ p	Bank £ p
2004					2004					
1 Jan	Balance b/d		78.50	567.20	2 Jan	Expenses – Co. Secretary			27.00	
2 Jan	P Simms Ltd	10.00		390.00	5 Jan	Ace Advertising	100559	9.50		378.00
7 Jan	Cash sales		120.00		12 Jan	Star Insurance	100560			89.00
8 Jan	Smart Trading			625.00	23 Jan	M Evans	100561			635.00
15 Jan	A Lucas	3.70		144.30	30 Jan	Travel Expenses			22.78	
19 Jan	J Jackson			220.00	31 Jan	Logan Products	100562	4.75		185.25
27 Jan	W Little Ltd	11.25		438.75	31 Jan	Balance c/d			148.72	1,098.00
		24.95	198.50	2,385.25				14.25	198.50	2,385.25
1 Feb	Balance b/d		148.72	1,098.00						

12.2

Dr				Cappers Crafts: Cash Book						Cr

Date	Details	Discount Allowed £ p	Cash £ p	Bank £ p	Date	Details	Discount Received £ p	Cash £ p	Bank £ p
2004					2004				
1 Mar	Balance b/d		252.00	1,300.00	2 Mar	Star Insurance 123466			50.00
3 Mar	St James School	3.25		126.75	4 Mar	Gary's Garage 123467			98.40
5 Mar	Arts & Crafts			57.20	4 Mar	Dobby Arts & Crafts	6.25	243.75	
6 Mar	T Ahmed		42.50		5 Mar	K Ashworth 123468	5.95		232.05
10 Mar	Banks Lane School		51.00		11 Mar	Akbar's Wholesale 123469	10.50		409.50
12 Mar	Judith's Art Materials		76.00		15 Mar	Burgess Supplies	2.00	42.00	
16 Mar	Goddards Limited	8.55		333.45	17 Mar	Business Supplies 123470			37.50
18 Mar	Beech Primary School	15.00		225.00	22 Mar	Southern Electric 123471			108.20
24 Mar	Worrall's Workshop		23.00		23 Mar	Matthews Paper 123472	1.50		62.00
25 Mar	Hobby Craft Co	3.20		115.00	26 Mar	Blakes Advertising 123473	3.00		117.00
30 Mar	Mellors Limited			63.00	29 Mar	Rates 123474			122.00
					31 Mar	Gee Wholesale 123475	12.30		570.00
					31 Mar	Patel Wholesale		27.50	
					31 Mar	Balance c/d		131.25	413.75
		30.00	444.50	2,220.40			41.50	444.50	2,220.40
1 Apr	Balance b/d		131.25	413.75					

CHAPTER 13 – BANK TRANSACTIONS

13.1 (a) debit column (b) credit column

13.2 (a) On 1 September the balance of the bank account was overdrawn by £450.95

(b) On 1 November the balance of the bank account was £1,096.70 in credit

13.3 (a) An example from cheques paid in, cash paid in, cheque paid out, cash drawn out, standing order paid.

(b) An example from bank giro credit received, direct debit paid, bank charges, interest received or paid. It is possible that the following will not have been advised to the account holder: BACS payment received, unpaid cheque.

13.4 Standing order, direct debit. See text for explanation.

13.5 It is sent by the customer to the supplier to advise the amount of money being sent to the supplier's bank account through the BACS payment system.

13.6 Interest entered in the credit column is interest received on a bank deposit, interest in the debit column is interest charged on bank borrowing, eg overdraft.

CHAPTER 14 – BANK RECONCILIATION STATEMENTS

14.1 FERN LIMITED

CASH BOOK (Bank columns only)						
RECEIPTS			PAYMENTS			
Date	Details	Bank	Date	Details		Bank
2004		£	2004			£
31 Aug	Balance b/d	2,284	31 Aug	Bank charges		55
30 Aug	Torr Bros (BGC)	92	31 Aug	City Finance SO)		1,000
			31 Aug	Balance c/d		1,321
		2,376				2,376
1 Sep	Balance b/d	1,321				

FERN LIMITED
Bank Reconciliation Statement as at 31 August 2004

		£	£
Balance at bank as per Cash Book			1,321
Add: unpresented cheque(s)			
	Harvey & Co	206	
	Hill Bros	22	
	Ashleys Ltd	137	
			365
			1,686
Less: outstanding lodgement(s)		520	
		82	
			602
Balance at bank as per bank statement			1,084

14.2 BROOKLYN LIMITED

CASH BOOK (Bank columns only)					
RECEIPTS			PAYMENTS		
Date	Details	Bank	Date	Details	Bank
2004		£	2004		£
28 Feb	Balance b/d	705	26 Feb	Rates (DD)	103
27 Feb	D Stead (BACS)	220	28 Feb	Bank charges	38
			28 Feb	Balance c/d	784
		925			925
1 Mar	Balance b/d	784			

BROOKLYN LIMITED
Bank Reconciliation Statement as at 28 February 2004

	£	£
Balance at bank as per Cash Book		784
Add: unpresented cheque(s)		
R Jackson Ltd	540	
Spencer Partners	42	
Shanklin Garage	110	
White & Co	120	
		812
		1,596
Less: outstanding lodgement		94
Balance at bank as per bank statement		1,502

14.3   O'CONNOR LIMITED

CASH BOOK (Bank columns only)					
RECEIPTS			**PAYMENTS**		
Date	Details	Bank	Date	Details	Bank
2004		£	2004		£
28 Oct	Bayley's (BACS)	114	30 Oct	Balance b/d	604
31 Oct	Balance c/d	588	29 Oct	Bank interest	53
			29 Oct	Bank charges	45
		702			702
			1 Nov	Balance b/d	588

O'CONNOR LIMITED
Bank Reconciliation Statement as at 31 October 2004

	£	£
Balance at bank as per Cash Book		(588)
Less: unpresented cheque(s)		
Kerr's Garage	32	
J Choudrey	28	
	60	
		(528)
Add: outstanding lodgement(s)	58	
	209	
	267	
Balance at bank as per bank statement		(795)

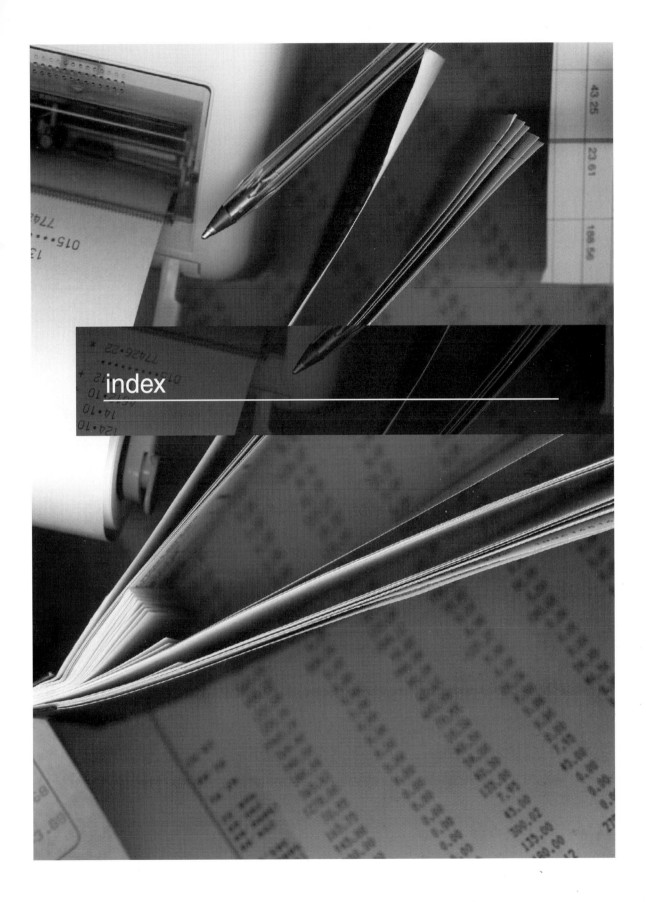

index